Journal of Various Visits to the Kingdoms of Ashanti, Aku, and Dahomi, in Western Africa

Thomas Birch Freeman
John Beecham

CAMBRIDGE UNIVERSITY PRESS

Cambridge, New York, Melbourne, Madrid, Cape Town, Singapore,
São Paolo, Delhi, Dubai, Tokyo, Mexico City

Published in the United States of America by Cambridge University Press, New York

www.cambridge.org
Information on this title: www.cambridge.org/9781108023306

This edition first published 1844
This digitally printed version 2010

ISBN 978-1-108-02330-6 Paperback

JOURNAL OF VARIOUS VISITS

INTO THE

INTERIOR OF WESTERN AFRICA.

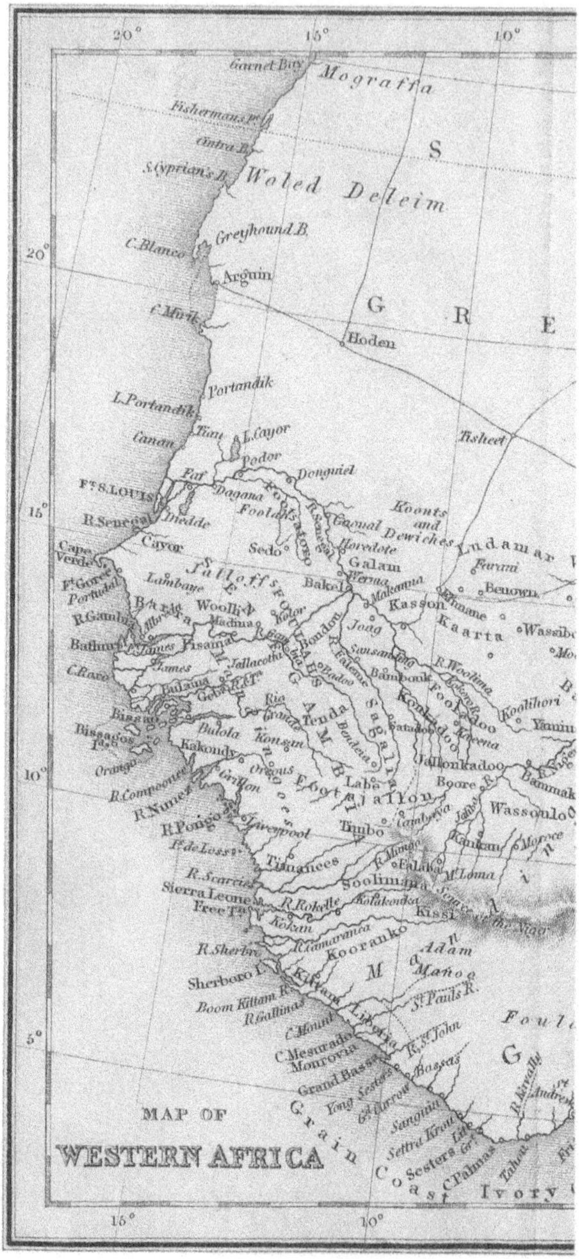

MAP OF WESTERN AFRICA

Garnet Bay
Mograffa
Fishermans Pt.
Cintra B.
S. Cyprian's B.
Woled Deleim
Greyhound B.
C. Blanco
Arguin
C. Mirik
Hoden
Portandik
L. Portandik
L. Cayor
Podor
Dongniel
Ft. S. LOUIS
R. Senegal
Dagana
Foolahs
Koonts and Dewiches
Ludamar
Cape Verde
Ft. Goree
Portudal
Cayor
Sedo
Horedote
Galam
Bakel
Lambaye
Jalloffs
R. Gambia
Woolli
Madina
Bondou
Kasson
Kaarta
Bathurst
Pisania
Jallacotha
Bambouk
C. Roxo
Bissao
Bissagos Is.
Tenda
Kakondy
Orango
R. Componee
R. Nunez
R. Pongo
Laba
Timbo
Wassoulo
Ft. de Loss
Timanees
R. Scarcies
Sierra Leone
Free Tn.
R. Rokelle
Soolimana
Kissi
Falaba
R. Sherbro
Kooranko
Sherboro I.
Boom Kittam R.
R. Gallinas
Liberia
St. Pauls R.
R. St. John
C. Mount
C. Mesurada
Monrovia
Grand Bassa
Grain Coast
C. Palmas
Ivory

20° 15° 10°
20° 15° 10° 5°

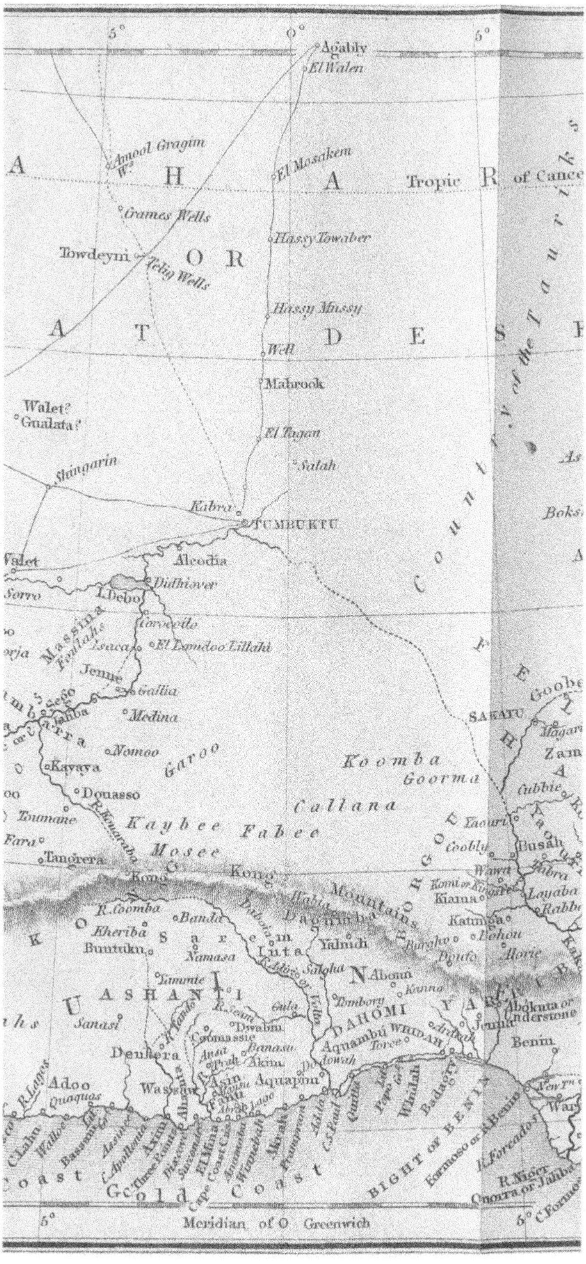

5°
0°
5°
Agably
El Walen
Amool Gragim Ws
El Mosakem
Tropic of Cancer
Grames Wells
Hassy Towaber
Towdeyni
Telig Wells
Hassy Mussy
Well
Mahrook
Walet?
Gualata?
El Tagan
Salah
Shingarin
Kabra
TUMBUKTU
Walet
Alcodia
Didhiover
Sorro
L. Debo
Corocoilo
Massina
Foulahs
Isaca
El Lamdoo Lillahi
Jenne
Sego
Gallia
Jamba
Medina
Nomoo
Garoo
Kayaya
Douasso
Toumane
Fara
Tangrera
Kaybee Fabee
Mosee
Callana
Koomba
Goorma
SAKATU
Goobe
Magari
Zam
Gubbie
Yaouri
Coobly
Busah
Wawa
Tabra
Komi or Kings Te
Kiama
Layaba
Rabba
Katunga
Bohou
Alorie
Kong
Kong Mountains
R. Coomba
Banda
Kheriba
Buntuku
Namasa
Dagumba
Yahndi
Luta
Salgha
Aboun
Kanna
Tambory
Tamnie
ASHANTI
Sanasi
Coomassie
Dwabin
Denkera
Akim
Aquapim
Wassaw
Asin
Fanti
Adoo
Quaquas
DAHOMI
Aquambu
WHIDAH
Ardrah
Jenna
Abokuta or Understone
Benin
BIGHT OF BENIN
R. Benin
R. Forcados
Formoso or R. Benin
R. Niger
Quorra or Joliba
Whidah
Badagry
El Mina
Cape Coast Castle
Apollonia
C. Three Points
Gold Coast
Meridian of 0 Greenwich
5°
5°

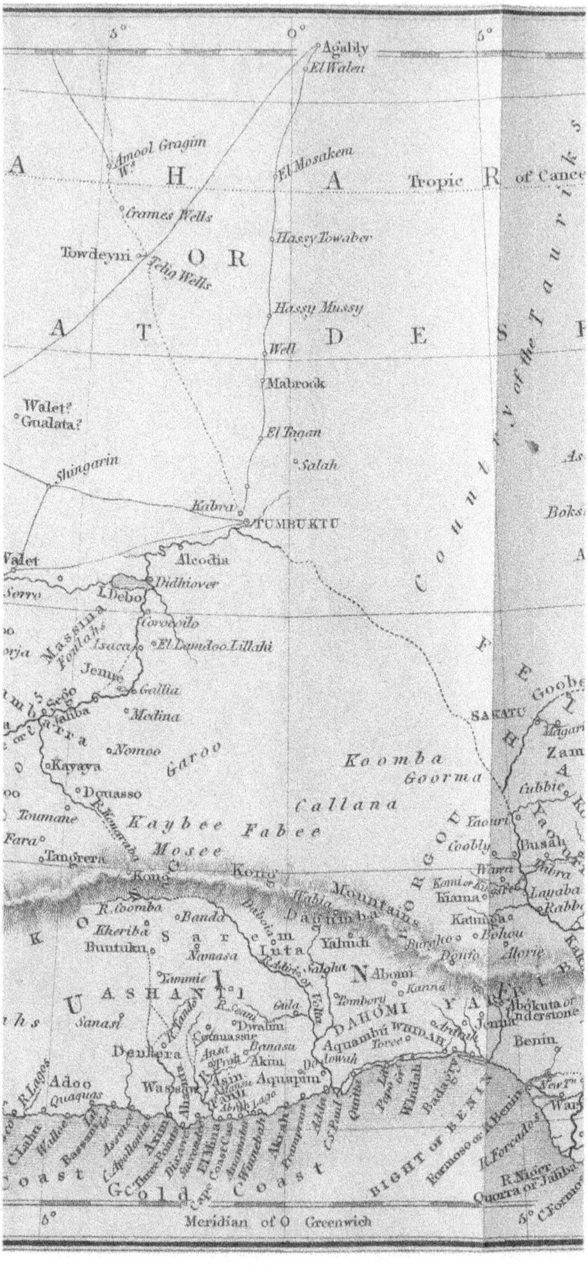

5° 0° 5°

Agably
El Walen
Amool Gragim Ws
El Mosaken
A H A Tropic R of Cancer
Grames Wells
Hassy Towaber
Towdeyni
Telig Wells
O R
Hassy Mussy
A T D E S
Well
Mabrook
Walet?
Gualata?
El Tagan
Salah
Shingarin
Kabra
TUMBUKTU
Walet
Alcodia
Didhiover
L. Debo
Sorro
Corocoilo
Massina Foulahs
Isaca
El Lamdoo Lillahi
Jenne
Gallia
Sego
Jalliba
Medina
Nomoo
Kayaya
Garoo
Douasso
Toumane
Fara
Tangrera
Koomba
Goorma
Callana
Kaybee Fabee
Mosee
Kong
Kong
Country of the Tuariks
F E L
SAKATU
Goobe
Magari
Zam
Gubbie
Yaouri
Coobly
Busah
Wawa
Layaba
Rabba
Kiama
Katunga
Bohou
Alorie
Mountains
Dagwumba
R. Coomba
Banda
Kheriba
Buntuku
Namasa
Luta
Yahndi
Saloha
Aboim
Kanna
Yammie
UASHANTI
Tombory
DAHOMI
YARRIBA
Abokuta or Understone
Sanasi
Gula
Volta
Aquambu
Whidah
Ardrah
Jenna
Benin
Denkera
Coomassie
Banasu
Akim
Aquapim
Adoo
Quaquas
Wassaw
Asin
Fanti
R. Lagos
Wallow
Bassam
C. Lahu
Assence
Axim
C. Apollonia
Three Points
Elmina
Cape Coast Castle
Annamaboe
Winnebah
Akrah
Prampram
C. St. Paul
Quitta
Popo
Whidah
Badagry
BIGHT OF BENIN
Formoso or R. Benin
R. Forcados
R. Niger
Quorra or Joliba
C. Formoso
Coast
Gold Coast

5° Meridian of 0 Greenwich 5°

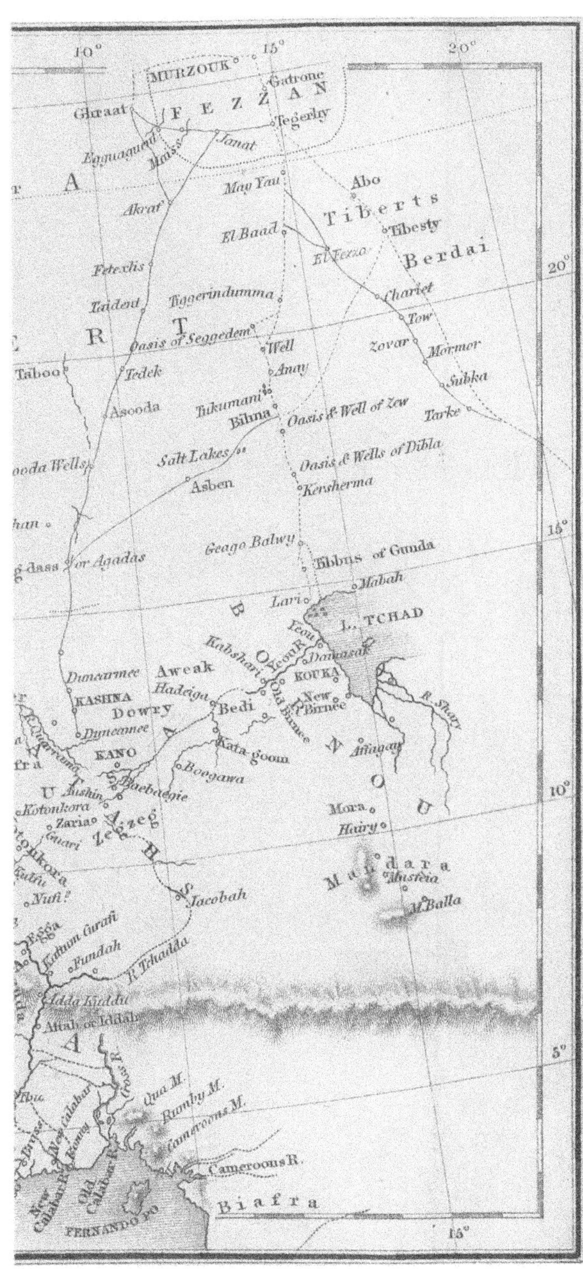

J. & C. Walker Sculp.

JOURNAL OF VARIOUS VISITS

TO THE

KINGDOMS OF ASHANTI, AKU, AND DAHOMI,

IN WESTERN AFRICA,

BY

THE REV. THOMAS B. FREEMAN,

TO PROMOTE THE OBJECTS OF THE WESLEYAN MISSIONARY SOCIETY.

WITH APPENDICES.

TOGETHER WITH

AN HISTORICAL INTRODUCTION,

BY THE REV. JOHN BEECHAM.

SECO D EDITION.

LONDON:
SOLD BY JOHN MASON, 66, PATERNOSTER-ROW,
AND AT THE WESLEYAN MISSION-HOUSE,
BISHOPSGATE-STREET WITHIN.

1844.

ROCHE, PRINTER, 25, HOXTON-SQUARE, LONDON.

CONTENTS.

Page

CHAPTER III.

CHAPTER IV.

CHAPTER V.

CHAPTER VI.

APPENDICES TO THE SECOND JOURNAL.

APPENDIX, A.

WOODCUTS.

Page

THIRD JOURNAL.

CHAPTER I.

CHAPTER II.

CHAPTER III.

CHAPTER IV.

Page

CHAPTER V.

CHAPTER VI.

APPENDICES TO THE THIRD JOURNAL.

APPENDIX, A.

APPENDIX, B.

APPENDIX, C.

APPENDIX, D.

APPENDIX, E.

INTRODUCTION.

ASHANTI* is a powerful kingdom contiguous to the Gold Coast, in Western Africa. Kumási, the capital, it has been calculated, is more than one hundred and thirty miles from Cape-Coast Castle in an horizontal direction, but the distance is much greater by the pathway through the forest. It is a very considerable place, and is surrounded by numerous towns and villages, which contain a great number of inhabitants. The entire population of Ashánti, with all its dependencies, has been estimated at upwards of four millions.

The martial exploits of the Ashántis in the countries on the coast, since the commencement of the present century, have rendered their national name familiar in Europe. The Fantis, who were originally an inland people, subject to the Ashánti crown, having, in the year 1807, afforded protection to Chibbu and Apoutai, two of the vassal Chiefs of Osai Tutu Quamina, King of Ashánti, who had rebelled against his authority, the King invaded Fanti with a powerful army. In the first instance, he appeared solicitous to obtain possession of the two rebel Chiefs by amicable means; but he

* Although we retain the aspirate and the initial A in Ashánti, they are scarcely sounded by the natives, who pronounce the name of their country very nearly as the English would express S-a-n-t-y.

The vowel signs of the Ashánti alphabet have the same sounds as in Italian.

became so exasperated by the insults and indignities which were offered to him, that he formed the resolution entirely to extirpate the Fantis. Orders were accordingly issued to spare neither man, woman, nor child; and the country in the rear of the advancing army became, in consequence, a scene of utter desolation. Having signally wreaked his vengeance upon Abrah, the seat of Government, where his messengers had been barbarously murdered, the King, with one half of his army, pursued the retreating enemy towards the coast; while the other half were employed in destroying the towns as they passed along, leaving none of the people alive, except some of the highest rank, who were reserved to experience more refined cruelties on the return of the conqueror to Kumási.

The advanced guard of the army, led on by the Viceroy or Tributary King of Denkera, first obtained sight of the sea in the neighbourhood of Cormantine. This town was destroyed, and the Dutch fort taken possession of, by the Ashántis. The successes of the invaders now began to excite uneasy apprehensions at Anamabu; and Mr. White, the Governor of the fort, humanely endeavoured to put a stop to the further effusion of blood, by friendly explanations. But vain was the attempt. The King had bound himself by "the great oath," that he would not go back to his capital without the heads of Chibbu and Apoutai; who, after the destruction of Abrah, had, in the first instance, taken refuge at Anamabu, which was then the largest town upon that part of the coast. As the Ashántis approached, they, however, retired to Cape Coast, on the invitation of the natives of that place. When the King presented himself before Anamabu, he found that the inhabitants had drawn out their forces to meet him; but they soon gave way, and were pursued to the very walls of the fort, which afforded them only slender protection. The cannon were shortly rendered useless, as the Ashánti marksmen picked off the soldiers as fast as they appeared at an embrasure, or showed their heads above the ramparts; and, before the close of the day, the efforts of the little garrison were exclusively confined to the defence of the gate, which the enemy attempted to force or burn. At least eight thousand of the natives perished in the contest, and Mr. White, the Governor of the fort, was severely wounded. After two or three days, the King prepared to renew the attack upon the fort, with six thousand men selected for the occasion; but in the morning of the day on which he had vowed to seat himself, "by the help of his gods," in the Governor's chair, a white flag was lowered from the walls. A negotiation ensued. The Chief Governor, Torrane, went over from Cape-Coast Castle, and concluded a treaty of peace. Apoutai made his escape, but Chibbu was delivered up to the King, who withdrew his army, carrying with him many of the surviving inhabitants, as his prisoners. In the rejoicing which afterwards took place at the capital, the wretched Chibbu suffered the most exquisite torments, and his head became one of the principal decorations of the death-drum of the King.

In the year 1811, Fanti experienced a second invasion from the Ashántis; and a third in 1816, when Cape Coast underwent a long blockade. These repeated attacks inflicted great miseries upon the Fantis, and thousands were dragged into the interior to be sacrificed to the superstitions of the conquerors.

To avert a continued succession of such calamities, an embassy was sent to Kumási; and Mr. Bowdich, who was placed at its head, after the recall of Mr. James, concluded a treaty with the King. Mr. Hutchinson was left behind as Resident in Ashánti, but returned to Cape Coast on the eve of the war with Gaman.

After this, Mr. Dupuis was sent by the British Government to Kumási, invested with consular powers. He concluded a second treaty, and returned to Cape Coast with numerous presents, accompanied by Ambassadors to the King of England.

New misunderstandings however arose, and an Ashánti army again marched towards the coast, at the close of the year 1823. Sir Charles M'Carthy took the field against them, with the most encouraging prospect of success; for, besides a strong body of regular troops which was under his command, many Chiefs threw off their allegiance to Ashánti, and all the districts on the sea-coast, west of the Volta, were in arms, to the amount of thirty thousand warriors. But disastrous was the result of the first campaign. The Governor, with a division of the army, having crossed the Prah, advanced into the Wassaw country, where he engaged the Ashántis, and experienced a complete defeat. Sir Charles himself, after having been severely wounded, fell into the hands of the enemy, who cut off his head, and preserved it in the usual manner. His heart was eaten by the principal Ashánti Chiefs, in order that they might, as they imagined, imbibe his bravery; and his flesh, having been dried, was divided, together with his bones, amongst the men of consequence in the army, who kept their respective shares about their persons, as charms to inspire them with courage.

In the month of May following, the new King, Osai Ockoto, (the brother of Osai Tutu Quamina, who had died soon after the commencement of the war,) came down to his army, at the head of a strong reinforcement, with the avowed intention to destroy Cape-Coast Castle, and drive the English into the sea. After some hard fighting, and when the Ashánti army had suffered the loss of many thousands of men, by the ravages of disease, and the want of provisions, the King drew off his forces in the direction of Anamabu. The last and decisive battle was fought about the middle of the year 1826, twenty-four miles north-east of Akráh; when the British and their allies gained the victory, and took the Ashánti camp and baggage. After this battle, negotiations were commenced; but, owing to various causes, it was not until the month of April, 1831, that a treaty of peace was signed, when the King sent one of his sons, and a son of the preceding King, as hostages, with six hundred ounces of gold, to be lodged at Cape-Coast Castle, as a security for the performance, on his part, of the conditions of the treaty, for the term of six years. At the end of six years, the gold was returned; and the present King, Quako Duah, who had in the mean time succeeded his brother, Osai Ockoto, consented that his nephews, who had been given up as hostages, should be sent to England for education.

It was shortly after the execution of this treaty, that the land which had been so awfully desolated by war, was visited, in the order of Divine Providence, with the blessings of the Gospel of peace. The Wesleyan Missionary Committee were led to accept the generous offer of Captain Potter, of Bristol, to take a Missionary in his vessel, free of expense to the Society; and, in the year 1834, the Rev. Joseph Dunwell was sent on a visit of observation to Cape-Coast Castle. He was welcomed by many of the natives with gratitude and affection; and his faithful labours among them were crowned with signal success. The work which thus so auspiciously commenced, since his lamented death has extended along the Gold Coast eastward, as far as Akráh, and westward to Dixcove; several chapels have been built; and upwards of six hundred converts from Heathenism have been united in church-fellowship.

Interesting as this Mission appears, when viewed in its beneficial effects upon the natives of the Gold Coast, it, however, rises in importance when regarded as the means by which the way has been opened for the introduction of the Gospel into Ashánti. A beneficial influence was exerted by Mr. Dunwell's ministry upon the two Ashánti hostages, before they were brought by the Government to this country, where they completed their education under the care of the Rev. Thomas Pyne, a Clergyman of the Established Church. And the establishment of the Mission at length furnished the facilities by which the Rev. Mr. Freeman was enabled to visit Kumási, in the commencement of the year 1839.

On the receipt, at the Wesleyan Mission-House in London, of Mr. Freeman's Journal of his visit, the question, "What shall be done?" became the subject of grave consideration on the part of the Missionary Committee, under whose direction Mr. Freeman acted. The ordinary annual income of the Society was already pledged for the support of existing Missions; and yet the Committee durst not take upon themselves the responsibility of refusing to *attempt*, at least, the establishment of a Mission in Ashánti. It was at length resolved, that Mr. Freeman should be allowed to return home for a time, partly for the purpose of recruiting his health, but more particularly with a view to a special effort being made, in order to raise the funds necessary for the new undertaking; and two Missionaries were immediately sent to relieve him, for a time, from his laborious duties at the Gold Coast. On the arrival of the Rev. Mr. and Mrs. Mycock, and the Rev. Mr. Brooking, Mr. Freeman, therefore, came to England, accompanied by Mr. William De Graft, a native convert, and was the bearer of a message from the King of Ashânti, who requested that his two nephews might be immediately sent home; the contemplated establishment of a Christian school at Kumâsi having rendered him very anxious to see them.

The results of Mr. Freeman's visit to several of the principal towns in Great Britain and Ireland were of the most gratifying description. Members of the Church of England, some of whom are in the higher walks of life, and Christians of other religious denominations, as well as the members of the Wesleyan community, responded to the novel and deeply-interesting appeal; and, by these united exertions, the proposed sum of £5,000 was placed at the disposal of the Wesleyan Committee, to enable them to send with Mr. Freeman, on his return, six additional Missionaries, in order to strengthen the existing establishments at the Gold Coast, and to commence a new Mission in the kingdom of Ashânti. Arrangements were made in due season for their outfit and departure; and, at Mr. Freeman's suggestion, the Committee agreed so far to comply with the established African custom of offering presents, as to send for the King's acceptance and use, a suitable carriage, which was noticed with approbation by Her Most Gracious Majesty and His Royal Highness Prince Albert, to whose inspection it was submitted by Mr. Sims, the builder. In the month of December, 1840, the Rev. Mr. and Mrs. Freeman embarked at Gravesend, on board the "Osborne," accompanied by the Rev. Mr. and Mrs. Hesk, the Rev. Mr. and Mrs. Shipman, the Revs. Messrs. Watson, Walden, and Thackwray, and Mr. William De Graft, whom the Committee had received as a regular agent of the Society, to be hereafter wholly employed in the work of the Mission; and, after a few days, the party left the Channel, followed by the best wishes and ardent prayers of thousands who had become deeply interested in their arduous enterprise.

On their arrival at the Gold Coast, Mr. Freeman began to make the necessary preparations for proceeding to Kumási, at the proper season of the year. While thus employed, he received a severe shock from the decease of his beloved wife, who was eminently calculated, by her piety and talents, to aid him in his important operations; and this bereavement was followed by other inroads of disease and death into the Mission family. At the close of the rainy season, he was enabled to complete his arrangements, and started for the Ashánti capital, accompanied by the two Ashánti Princes, William Quantamissah and John Ansah, (who had returned to the Coast in one of the vessels of the Niger expedition,) Henry Smith, Esq., a resident at Cape-Coast, and the Rev. Mr. Brooking.

The results of this journey, as detailed in Mr. Freeman's Second Journal, are of a very gratifying character. The Mission in Ashánti has been commenced under circumstances still more satisfactory than could have been reasonably anticipated, from the narrative, encouraging as it was, of his former visit to Kumási; circumstances which warrant the hope, that a considerable measure of success will be realized at no distant period. After the reader has perused the heart-stirring description which Mr. Freeman gives of his reception, and the opening prospects of the new Mission, he will not be surprised that Mr. Freeman should manifest an intense desire, that adequate means should be provided to improve the opportunities which present themselves. He will not wonder that the Missionary who nobly "jeopards his life unto the death in the high places of the" West African Mission "field," and who has the most vivid perception of the glorious victories which are likely, with suitable aid, to be effected in furtherance of the kingdom of Christ, should thus give expression to his benevolent feelings, in one of his recent letters addressed to the Wesleyan Missionary Committee:—

"O that we had more help here! What distressing obstacles it throws in the way of our usefulness! England is doing nothing, as yet, compared with what she ought to do. O that God would raise up another successful 'Peter the Hermit,' to call Christian England, and her Christian allies of Europe, to engage more effectually in a grand spiritual warfare; not in order to rescue a lifeless sepulchre from the hands of heretics, but to snatch millions of immortal spirits, in Africa, from the iron grasp of Satan, and thus transform the ancient chivalry of Britain into burning zeal for the glory of the God of heaven, in the evangelization of the degraded posterity of Ham! In this, success would be certain; and the Christian Crusader, if I may be allowed to call him by that name, would enjoy a present reward, in the happy consciousness that he was saving souls from death. I trust the day is not far distant when some mightier movements will take place in the Christian camp, and when England will do something for Africa worthy of her knowledge, her piety, and her greatness. Her energies are inexhaustible, and she is at present *doing comparatively nothing.*"

FIRST JOURNAL

OF THE

REV. THOMAS B. FREEMAN.

(*Addressed to the Secretaries of the Wesleyan Missionary Society.*)

CHAPTER I.

OBJECT OF THE JOURNEY—DIFFICULTIES, AND REMOVAL—ANAMABU—DOMONASI—YANKUMASI—ASIN CHIBBU—MANSU—PREACHES TO THE CHIEF—FESSU—BERAKU—RIVER PRAH—ENTERS THE ASHANTI TERRITORY—ASINS—ANSO—QUISAH—FOMUNAH—PREACHES TO KORINCHI, THE CHIEF—HUMAN SACRIFICES—SUPERSTITIOUS OBSERVANCES.

REV. AND DEAR SIRS,

ACCORDING to the promise in my last, I embrace the opportunity of sending you, per brig "Maclean," a copy of my Journal during my recent Mission to Ashánti, with a few accompanying remarks.

Before I commence, however, I beg leave briefly to state my object in undertaking such a work, and the prospects I had at my setting out.

Ever since my arrival on this Station, I had felt very anxious to visit Kumási, the capital of Ashánti, and residence of the King. The tales of horror, wretchedness, and cruelty which I had often heard respecting the Ashántis, wrought in my mind the deepest commiseration, and a constant restlessness to commence Missionary operations among them.

Opposed to this project were, First, The fears of a large majority of our members, as to the results of such an enterprise, concerning my health. Secondly, The very heavy expenses attending such a journey. Thirdly, The doubts of many with whom I conversed on the subject, that I should not succeed even in an attempt to get to Kumási, on account of the almost unconquerable jealousies of the King. Fourthly, The strong claims of our societies on the coast; from which, in the event of my undertaking the journey, I must in all probability be absent from two to three months. And, lastly, The importance of my being at Cape Coast on the arrival of a fellow-labourer, whom I had for several weeks been expecting.

The first obstacle was removed by our members gaining a steady and increasing confidence, that God would preserve me, (if I endeavoured to take care of my health,) and bring me back in safety.

The second obstacle was removed by a promise, on the part of our societies on the coast, to render me all possible assistance by their prayers and contributions.

The third obstacle was removed by a promise of all necessary assistance on the part of His Excellency President Maclean.

My fourth obstacle was removed, by the expectation that a new Missionary would arrive in the course of a few weeks at the latest; and also by my obtaining the assistance of an excellent young man, (Mr. W. De Graft,) who was ready to take charge of the Mission-house, of our societies, &c., during my absence; and,

My fifth obstacle was, in a measure, removed by considering that I could write a long letter, by way of information and instruction, and leave it at the Mission-house for my fellow-labourer on his arrival.

Having, therefore, determined on commencing my journey without delay, I immediately began to prepare myself, by packing up a supply of provisions, hiring hammock-men, carriers, &c.; while President Maclean kindly provided me with two soldiers, (a Sergeant and a private,) to conduct me; and also placed in my hand a letter of recommendation to the King of Ashánti.

Deeply sensible of the difficult and dangerous nature of my undertaking, and not forgetful of that eternal Source from whence I must receive all my strength, both physical and spiritual, I took an affectionate leave of our society at Cape Coast, on Tuesday evening, January 29th, 1839; and on the following morning, January 30th, at half-past seven, I left Cape Coast for Kumási, and reached Anamabu at noon.

In the afternoon I made arrangements for starting for Domonási the following morning. Domonási is not in the direct road to Ashánti; but as it is not far out of the way, I chose to call and visit our societies there, before I left the Circuit.

Thursday, 31st.—At eight, A. M., I proceeded on my way to Domonási, where I arrived early in the afternoon, a little unwell; the heavy anxieties which I had felt for several days, on account of leaving for the interior, having brought on a slight fever. Here I rested until the following afternoon, hoping to recover strength.

February 1st, Friday.—At three, P. M., I proceeded to Yankumási, where I arrived at a quarter past five, and immediately repaired to the residence of Asín Chibbu, the Chief of the town and surrounding country. He received me very kindly, provided me with lodgings for the night, and made me a present of a sheep and some green plantains.

Saturday, 2d.—At ten, A. M., I again resumed my journey, Asín Chibbu providing me with four men and a boy, to assist in carrying my luggage to my next lodging-place, gratis.

Yankumási is one of the largest native towns I have

yet seen in Fanti, and it is kept remarkably clean. Asín Chibbu is a young man of more respectable appearance than many of the Chiefs of the country. During my short stay, I had some conversation with him concerning the worship of the true God. He paid attention to what I said, and appeared to be void of that obstinacy which characterizes many of the Fanti Chiefs and Kabosirs, when conversed with on religious subjects. There are many hundreds of souls in Yankumási, to whom much lasting good might be done, by a Teacher residing among them, who is zealous for the glory of God, in the eternal welfare of the people.

At three, P. M., I reached the town of Mansu, and was very kindly received by the Chief and his Captains. Finding myself feverish, with a violent headache, I thought it prudent to have recourse to medicine. Before I retired to rest, Gabri (the Chief) sent me a present, consisting of a good sheep, some plantains, and pine-apples. His mother also sent me some yams and plantains.

Sunday, 3d.—Much better in health, and my fever nearly gone. At four, P. M., I preached the word of life to the Chief and his Captains, and to many of the people, on, "Go ye into all the world, and preach the Gospel to every creature." Considering their ignorant condition, they behaved very well. I do not remember that I ever witnessed a more soul-refreshing and interesting scene, than that which took place at the close of the sermon. The sublime truths concerning the mysterious plan of human redemption,—God becoming incarnate and dying to save his rebellious creatures, and to bring them to eternal glory,—made such an impression on the minds of the Chief and his Captains, that they could not contain themselves; but spreading abroad their hands, and lifting up their voices, they acknowledged the lovingkindness of God, and declared before many of their people who were present, that they would worship Him; and I verily believe they would, if they could be watched over, and attended to continually, by a Missionary or Teacher. "The harvest truly is great, but the labourers are few." O God of love! wilt thou not undertake for these souls? Save them from the power of the enemy, and strengthen the hands of the few, very few, labourers in this extensive vineyard! Is it not of thine own planting?

"Art thou the God of Jews alone,
And not the God of Gentiles too?
To Gentiles make thy goodness known;
Thy judgments to the nations show;
Awake them by the Gospel call:
Light of the world, illumine all!"

They are as the dry bones in the valley. But, O, thou Fountain of Life! thou Spirit of eternal truth! breathe upon these slain, that they may live!

Monday, 4th.—At a quarter past seven, A. M., I left Mansu, and proceeded on my way to Fessu. Our path lay through a dense forest, abounding in lofty silk-cotton and other trees, and many handsome varieties of Fern. Many small rivulets nearly dried up by the long drought, remind me that I am in a torrid clime. At five, P. M., I reached Fessu.

Tuesday, 5th.—At seven, A. M., I left Fessu, and reached my next resting-place, Beraku, at five, P. M. Fessu and Beraku are both small crooms, or villages, belonging to Mansu.

Wednesday, 6th.—At a quarter past six, A. M., I started from Beraku for the river Prah,* which I reached nine minutes before nine. The river, the largest I have yet seen in Africa, with its thickly-

* Boosemprah of Bowdich.

wooded banks, abounding in Palm-trees and Mimosæ, presented a beautifully picturesque and interesting scene. When it is at its greatest height, its depth may be about thirty or forty feet, and its breadth about ninety yards. Near the crossing-place, its bed is rocky. As it was very low, I could see many large pieces of granite above the surface of the water. The river Prah forms the boundary, between the Fanti country, and the dominions of the King of Ashánti. On the Fanti side of the river is a small town, called Prahsu. Here I halted until the following morning, that my people might have an opportunity of refreshing themselves by bathing, &c.

In the course of the day, my interpreter had the misfortune to cut his foot with an oyster-shell, while bathing in the river, which made him almost incapable of walking for two or three days. I was, therefore, obliged to relieve him, by walking more than usual myself, that he might ride in my travelling-chair. I was soon, however, obliged to hire four extra men, to carry him in a basket, which I had the precaution to take with me, besides my chair, as my heels became so sore with boils, occasioned by the intensity of the heat, that I was little able to walk myself. The road also was exceedingly bad, being in many places not more than nine inches wide, full of holes, and roots of trees rising above the ground.

The whole of the Fanti country through which I passed, from within a mile or two of Cape-Coast Castle, as far as the river Prah, a distance of about eighty-five miles, is covered with luxuriant vegetation, consisting of Plantains, Bananas, Palms, Bamboos, Pines, many large forest-trees, covered with climbers, *Epiphytical Orchideæ*, and Ferns. Among the shrubs and herbaceous plants, I noticed a very pretty variety of *Croton*; also

Lantana Odorata, and a species of *Gardenia Hedychium*, or garland-flower, *Canna Indica*, and a handsome blue variety of *Maranta*, the leaves of which were, on the upper side, of a pale green colour, and underneath a bright purple. My ears were charmed with the notes of some of the feathered songsters of the forest; * and my attention was also arrested by the well-known sound of the woodman's hook and axe, employed to clear small tracts of ground in the forest, for the cultivation of yams, &c.

Thursday, 7th.—At seven, A. M., I crossed the Prah in a large, heavy canoe, and journeyed through a country formerly inhabited by the Asins, a people who were incorporated with Ashánti, until the late war between the Ashántis and the British, when they threw off their allegiance, and took refuge in Fanti, under the protection of the latter. In the evening I reached Anso, a small croom, where I halted for the night.

Throughout the day the *harmattan* was very strong, painfully affecting my eyes, and producing a sensation like what is felt with a violent cold in the head.

During the night I slept in a small hut; and having nothing but thin strips of Bamboo tied close together, to supply the place of walls, I felt the cold damps severely, although I lined this frail dwelling with a blanket and sheet. I was also mortified in the morning, to find that a rat had eaten some of my hammock-strings, which almost rendered it unfit for use.

Friday, 8th.—At seven, A. M., I started for Quisah, the first town of any importance on the Ashánti side of the Prah, where I arrived at five, P. M. Immediately before entering Quisah, I passed over a hill, the

* The general remark, that the notes of the birds of tropical climes are not harmonious, is not applicable to this part of the world: many of them sing melodiously.

ascent of which occupied seventeen minutes. This hill is, I think, the highest of a long chain, which forms the boundary between Ashánti Proper, and the Asín country. Were it not for the thick bush which covers the summit of this hill, a very extensive prospect of part of the Ashánti and Asín countries might be obtained. Its soil is very rich, consisting of a mixture of yellow loam and clay. A spring of the most delicious water I ever tasted, rises about half-way up the hill, as far as I could judge; and after tumbling down its rocky bed of granite, flows by the small town of Quisah. The Asín country, though possessing a very rich and fertile soil, and covered with luxuriant vegetation, presents one unbroken scene of desolation, except here and there a few huts occupied by Ashántis, whom the King sends to take care of the path.*

I had not been in Quisah more than an hour, when I was informed by the Chief, that I could proceed no farther into the Ashánti country without obtaining permission from the Chief of Adansi, who resides at Fomunah, a neat little town, about a mile distant from Quisah. Being provided with a lodging-place, I halted here for the night. I was delighted to find in Quisah several Fantis, members of our society, who had come hither for trading purposes.

Saturday, 9th.—This morning the Chief informed me that Korinchi, the Chief of Fomunah, had sent for him, in order to converse with him respecting me; and shortly afterwards a messenger arrived requesting

---

* If we compare this brief account of Fanti and Asín with that given by Bowdich, (pages 23, 24,) we shall perceive, that the Fanti country is rapidly improving under the fostering care of the local Government of Cape Coast; while the Asín country, abandoned by its rightful owners, is in ruins.

PREACHING TO KORINCHI AND HIS CAPTAINS.—Page 19.

me to go over and visit him, which I immediately prepared to do. When I entered the town, Korinchi was sitting before the front of his house, under his large umbrella, waiting to receive me; his Captains and people occupying the ground on his right and left. After the usual compliments on meeting, he asked me what object I had in view, in wishing to pass up to Kumási. I told him I had nothing to do with trade or palavers, but was come into the country to promote the best interests of the King of Ashánti and his people, by directing them in the way of peace and happiness, through the preaching of the Gospel. He said he should like to hear the Gospel in his town, before I proceeded any farther into the country. I hereupon proceeded to speak to him, and all present, on the being of a God. I commenced, by taking into my hand a leaf which had fallen from a Banyan-tree, under which I was standing, and asking them if they could make one like it; and they answered, *Debida,* "No." I then asked them, if they thought it possible for all the wisdom, power, and genius in the world, united, to make such a leaf: they answered again, *Debida.* Having brought them to this conclusion, I directed their attention to the almighty power, mercy, and truth of "God, who made the world and all things therein;" and spoke to them on the nature of the Christian religion. They readily assented to all I said; and Korinchi requested me to pay them a visit on the morrow, that they might hear more from me concerning the Christian religion. On my remarking, that as I was a Minister of Christ, I could not prudently make them presents according to the usual custom, it being beneath the dignity of Christianity, so truly excellent in itself, that it requires no recommendation, except a conviction of its value; he answered, "We do not desire any of the customary presents from you, but wish rather to become acquainted with the Gospel." I then asked him, when I could proceed to Kumási, to which he answered that I should know more about it on the morrow.

Sunday, 10th.—At three, P. M., I again went over to Fomunah to preach the word of life, followed by the Chief of Quisah. I took my station in the same place on which I stood the preceding day. Korinchi and his people soon made their appearance, and I commenced divine service, by giving out some verses of the hymn,—

"Plunged in a gulf of dark despair," &c.

I had a goodly number of our people with me, who assisted in singing the praises of God. After a short prayer in Fanti by my interpreter, we sung the first verse of the hymn,—

"Lord over all, if thou hast made,
Hast ransom'd, every soul of man;"

after which I preached from Mark xvi. 15; when I explained more fully the nature of the Gospel, and gave them many arguments to prove the divine origin of the Bible. Solemnity sat on their faces, and the deepest attention was paid to the grand and awful truths which were laid before them: every minute almost did they utter a hearty *Eou*, "Yes," by way of giving their assent. At the conclusion of the sermon, Korinchi and his Captains said it was a "good palaver." On my telling them, that I had not laid before them a thousandth part of the sublime truths contained in the Bible, they said they should like to hear more of them; and especially what *Yankumpon*, "God," liked, and what he disliked; and seemed much pleased when I told them, that I should be happy to preach to them again whenever they pleased.

Knowing their jealous disposition, I thought it prudent to make them as sensible as I possibly could of the disinterested character of my Mission. I therefore told them, that it was my love to God, and the souls of my fellow-creatures, which caused me to leave my happy native land, and come among them; and that this love was the fruit of my having embraced Christianity, as I was once as ignorant of practical religion as they were, and did not feel the desire to benefit my fellow-men, until I had repented of my own sins, and turned to God. On hearing this, they were struck with astonishment, and said that the religion which I thus recommended to them from practical experience was good. There were about five hundred persons present.

Monday, 11th.—I am still detained at Quisah, waiting for an answer from the King of Ashânti, to the information sent him the other day concerning me. I find this delay to be a heavy trial, as I am anxious to return to our societies on the coast as early as possible. I trust, however, that it is the Lord's doing, and will be productive of future good.

Tuesday, 12th.—The *harmattan* is very strong, and the air so cold, that the thermometer has been down as low as 66° (Fahrenheit) at eight o'clock in the morning for several days past. This I find very trying to my constitution; my lodging-place being a small hut, or open shed, with a thatch of Palm-leaves, so thin, that I can see through it in many places. I am continually taking cold; but I trust that I shall be preserved for usefulness in this dangerous climate. I often see many of my people shivering with cold at six o'clock in the morning, much more than I have seen in England in the month of January. To-day Korinchi again sent for me; and shortly after my arrival at his residence, a messenger arrived from Kumási with the King's compliments; also a present of nine ackies of gold-dust, £2. 5*s*. currency, and a promise from the King, that he would send for me in a few days, during which time the messenger is to stay with me. Korinchi having made me the offer of waiting the King's pleasure at Fomunah, instead of Quisah, I readily embraced it, as Fomunah is much larger, more open, and healthy. I consequently removed to Fomunah in the evening.

Wednesday, 13th.—Since my arrival in Ashánti, the Fetishmen seem to have taken the alarm. A day or two back, the Quisah Fetishman said, that the town was in danger of being destroyed by fire, and that they must make Fetish to ward off the danger. On my way to Fomunah on Sunday last, I saw the path literally strewed with offerings to Fetish; consisting of boiled eggs, beads, plantains, &c. This is the work of those wretched Fetishmen, whose employment is to impose on the ignorance and weakness of the poor deluded people.

Thursday, 14th.—At eight, A. M., Korinchi sent to my lodgings, requesting me to pay him a visit. I immediately repaired to his house, where I found him seated with his Captains, ready to receive me. He informed me that they were waiting to hear me explain some of the truths of Christianity. Knowing the injurious effects of talking much in this climate with an empty stomach, I asked Korinchi to excuse me for a few minutes, while I stepped home to take my breakfast, which I was about to do at the moment he sent for me. After hastily doing this, I again repaired to Korinchi's house, and conversed with him and his Captains on the doctrine of the general resurrection;

PREPARATION OF A FETISH.

on which subject their minds seemed very much confused. By divine assistance I succeeded in convincing them of the possibility of such an event; after which I directed their attention to the doctrine of future rewards and punishments.

Friday, 15th.—About eight, A. M., Korinchi sent to make every inquiry respecting my Mission, as he was about to send another messenger to the King; upon which I furnished him with all necessary information, and handed to him my letter of recommendation from President Maclean to the King, with which he despatched the messenger in the course of the day.

Saturday, 16th.—At eight, A. M., Korinchi paid me a visit at my lodgings. I swung my hammock (having repaired it, so as again to be fit for use) under a large Banyan-tree in the principal street in the town; where a group of the natives soon collected around me. I fell into conversation with them concerning some superstitious offerings, which consisted of soup made with the palm-nut, eggs, &c., which I saw preparing near me, for a present to the Fetish. Upon my questioning them on the subject, they seemed confident that it was just and right for them to do so; but when I pointed out to them the folly of these heathenish observances, &c., they seemed convinced of it, and said their Fetish-men told them nonsense, and deceived them.

Sunday, 17th.—Blessed be God, through whose good providence I was born in a Christian country!

> "Thine 's the sabbath-peace, my land!
> And thine the guarded hearth."

How amazing the difference between England and Ashánti! Here no village bell, sweetly sounding "across the daisied mead," invites the humble Christian to the sanctuary of God! Here (it may be presumed) no hymn of praise ascends from the natives of this country to their Creator; no house of prayer is seen standing with its doors wide open, inviting man to share in its sacred immunities! May the happy day soon arrive, when even over this sanguinary country, the olive-wand of sacred peace shall be triumphantly extended!

In the afternoon I sent to inform Korinchi that we were about to commence the worship of God at my lodgings; and that I should be glad if he would join us. He immediately came, attended by his Captains, &c. God was present with us, by the gracious influence of his Holy Spirit on our hearts, and the minds of many present appeared deeply impressed with the solemnity of the service.

Monday, 18th.—In the evening, one of Korinchi's Captains made me a present of a pot of palm-wine.

Tuesday, 19th.—Last night a sister of Korinchi died, after a long sickness. Her death was announced by the firing of muskets, and the "mourners going about the streets." When an Ashánti of any distinction dies, several of the deceased's slaves are sacrificed. This horrible custom originates in some shadowy ideas of a future state of existence; in which they imagine that those who have departed hence, stand in need of food, clothing, &c., as in the present world; and that as a vast number of concubines, slaves, &c., are the chief marks of superiority among them here, so it must also be in a future state. Accordingly, as I walked out early in the morning, I saw the mangled corpse of a poor female slave, who had been beheaded during the night, lying in the public street. It was partially covered with a common mat, (made from the stem of the Plantain-tree,) and, as this covering is unusual, I concluded that it was thrown over, in order to hide it from my view. In the course of the day I saw groups of the natives dancing round this victim of superstitious cruelty, with numerous frantic gestures, and who seemed to be in the very zenith of their happiness. In the evening I was informed, that as Korinchi and his Captains did not wish me to see any more headless trunks lying in the streets, they have not sacrificed others during the day, but would most probably do so in the night. I am happy to say, however, that I could not ascertain that any more sacrifices were made. That only one person was immolated, I believe, resulted entirely from my presence in the town.

In the afternoon I received a present of palm-wine, plantains, yams, and pine-apples, from one of the King of Ashánti's sisters, who is paying a visit in a distant croom, her place of general residence being Kumási. Throughout the day, I saw females fantastically dressed, with their faces and shoulders daubed over with red ochre, parading the town as mourners for Korinchi's sister.

Friday, 22d.—My interpreter informed me, that, as he was going from Fomunah to Quisah, he saw the mangled trunk of the poor female slave lying in a ditch, a few hundred yards from the town; and that at the time she was beheaded, she was in the prime of her days Thus exposed to public view, in a ditch near the common road, the corpse, deprived of its head, must lie and putrefy, unless the turkey-buzzards, or some beast of prey, devour it.

O thou God of Missions, who willest not that any should perish, but that all should come to the knowledge of the truth, have mercy upon these benighted people! May thine everlasting Gospel speedily spread itself through the length and breadth of this land, and chase the demon from these his dark abodes of cruelty!

Saturday, 23d.—Early in the morning, the Fetish

tune was played through the town, to collect the people together for the finishing of the "custom" for Korinchi's sister. In the afternoon, nearly all the principal persons in the town were dressed in their gayest attire: a large group of them was collected under the Fetish-tree, to see and hear the Fetishman, while he made his orations, and danced to the sound of several drums, which were played by females. The appearance of the Fetishman was very much like that of a "clown:" his face was daubed with white clay; he had a large iron chain hanging around his neck,* which seemed to be worn as a necklace; around his legs were tied bunches of Fetish; and he held in his hand an immense knife, about fifteen inches long, and two and a half broad. Sometimes he danced with many frantic gestures; and at other times stood, gazing around him with every indication of a vacant mind. While I was at a distance, looking at him, he set out, and ran to a distance of about a hundred yards. Anxious to keep him in sight, I walked forward, past a small shed, which would have concealed him from me, and saw him standing with a musket at his shoulder, taking aim at a turkey-buzzard on a tree hard by. Having fired without hitting his mark, he returned to the tree from whence he started, and began to make a speech to the people.

It is at these public meetings, that such men deliver to the poor credulous people, the messages which they pretend to have received from the Fetish; which messages are esteemed by the great body of the inhabitants as sterling truth. O man, into what an awful state of degradation art thou fallen!

---

* I tried some time afterwards to get this chain of the Fetishman as a curiosity, but could not succeed.

Sunday, 24th.—At a quarter past seven, A. M., I conducted divine service at my quarters. Several of our members from Cape Coast (who are trading in the neighbourhood) attended. During the service, Korinchi came to pay me a visit, but did not stay until the conclusion. He looked wild and confused, having been up during the whole of the last night, finishing the "custom" for his sister. I believe that almost every person in the town was up also. All whom I saw, as I walked out in the evening, had a sottish appearance. At half-past four, I again conducted divine service at my place of abode. To screen myself from the oppressive heat of the day, I went to my usual spot for retirement, on the skirts of the forest, intending to swing my hammock to some of the trees, and remain there until towards evening. As I approached the place, I found that the air had a putrid smell; which reminded me, that I was not far from the ditch where the body of the sacrificed female was thrown: prudence, therefore, obliged me to return, as I could find no other place sufficiently quiet on the one hand, and free from large ants and snakes on the other.

Tuesday, 26th.—I went into the forest, where I saw some large monkeys, and several kinds of birds of the most exquisitely-beautiful plumage.

Wednesday, 27th.—I had a long conversation with some of the natives on the subject of the general resurrection, and of the injury done to their country by human sacrifices. Many of them seem to have an utter dislike to this horrid practice; while others are sunk into such a state of apathy, that they are altogether indifferent about it, though their lives, as well as others', are continually in danger.

Thursday, 28th.—I paid Korinchi a visit, and reasoned with him closely on the painful consequences of human sacrifices, and "customs" for the dead. He readily acknowledged the evil, and expressed himself ready to abolish it, if he were at full liberty so to do; but he feared the King. The only reason he could give for making "customs" in addition to human sacrifices, for the dead, was, that they felt very unhappy when they lost their relatives and friends, and were glad to have recourse to drunkenness, or any thing which would drive gloomy thoughts from their minds for a season. As he thus gave me a good opportunity of directing him to the only refuge for a troubled mind,—the consolations of true religion,—I told him, God alone was able to sustain under afflictions and bereavements. He seemed affected with what I said to him. In the evening he sent me a present, consisting of a sheep, yams, and plantains.

March 1st, Friday.—Early last evening the Fetish-man called many of the people together, and continued beating his drum all night; the noise of which disturbed me so much, that I had little sleep; consequently, I arose this morning so unwell, that I was under the necessity of retiring to bed immediately after breakfast.

Saturday, 2d.—To-day another human victim was sacrificed, on account of the death of a person of rank. As I was going out of the town, in the cool of the evening, I saw the poor creature lying on the ground. The head was severed from the body, and lying at a short distance from it: several large turkey-buzzards were feasting on the wounds, and rolling the head in the dust. He appeared to be about eighteen years of age; a strong, healthy youth, who might, in all probability, have lived forty, fifty, or even sixty years longer. As I returned into the town, I found that they had dragged the body to a short distance, and put it into the ditch where the female was thrown the other day. On my

HUMAN SACRIFICE.

conversing with the natives concerning the horrible nature of human sacrifices, they said, they did not like them, and wished they could be done away. While the body was lying in the public street, many of the people were looking on, with the greatest indifference: indeed, they are so familiar with these awful and bloody scenes, that they think as little of them, yea, not so much, as they would of seeing a dead sheep, monkey, or dog.

Sunday, 3d.—About half-past seven, A. M., I conducted divine service at my lodgings, and also at half-past four, P. M. God was in the midst of us.

Tuesday, 5th.—This afternoon I received letters, containing some very interesting intelligence concerning our societies on the coast. Blessed be God, all is well with them.

Thursday, 14th.—As I was returning home from my afternoon exercise, (a walk in the forest,) I saw a splendid species of *Epidendrum* clinging to a tree, at a considerable height from the ground. Anxious to obtain it, I sent a person up the tree for that purpose, who, while in the act of pulling it off, espied a venomous snake in a hole nearly close to his hand. It did not, however, attempt to bite him, (though one of the worst kind of snakes,) and the man, having obtained the plant, descended in safety. The country abounds in such reptiles.

CHAPTER II.

APPETITE FOR BLOOD—PREACHING, AND FURTHER PROCEEDINGS AT FOMUNAH—OBSTACLES TO ADVANCING FURTHER IN ASHANTI—RETURN TO QUISAH.

SATURDAY, 16th.—The Ashántis are very fond of eating the blood of beasts. This I learned from a scene which I witnessed this morning. Having agreed to purchase part of an ox, which was brought into the town for sale, I felt curiosity to see their method of slaughtering. Soon after break of day, the owner sent to inform me, that they were ready to slaughter the ox; but as I was afraid of the damps, (much rain having fallen during the night,) I sent my interpreter to see it killed, who returned to inform me, that the beast was too strong for them; and that, instead of tying it down, and cutting the throat, they would be obliged to shoot it. I put on my cloak, and repaired to the place where the beast was, to see how they would proceed: it was standing about twenty yards from the man who was preparing to shoot it. The first shot was fired without effect; the second wounded it in the shoulder; which they no sooner perceived, than forty or fifty men surrounded it; some caught it by the horns, others by the tail, and endeavoured to drag it along the ground to a convenient place for cutting it up. The beast, however, soon recovered strength, and, rising up, kicked one man down, and made the others escape in every direction. On seeing this, I loaded my fowling-piece with a ball, and shot it in the head, which soon arrested its progress. It was no sooner on the ground, than the greatest uproar ensued. A number of them (ten or twelve) stood over the animal with immense knives, which they flourished around them, while quarrelling about the blood; a few of them wished to cut off the head immediately, while the others were desirous of catching as much blood as they could before it died. I verily believe, for the sake of the blood, they would have allowed the ox to bleed and suffer for half an hour, if I had not been present urging them to kill it. On inquiring why they clamoured for the blood in such a manner, I learned that they are fond of it, and make stews with it. Their chief food, however, is soup made from the palm-nut, boiled with dried fish, or the flesh of the monkey; to which they add a kind of pudding, (native name, *foofoo*,) made with the green fruit of the Plantain-tree, (*Musa Paradisiaca*,) which they first boil, and then pound with a large wooden pestle in a mortar. These mills are to be heard going in almost every house, during certain hours of the day. This work is generally performed by females, one of them using the pestle, and the other keeping the food in a lump, by plying it with her hands, that the pestle may act more effectually. The same method is practised in Fanti; but the Fantis are not obliged to use the Plantain so much as the Ashántis, as they have plenty of Indian corn, (*Zea Mays*,) with which they make both bread and puddings. The Ashántis have a tolerable supply of sheep, which they seldom use for any other purposes, than making sacrifices to Fetish. They have also much fine poultry, which they keep for the sake of the eggs, abundance of which they also offer to Fetish. While travelling through the sombre gloom of the forest, the crowing of chanticleer, a sure indication that a croom is at hand, is very pleasing. The average price of a fowl in Ashánti is 1*s*. 3*d*., of an ox £5, and of a sheep, £1. 15*s*.

Sunday, 17th.—At half-past nine, A. M., I conducted divine service at my lodgings: after which I felt the air so cold, (occasioned by a strong *harmattan*,*) that I was obliged to put on a warm dress. In the afternoon I again conducted divine service, and preached from Matthew xix. 17: "If thou wilt enter into life, keep the commandments." Korinchi and several of his Captains were present, and appeared much excited during the sermon; but more especially during that part, in which I explained to them the Commandments contained in the Decalogue. They often stopped me in my discourse, to ask questions, among which was the following:—"Is the offering of human sacrifice murder?" I answered, "It is even so; and you will henceforth be left without excuse, if you persist in that horrible practice." After I had directed their attention to the excellency of the Ten Commandments, especially describing the temporal and spiritual blessings, which the consecration of the Christian Sabbath is calculated to introduce among mankind, I proposed to them the following question: "Who are the happiest persons; those who conscientiously keep God's commandments, or those who wilfully break them?" They answered, without hesitation, "Those who keep them;" and I verily believe, that this answer was given in sincerity, as they appeared to be deeply impressed with the solemnity of the discourse.

Monday, 18th.—"How excellent is thy loving-kindness, O God!" Truly God is good. Although I am in a sickly clime, and exposed to many peculiar dangers, yet how trifling are my sufferings! Indeed, they are not worthy to be mentioned. "Bless the Lord, O my soul!"

* A keen easterly wind which prevails in December, and the early months of the year.—Ed.

Tuesday, 19th.—Korinchi came to pay me a visit, when I embraced the opportunity of refreshing his memory concerning the discourse which he heard on Sunday. Remembering the Fourth Commandment, he said, he had always thought that God had appointed different days, to be kept sacred by different nations; such as one day for the Ashántis, another for the Fantis, another for the Wassaws, &c.; and if so, the keeping of the Christian Sabbath was not binding upon the Ashántis. I told him, there is now but one day which God has consecrated, and set apart for his special worship; and that the observance of that day is binding upon all who are favoured with information concerning it.

Wednesday, 20th.—This morning Korinchi paid me another visit, when the subject on which we conversed yesterday, was resumed. During our conversation, he appeared more deeply convinced of the truth, than he did yesterday, and requested me to accompany him to his residence. After we had taken our seats in his house, our former topic of discourse was discussed. While we were thus engaged, several of his Captains, and the King's messenger, (a respectable old man,) joined us. As some of them thought yet, that the Christian Sabbath was not intended for them, I asked them to prove the truth of what Korinchi stated yesterday, namely, "That God had set apart different days for different nations." They said, that there was a person in the interior, who had lived ever since the creation of the world, and that he knew these things, and could prove them. I told them, I should very much like to see him. On their observing, that they feared they would expose themselves to much danger, as a nation, by giving up their Fetish days, and keeping the Sabbath, I endeavoured to convince them, that their fears were groundless, and that so far from bringing a curse upon the nation, God would abundantly bless them; and referred them to England, as a proof of my assertion. I told them what England was once, in its state of heathen barbarism, and of the mighty change which has been experienced since the introduction of Christianity. This argument was too strong for them, and they gave up the point.

Thursday, 21st.—This morning I paid Korinchi a visit, and found him seated in company with several of his Captains, and the King's messenger. I entered into conversation with them concerning my long detention at Fomunah, and the importance of my seeing the King, and returning to Cape Coast, before the commencement of the rainy season. I told them, that I fancied some bad persons about the King, were endeavouring to frighten him, by telling him that I was come into the country as a spy; and that it would be my duty to turn aside, and carry the glad tidings of salvation to another nation, if I found them averse to receiving the truth. At this they seemed very much concerned, and said, they felt no disposition to oppose the introduction of Christianity among them, and that they believed the King would also be glad to hear the truths of the Gospel, and that he would wish me to stay a long time in Kumási, after my arrival and first interview.

In the afternoon, I rambled through the thicket to the summit of a distant hill, where one of the most splendid pieces of scenery I ever saw, burst on my view. The bush on the summit being rather low, I had an opportunity of viewing the surrounding country, in some directions, to an extent of several miles. Down the sloping sides of the hill, the splendid Plantain-tree was luxuriating, and waving its beautiful foliage before the balmy zephyrs which whispered around. Then followed the delightful vale, winding to the right and left, studded with gigantic Silk-cotton trees, *Acaciæ*

Mimosæ, with an endless variety of climbers, (chiefly papilionaceous,) running up and reclining on the top-most branches, descending and embracing the earth, and again ascending to the top,—that portion of their stems between the ground and the high branches of the trees, appearing like immense cables.* Beyond the valley were seen other hills in the distance, clothed with most beautiful verdure to their very summits, except here and there a small spot, cleared by the natives, for the purpose of cultivating yams, &c. While I stood gazing on this scene of splendid, though wild luxuriance, "I felt an inward bliss spring o'er my heart." Even the Fantis who were with me, whose ideas of the beauties of nature are generally bounded by the skirts of the forest which girt their little crooms, expressed their participation in the satisfaction which I enjoyed, by exclaiming, in the native tongue, *Oya fieu doodo*, "It is very handsome." "These are thy glorious works, Parent of good! Almighty." But, alas! how painful is the reflection, "Man seems the only growth that dwindles here!" What dark lines on these fair colours are the habitations of cruelty, superstition, and death! In vain do the pretty Jessamine, (*Jasminum Gracile*,) and other odoriferous flowers, perfume the air, while man murders his brother, and taints the atmosphere with the noxious effluvia arising from the putrefying carcase of the mangled victim of his superstition and cruelty.

O thou Almighty Being! hasten the day when even sanguinary Ashánti shall be evangelized; when its repentant inhabitants "shall go out" of captivity "with

* These stems are so strong, that a man may climb them with the greatest ease and safety. In more than one instance, I have sent a man up to procure some of the numerous *Orchideæ*, growing on the large trees.

joy, and be led forth with peace;" when these "mountains and hills shall break forth before them into singing;" and, when "all the trees of the field shall clap their hands."

During this interesting ramble, I found a pretty variety of *Amaryllis Albus* in full bloom. I also saw a tree, or rather a shrub, at a short distance, which I could not conveniently approach, on account of the thick underwood, but which appeared, by its almost naked stem, and beautiful scarlet flowers, to be a species of *Crythrina.* At the foot of the hill is a small rivulet, overhung by trees covered with Mosses and Ferns, some of the latter being very fine.

Friday, 22d.—I informed Korinchi that I should soon be under the necessity of returning to the coast. In answer to this, he said, that he expected a messenger down from Kumási on Tuesday; but was not quite certain of his coming so early. I consequently agreed to wait until after Sunday, before I made any arrangements for returning.

Saturday, 23d.—How true and faithful is the Lord! In what a large degree do I realize the truth of the promise, "As thy days, so shall thy strength be!" Notwithstanding my long detention in this place, I feel no tedium:—

"With me no melancholy void,
No period lingers unemploy'd."

Sunday, 24th.—At half-past nine, A.M., I read prayers and preached from Prov. xii. 21. Our little congregation was very attentive. In the afternoon I held a long conversation with several Heathens and Christians, (who are travelling with me,) concerning the salvation of their souls. It was a solemn and delightful service, and lasted about two hours. In the evening I administered the holy sacrament of the Lord's Supper to the members of our society. In this sacred ordinance I found my soul strengthened; and I believe many felt it to be a refreshing service. A heavy tornado was raging around us, and the lightning was glaring into our little sanctuary; but while the elements were raging, we were in peaceful and happy serenity.

Monday, 25th.—I called on Korinchi, and informed him, that I had made up my mind to commence my return on Wednesday morning, if I did not see a messenger from the King before that time. As he appeared careless about what I said, I began to suspect him of a treacherous intention to keep me longer on the way than was really necessary, and therefore deemed it prudent to teach him, that I would not be detained and trifled with in such a manner. Consequently, in the course of the day, I packed my boxes, and put myself in a state of readiness for returning. In the evening he (Korinchi) came with his two linguists and some of his Captains, to intreat me to wait another day or two, before I made up my mind to leave; which I agreed to do, on the condition, that he should provide a messenger, who should accompany the Sergeant to Kumási, with a letter which I intended to write to the King, on the following morning; and after he had used every means to persuade me to the contrary, he consented with much reluctance.

Tuesday, 26th.—Early on this day I wrote a letter to the King, ordered the Sergeant to prepare for starting to Kumási, and sent to Korinchi to inquire if his messenger were ready. In answer to this, he said, he had sent to Quisah for the King's path-keepers, and as soon as they arrived, he would consult with them, and let me have a messenger. Shortly after this, I sent a second time, and received the same answer. Feeling satisfied that this delay was intended for the purpose of frustrating my design, I thought it prudent to act with as much promptitude as the circumstance of the case would allow, and therefore repaired to Korinchi's house, and inquired for him, but was informed that he was not within. Every thing which I saw confirmed my suspicions. I went from thence to the residence of the King's messenger, and inquired of him the reason of the delay; in answer to which he said, that they were waiting for the linguists belonging to other Chiefs on the way to Kumási, to speak with them also, before they prepared a messenger. At this I felt displeased, seeing plainly that all this was said on purpose to hinder me from sending to the King, or from going either backward or forward. I returned to my lodgings, and ordered my people to make ready for going to Cape Coast immediately; and then repaired to Korinchi's house again, taking the precaution of sending one of my attendants towards the back-door of his house, to see if he would attempt to make his escape from me in that direction, as I went in at the front.* When I arrived at the door, I saw one of the linguists, who said Korinchi was not within. Not satisfied with this answer, I stepped into the house, before any one could get to the Chief to tell him that I was coming; when I found him leisurely taking his breakfast. I upbraided him for his unjust conduct, and requested a messenger as soon as he had finished his repast. On his promising to settle the matter immediately, I withdrew into another apartment, and waited for him nearly half an hour: I then sent my interpreter to see if he was ready, who

* As the despotic nature of the Government under which this people live, often places their lives in danger, all the Ashánti Chiefs, Captains, &c., build their houses in such a manner, that they can readily escape at one door, the moment in which a person enters another.

returned to inform me, that Korinchi had finished his breakfast, and had escaped. Finding that he was trying to get the mastery over me, I saw the necessity of securing his compliance with my wishes, by coming to the determination, that if he would not let messengers go forwards, I would immediately return. Accordingly I sent to one of the linguists to inform him of my intention, returned to my lodgings, and began to send my people off with the luggage. While I was busily engaged in doing this, one of the linguists came, and begged of me to stop; promising that a messenger should be immediately despatched to Kumási. I answered, "Let me see him ready to commence his journey without delay, or I will soon be out of the town." He then left, saying he would get one immediately; but I did not believe him, and therefore continued sending off my luggage. He came again, saying, "The messenger is nearly ready." I answered, "Let me see him:" but none came. Having sent off all my people, informing them where I wished them to wait for me on the road, I again walked to Korinchi's house, to take my leave of him: he appeared stupid, brutal, and sullen, and would not give me his hand: I consequently turned from him, and waited a moment to tell the King's messenger I was going. Before I parted with him, I asked whether he did not think forty-six days a sufficient length of time for me to wait patiently, especially as I was getting short of provisions, and the rainy season was fast approaching. He candidly acknowledged that I had been detained too long, and that he could not blame me for returning. I had proceeded but a short distance on my way, when Korinchi sent, begging me to stop and speak with him; to which message I thought it right to pay no attention.

When I arrived at Quisah, I found my people waiting

for me in the street; and I again desired them to proceed. While so doing, the Chief (one of Korinchi's Captains) came to entreat me to stay a day or two at Quisah. This I should have had no objection to do, had I not been aware that it was a scheme of Korinchi, devised on purpose to hinder me from proceeding homewards: being aware of this, I proceeded, and began to ascend the high hill, which separates the Ashánti and Asín countries. When about half way up the hill, one of Korinchi's linguists came running after me, entreating me to return, saying that his master was very sorry for what he had done; that if I would go back, the messenger should be provided instantly; and that he should travel to Kumási during the night by torch-light:* but as I thought he was not sufficiently frightened, I still proceeded on my way. Korinchi no sooner found out his mistake, in supposing that I would allow myself to be played with, than he became very much alarmed, and applied to a Fanti residing in Quisah, whom I knew well, entreating him to follow after me, and to tell me, that he sincerely begged my pardon, and hoped I would forgive him, and return; and that he would send messengers to conduct me back. Notwithstanding this, I still went forward, and took up my lodgings for the night in a small croom, about nine miles and a half from Fomunah. I had scarcely arranged my people for the night, when several messengers arrived from Fomunah and Quisah, (among whom were Korinchi's two linguists,) entreating me to return in the morning.

The croom in which I lodged was very small, containing about eight or nine little huts, scarcely affording us shelter from a tornado, which commenced soon after

* Travelling this road in the dark is very dangerous, on account of the serpents and panthers which infest the country.

our arrival. The hut which I had chosen to sleep in, was little more than six feet square. Into this place I received the messengers, to screen them from the rain, and to hear their tale. They represented Korinchi as very unhappy because I had gone from the town; * and said that all their lives would be in danger, if I left the country. They also reminded me, that I came into the country on purpose to promote their happiness; and hoped I would think of the thousands of their fellow-countrymen who would be benefited by the introduction of Christianity among them, rather than of the insult which Korinchi had offered me. These were, of course, my own feelings: personally I cared nothing about that man's bad conduct; but I knew very well, that if they saw anything in my behaviour like indecision, they would give me a great deal of trouble, and consequently thought I had better put a stop to their trifling at once. I therefore continued to conceal as much as possible any wish on my part to return with them, and told them, I would still proceed homeward, until I had crossed the Prah, and entered Fanti; which I thought of doing, and there waiting for a message from the King.

Fearing lest I should put this design into execution the following morning, they said, that if I would return, Korinchi would allow me to proceed to within a few miles of Kumasi. This satisfied me that he was at last sincerely sorry for what he had done, and that he would behave better for the future. I now agreed to go back, on the condition that they (the messengers) should provide people to carry my luggage, so that my

* I believe this to have been the truth, as I found on my return that Korinchi had actually made "custom," and had sat up during the whole night, playing his drums, drinking, dancing, &c., on purpose to keep the thought of my departure out of his mind.

hammock-men might be at liberty to bear me to the base of the hill, as the journey on foot would otherwise have been exceedingly trying to me, on account of the immense hill over which I must walk, it being too steep to admit of my being carried over it.* To this they readily consented; and further, as a proof of their sincere anxiety to get me back, they were ready even to carry my luggage themselves, thanking me very much for my kindness in returning with them.

* The labour of ascending this hill is so great, that I was obliged to clothe myself in flannel, to avoid taking cold from the violent perspiration, occasioned by exertion, being checked by the keen wind on the summit; which I had no sooner reached, than I found it necessary, in addition to the flannel, to wrap myself in a cloak.

CHAPTER III.

JOURNEY TO ASHANTI RESUMED — DUMPASI — AKWANKOWASI — EDUABIN— ESARGU—FRANFRAHAM—ENTRANCE INTO KUMASI—RECEPTION BY THE KING—HUMAN SACRIFICES—APOKO—TOWN OF KUMASI DESCRIBED.

WEDNESDAY, 27th.—Early after break of day, I returned with Korinchi's messengers, and had only been in the town half an hour, when a despatch arrived from the King, requesting me to proceed, and with him two or three persons whom Korinchi had expressly sent to Kumási as soon as he found me determined to go back, if I were not permitted to proceed. Korinchi having personally acknowledged his fault, I, of course, freely forgave him; and every thing was finally arranged for my starting for Kumási the following morning. Though Korinchi was evidently deserving of censure in this affair, I believe that much of his conduct arose from jealousy on the part of the King; who is not so much to be blamed, when we consider the confused notions which he must entertain concerning the real objects of a Missionary, together with the fact, that he is surrounded by Moors, whose great object would be, without doubt, to poison his mind, and to put a false construction on every thing connected with the idea of introducing Christianity into his dominions.

Thursday, 28th.—About eight, A. M., I commenced my journey, and travelled through a fine fertile country of hill and dale, full of luxuriant vegetation, and studded with immense Silk-cotton and other forest trees, covered with many varieties of *Orchideæ* and *Cryptogamiæ*. At nine, A. M., I halted in a pretty little town called Dumpási, to take my breakfast. I had no sooner taken my seat, than a large group of the natives collected around me; but on my taking a telescope to look at some *Orchideæ* on a distant tree, they all began to run away, supposing that I was going to shoot at them.

At half-past three I reached the small town of Akwankowási, and took lodgings for the night.

Friday, 29th.—At a quarter past eight, A. M., I proceeded on my way through a country very similar to that over which I passed yesterday, crossing several small rivers, the largest of which was about nine yards broad, and three feet deep. About half-past four, P. M., I passed through Eduabin, one of the largest towns I have hitherto seen in Ashanti; but in a very dilapidated state, many of the houses being tenantless, and tumbling down. At half-past five, P. M., we reached the small croom of Esargu, about nine miles distant from Kumási, having had a long and trying day's journey, which had tired the carriers, &c., so much, that several of them appeared quite exhausted. As for myself, I am mercifully blessed with extraordinary strength, so that I could have proceeded several miles farther, though I had already walked many, in order to rest the hammock-men. A Missionary passing up to Kumási, is so strange an occurrence, that nearly all the people in the different towns and crooms through which I go, come out to see me; and so totally ignorant are they of Christianity, or rather, of any reasonable way of worshipping God, that they actually run away, when they see us engaging in that solemn duty. On my arrival at this place, a female relative of the King brought me some palm-wine in a calabash; and being very thirsty, I took a hearty draught. It was, I think, the best palm-wine I have tasted since I have been in Africa. Many of the natives are truly kind. Every day I receive presents from some of them, consisting of palm-wine, yams, plantains, bananas, ground-nuts, &c. The banana is a delicious fruit, and not so likely to cause indisposition as some other fruits.

Saturday, 30th.—No travelling to-day. Preparing for the Sabbath, and for starting forward, immediately after the arrival of another message of invitation from the King. I do not expect to leave this place until Monday morning, the King being fully aware, that I will not travel on the Sabbath-day.

Sunday, 31st.—At half-past eight, A.M., I conducted divine service. During the day, which was excessively hot, I saw troops passing up to Kumási, from different parts of the country. The presence of these soldiers, together with a heavy tornado in the evening, hindered us from holding any afternoon or evening service. About six, P.M., a messenger arrived to inform me, that His Majesty wished me to proceed early the following morning.

April 1st, Monday.—Throughout the night I was disturbed by the noise made by the troops as they passed up to the capital. At four, A.M., we commenced our journey. The morning was so very moist, that a thick November fog in England could scarcely equal it; notwithstanding which, the heat was so great, that I could scarcely bear a light Mackintosh thrown over me, which was necessary to keep out the damps, though I was only clothed in a light linen dress.

About eight, A.M., we reached Franfraham, a small croom, about a mile and a half from Kumási, (built for the accommodation of strangers travelling to the capital,) having halted an hour, at least, on the road. Here I took some refreshment, and waited for another invitation from the King. While we remained, we held a prayer-meeting, for the purpose of imploring the blessing of the God of Missions upon our undertaking.

For several days past I have felt an indescribable sensation, best known, I presume, to those whose awful employment it is to bear the standard of the Cross, "to proclaim the acceptable year of the Lord, and the day of vengeance of our God." "Simon, Simon, behold, Satan hath desired to have you, that he may sift you as wheat; but I have prayed for thee that thy faith fail not." "Lo, I am with you alway, even unto the end."

At two, P.M., a messenger arrived from the King, requesting me to proceed as early as possible. I immediately dressed myself; and while so doing, three others arrived, each bearing a gold sword, requesting me to hasten forward. I then advanced towards the town, preceded by the messengers and some soldiers bearing arms. Having reached the outskirts, we halted under a large tree, and there waited for another royal invitation. In a short time, His Majesty's chief linguist, Apoko, came in a palanquin, shaded by an immense umbrella, and accompanied by messengers bearing canes nearly covered with gold, to take charge of my luggage, and to see it safely lodged in the residence intended for me. All these things being properly arranged, another messenger arrived, accompanied by troops, and men bearing large umbrellas, who requested me to proceed to the market-place. "The King's commandment" being "urgent," we pushed along with speed, preceded by a band of music. As soon as we arrived at the market-place, I got out of my travelling chair, walked through the midst of an immense concourse of persons, a narrow path being kept clear for me, and paying my respects to the King and his numerous Chiefs and Captains, who were seated on wooden chairs, richly decorated with brass and gold, under the shade of their splendid umbrellas, some of them large enough to screen twelve or fourteen persons from the burning rays of the sun, crowned with images of beasts covered with gold, and surrounded by their troops and numerous attendants. I was occupied for half an hour in walking slowly through the midst of this immense assembly, touching my hat and waving my hand, except before the King, in whose presence I of course stood for a moment uncovered. I then took my seat at a distance, accompanied by my people and several respectable Fanti traders, who are staying in the town, to receive the compliments of the King, &c., according to their usual custom. After I was seated, the immense mass began to be in motion: many of the Chiefs first passed me in succession, accompanied by their numerous retinue, several of them cordially shaking me by the hand. Then came the officers of the King's household, his Treasurer, Steward, &c., attended by their people; some bearing on their heads massive pieces of silver-plate, others carrying in their hands gold swords and canes, native chairs and buffets, neatly carved and almost covered with gold and silver, and tobacco-pipes richly decorated with the same precious materials. Amidst this ostentatious display, I saw what was calculated to harrow up the strongest and most painful feelings,—the royal executioners, bearing the blood-stained stools on which hundreds, and perhaps thousands, of human victims have been sacrificed by decapitation, and also the large *death-drum*, which is beaten at the moment when the fatal knife severs the head from the body, the very sound of which conveys a thrill of horror.* This rude instrument, connected with

* The language of this drum is understood by the natives whenever they are within hearing; so that they are well aware of the moment when a sacrifice is made, as though they were on the

which are most dreadful associations, was literally covered with dried clots of blood, and decorated with the jaw-bones and skulls of human victims. Then followed the King, Quako Duah, under the shade of three splendid umbrellas, the cloth of which was silk-velvet of different colours, supported by some of his numerous attendants. The display of gold which I witnessed, as His Majesty passed, was astonishing. After the King, followed other Chiefs, and lastly the main body of the troops. This immense procession occupied an hour and a half in passing before me. There were several Moors in the procession, but they made by no means a conspicuous appearance. While I was sitting to receive the compliments of some of the first Chiefs who passed, His Majesty made me a present of some palm-wine.

I suppose the number of persons which I saw collected together exceeded forty thousand, including a great number of females. The wrists of some of the Chiefs were so heavily laden with golden ornaments, that they rested their arms on the shoulders of some of their attendants.

The appearance of this procession was exceedingly grand and imposing. The contrast between the people themselves, and their large umbrellas, seventy in number, and of various colours, which they waved up and down in the air, together with the dark green foliage of the large Banyan-trees, under and among which they passed, formed a scene of that novel and extraordinary character, which I feel unable to describe.

---

spot. While the King was making sacrifices during the "custom" for his brother, I was in a distant part of the town, conversing with my interpreter, who, knowing the fatal meaning of the sound of the drum, said, "Hark! do you hear the drum? A sacrifice has just been made, and the drum says, 'King, I have killed him!'"

I gazed on this concourse of Heathens with feelings of sorrow and joy. I sorrowed in the reflection, that most (perhaps all) of them were totally ignorant of the great Author of their being, and without one ray of divine consolation, to cheer them amid the changing scenes of this visionary world. Are they laid on a bed of languishing? They have nothing to comfort them, or to buoy up their drooping spirits. Does death, which stalks through the land in such horrid forms, rob them of their friends? Alas! they must sorrow as men without hope! They do not see, with the eye of faith, the blood-bought throng standing in the presence of God, "clothed with white robes, and palms in their hands." Does death stare them in the face? Alas! they have no prospect beyond the grave, blooming with immortality! Is it not so? Tell it, ye murdered human victims, whose blood disfigures the streets, and whose putrefying bodies taint the air! Tell it, ye midnight revellers, who vainly strive to banish the agony from your hearts, by the fumes of intoxication! Tell it, ye carnivorous birds, and ye wild beasts of the forest, that feed on the mangled corpses of thousands of these victims of superstitious cruelty! And, lastly, tell it, ye human bones, that lie bleaching in the open day!

Have these poor sufferers no voice? no tale of woe to relate? Methinks I hear them crying to British Christians especially, "Come, pray come, and look on our unhappy country! See how it groans beneath the iron despotism of the prince of darkness! True, it is a beautiful country, its fertile soil produces an hundred fold! but what avails its beauty or fertility, when it is converted into one immense slaughter-house? O ye who enjoy the high blessings of Christianity, allow us to entreat you to direct your energies towards this scene of moral desolation!" Brooding in melancholy over the blood-stained wilds, fancy carries me to my native land, where, entering a well-known place in the metropolis, I hear the cause of Christian Missions advocated, in the presence of thousands, whose hearts burn with love towards their perishing fellow-creatures. I hear them speaking of unhappy, degraded Africa; of the pressing wants of its millions; and of the vital importance of increased exertions on the part of British Christians, for the extension of the blessings of Christianity among this mass of immortal men. I hear a Resolution moved and supported, that much more shall be immediately done for Africa; and especially for Guinea. Returning again to this immense field of labour, I feel encouraged to cry, "O ye dry bones, hear the word of the Lord!" "The captives of the mighty shall be taken away, and the prey of the terrible shall be delivered." Yea, "He that sitteth upon the circle of the earth, and the inhabitants thereof are as grasshoppers; that stretcheth out the heavens as a curtain, and spreadeth them out as a tent to dwell in," He hath said, "Ethiopia shall stretch out her hands unto God." "Enlarge the place of thy tent, and let them stretch forth the curtains of thine habitations; spare not, lengthen thy cords, and strengthen thy stakes. For thou shalt break forth on the right hand and on the left; and thy seed shall inherit the Gentiles, and make the desolate cities to be inhabited." O ye dry bones, hear the words of the Lord's people! Their prayer for you to God our Saviour is,—

"The servile progeny of Ham
Seize, as the purchase of thy blood."

Yes, for Africa they pray, and over Africa they weep! A brighter day is approaching; a day, when the death-drum shall give place to the heralds of the cross; and, instead of feeling the terror and dismay conveyed by the footsteps of the bloody executioner, the peaceful native shall exclaim, "How beautiful upon the mountains are the feet of him that bringeth good tidings, that publisheth peace, that bringeth good tidings of good, that publisheth salvation; that saith unto Zion, Thy God reigneth!"

"The watchmen join their voice,
And tuneful notes employ:
Jerusalem breaks forth in songs,
And deserts learn the joy."

The arduous duties of the day being over, I immediately repaired to my quarters; and, spreading a cloth upon the floor, sunk, tired and weary, into the arms of sleep.

Tuesday, 2d.—I rested, and arranged various things in my new apartments.

Wednesday, 3d.—This being the King's Fetish day, I heard nothing from him. Two Moors visited me, and told me they came from Mosu.

Thursday, 4th.—This morning the King sent his linguists (some of whom were heavily laden with golden ornaments) to make every inquiry as to my object in visiting him. I gave them all necessary information; but found much difficulty in making them understand me. And no wonder; for how can those who are buried in superstition, and who witness scarcely any thing, but scenes of cruelty arising from that superstition, form any just idea of the motives which stimulate the Christian Missionary to visit them? "O that they were wise, that they understood this!"

Friday, 5th.—Finding the place where I am located intensely hot, I sent my people into the forest to obtain materials for erecting a bower, to protect me from the burning rays of the sun.*

This morning I received information, that the King had lost one of his relations by death, and that, in consequence, four human victims were already sacrificed, and their mangled bodies lying in the streets. I therefore concluded that I should not have an opportunity of seeing the King for a day or two. Shortly afterwards I saw Apoko, the chief linguist, and told him, I was aware that there was bloody work going on, as I saw a number of large hawks and turkey-buzzards hovering over a certain spot, where I judged these poor creatures were lying. "Wheresoever the carcase is, there will the eagles be gathered together." He said it was even so, and, in consequence thereof, I should not have an opportunity of seeing the King to-day, and perhaps not to-morrow. I told him, that I did not like being confined to one place, in a low, unhealthy part of the town; and that I must walk out and take exercise, otherwise my health would suffer. I also said, that I was anxious to commence my journey home to the coast on Monday next. On hearing this, he went immediately to the King, and informed him of what I

* My lodgings were very small, containing about ten little sheds, of the average size of six feet by seven, each having only one opening, and that into a yard, about nine or ten feet square, in which no breeze could be felt. Surrounding one of these yards, there are generally from two to four of these sheds, the whole premises being connected by narrow doors leading out of one yard into another. In this contracted place I had about twenty persons; such as carriers, hammock-men, &c. And what tended to increase the heat was, that they were obliged to make their fires for dressing food, &c. This place, bad as it was, was one of the best that could be procured for me, unless I had gone up into the very heart of the town, which, for many reasons, would not have been prudent.

had stated; shortly after which, he returned, accompanied by two messengers, (one of them bearing in his hand an immense gold sword, to which was fastened a golden decanter, holding about a pint,) informing me, that His Majesty begged of me not to go out into the town to-day, as he was making a "custom" for a departed relative, and he knew Europeans did not like to see human sacrifices; that he did not wish to keep me from seeing his capital; that he was fully satisfied my object was to do good; and that he would see me as soon as the "custom" was over. I, of course, complied with his wishes, and made up my mind to wait patiently.

Throughout the day I heard the horrid sound of the death-drum, and was told in the evening, that about twenty-five human victims had been sacrificed, some in the town, and some in the surrounding villages; the heads of those killed in the villages being brought into the town in baskets. I fear there will be more of this awful work to-morrow.

Saturday, 6th.—This morning I again talked of going out into the capital, when Apoko informed me, that more sacrifices would be made during the day, and that I must not do so until to-morrow. I therefore remained where I was until the afternoon, when, finding myself in an unhealthy state for want of exercise, I insisted upon walking out at one end of the town for half an hour. In the evening I learned that several more human victims had been immolated during the day, but could not ascertain the exact number. The most accurate account I could obtain was, that fifteen more had suffered; making a total of FORTY, IN TWO DAYS!!

While speaking to Apoko, I did not fail to remind him, that the law of God forbids this fearful practice;

and that they were under great error, in supposing that the persons sacrificed would attend on the deceased relative of the King, in some other state of existence.

These poor victims were allowed to lie naked and exposed in the streets, until they began to decompose; and such is the callous state of mind in which the people live, that many were walking about, among the putrefying bodies, smoking their pipes, with amazing indifference.

Sunday, 7th.—At nine, A.M., I conducted divine service at my abode: many Ashántis were present, some of whom paid deep attention. At four, P.M., I again commenced the worship of God, but was compelled abruptly to close the service by a tornado.

Monday, 8th.—This morning His Majesty sent me a handsome present, consisting of a cow, a sheep, a pig, a quantity of palm-nuts, yams, and plantains, and one ounce and four ackies of gold-dust, (£5 currency,) also three ackies for my interpreter, and five ackies for my other attendants. The gold was brought in a golden blow-pan, weighing several ounces.

Having asked His Majesty to allow me to see the town to-day, he readily gave me liberty to go wherever I pleased. I therefore embraced the opportunity of looking over it, which occupied about an hour. The streets are large, and more clean and uniform than I have seen in any other native town since my arrival in Africa. The breadth of some of them is at least thirty yards, and the average length from three hundred to six hundred yards. The town is situated on a bed of granite; fragments of which are strewed in abundance over the finest streets; the average size of them being about twenty inches square (cube). A row of splendid Banyan-trees, planted at a considerable distance from each other, occupies some of the large streets, affording a delightful shade from the burning rays of the sun.

The streets differ also in appearance from those of other towns which I have seen in the interior, by the houses on each side having open fronts, the floor being raised from two to three feet above the level of the ground. The space between the ground and the level of the floor, and in some houses a foot or two even above that level, presents a front of carved work, beautifully polished with red ochre. In several, the carved work is continued up to the roof; and where that is the case, it is covered with white clay, which has the appearance of a lime white-wash. The roofs are made chiefly with bamboo-poles, or sticks, with the bark stripped off, and thatched with palm-leaves.

Behind each of these open fronts, are a number of small houses, or rather, open sheds, in which the people dwell, (the room open to the street being more of a public seat, than a private room,) averaging in number from thirty to forty. These small dwellings in the background are in many cases entirely hidden from the observation of any one passing along the streets; the only indication of them being, a small door on the left or right of the open front. The houses are all erected on the same plan, from that of the King, down to the lowest rank of Captains; and these are, with a few exceptions, the only persons who are allowed to build in any public situation. The rocky bed on which the town is placed, is, in many parts, very irregular and unlevel. Some of the streets are so full of holes, occasioned by the heavy rains washing the earth out of the fissures of the rocks during the rainy season, that any one attempting to walk through them in the dark, would place his neck in danger.

There is only one stone-built house in the town, which stands on the royal premises, and is called the "Castle." All the other buildings are of wood and *swish*, and by no means durable.

The market-place is a large open space, about three-quarters of a mile in circumference. There is no regularity in its form, but it approaches nearest to that of a parallelogram. On one side of it, is an extensive dell, surrounded by large trees and high grass,* into which they finally throw the dead bodies of sacrificed human victims. As I passed by this dell, I smelt a most intolerable stench, proceeding from the poor creatures who were thrown there on Saturday last. My feelings would not permit me to look into this horrid receptacle of the dead; but the very idea of it is dreadful. Yet even "there the prisoners rest together; they hear not the voice of the oppressor."

There are no regularly-built stalls in the market-place. Many articles of merchandise were laid on the ground; and others, on little temporary railings, which might be put up, or taken down, in a few moments. Among the commodities exposed for sale, I saw Manchester cloths, silks, muslins; roll-tobacco from the interior; large cakes of a kind of pomatum, made from the fruit of a tree found in the centre of the country, and used by the Ashántis for anointing their bodies, to give a polish to their skins; native tobacco-pipes, of very neat manufacture; cakes of a kind of whiting, used by the natives for marking their bodies; kankie, (native bread,) yams, plantains, bananas, pines, ground-nuts, fish, and the flesh of monkeys and elephants.

---

* There is a kind of grass in the immediate neighbourhood of Kumási, which grows to the enormous height of twenty feet, the stalk of which is about three-quarters of an inch in diameter.

CHAPTER IV.

BANTAMA—HEATHEN JEALOUSIES—INTERVIEW WITH THE KING—PREPARATIONS FOR RETURNING TO CAPE COAST—KINDNESS OF APOKO—LEAVES KUMASI—EMANCIPATION OF A SLAVE—FOMUNAH—CONDUCT OF KORINCHI—JOURNEY TO THE COAST—PRACTICABILITY OF A MISSION TO ASHANTI—LETTER OF PRESIDENT MACLEAN.

In the afternoon I asked His Majesty to allow me to visit Bantama, or the "Back Town;" to which he readily consented. I found it to be a small place, nearly one mile distant from Kumási, and connected with it by a long street, which runs from one town to the other. The only difference between the two towns is, that the streets of Bantama are much more noiseless than those of Kumási; which difference arises from the former being looked upon as sacred, on account of the Fetish-house, which contains the bones of the former Kings. Very few Europeans, or even Ashántis, are allowed to visit Bantama. Some of Apoko's men, who conducted me thither, informed me, that I was the only European who has been permitted to visit it during the reign of His present Majesty; and that the people of Kumási are only allowed to go there, when the King himself goes (which he does every forty days) to visit the tombs of his ancestors. Several splendid Banyan-trees are luxuriating in the centre of the main street; on one of which I saw a pretty variety of *Epiphytical Orchideæ*, in full bloom.

Before I left Bantama, I visited the Chief, (one of the greatest men in the kingdom,) who received me very kindly, and regaled me with some palm-wine.

As we were proceeding homewards, two or three men,

belonging to the Chief, came running after us, requesting us to stop. As soon as they came up, I learnt that they had been watching to see if we gathered anything from the Banyan-trees as we passed under them; and, on seeing my interpreter (who was riding in a palanquin) raise his hand to protect his face from the leaves, &c., they thought he had plucked some by my direction, and that I intended to make a medicine from them, for the purpose of poisoning the King! They seemed fully satisfied, however, from an explanation on the part of my attendant, that they were under a mistake. I believe their jealousy was excited by seeing me look up into one of the Banyans, where a variety of the *Orchideæ* was flowering; and as they have scarcely any idea of the beauty of a flower, they thought I must have some sinister intention in thus closely examining the tree.

As I passed by the King's residence on my way home, a small group of Physic-nut trees, thirteen in number, was pointed out to me as being the memorials of the former Kings; an additional tree being planted at the decease of every Monarch.

On arriving at my habitation, which is on Apoko's premises, I told him of the affair at Bantama, concerning the Banyan-leaves, &c., and asked him if they saw anything in my conduct, which authorized them to suspect me of any evil motive in visiting Bantama. He answered, "No;" and seemed to pay very little attention to the matter. However, to convince him more fully, I showed him some drawings of different varieties of *Orchideæ* in flower; and told him that the English are very fond of cultivating flowers from all parts of the world, and that I was very fond of studying their nature, character, &c. Apoko seemed much pleased with the plates, as they were laid open before him.

Tuesday, 9th.—The sudden change of temperature

on Sunday last being very great, (from 91° Fahrenheit, in the shade, to about 74°, or 75°,) accompanied with heavy rain, I caught a violent cold, although I took the precaution to cover myself partially with a cloak, as soon as the transition took place. I began to feel the evil effects of the cold this morning.

About half-past nine this forenoon, I went to the King's residence, to thank him for the handsome present which he made me yesterday. He appears to be about thirty-six years of age. He is of middle stature; his complexion is not so dark as that of many of his subjects; his manners are pleasing and agreeable. He has an aversion to drinking and smoking, a quality quite unusual among the Ashântis.*

Thursday, 11th.—Feeling better to-day, I walked out for air and exercise. As I passed the end of one of the streets, I saw a group of persons surrounding a large Kabosir's umbrella. A band of music was playing, and a human victim was lying on the ground before them, exposed to public view. I turned from the sickening sight with painful feelings. Coming round to the further end of the same street, I saw it crowded with people, and numbers more joining them in rapid succession. The King was seated in the street under his umbrellas, to drink palm-wine with his Chiefs, &c., previous to a week's partial retirement in his palace, immediately after the conclusion of the "custom" for his relation, who died on the 4th instant; this being the last day of the ceremony.

I reminded Apoko of my anxiety to obtain an

---

* While I was staying at Fomunah, I reproved Korinchi for drunkenness; when he said, that the King had checked him for it once; and since I also had done it, which was the second reproof he had received, he would endeavour to avoid it for the future.

answer from His Majesty, respecting the establishment of Schools, &c., in Ashánti; who replied, "The King will speedily give you an answer; and we hope you will come to Kumási again, and pay us another visit, for we shall be always glad to see you. The King believes that you wish to do him and the people good."

Saturday, 13th.—I again reminded Apoko, that I must speedily return to the coast, as the rains were becoming frequent and very heavy. He immediately went to tell the King; and returned to inform me, that His Majesty had been so busily engaged throughout the morning, that he could not see me and make me ready to start to-day, but that he would do so to-morrow.

From the general aspect of things, I became sensible, that though I should not meet with anything to discourage me, yet it would cost me another journey to Kumási, before the confidence of the King would be fully secured; his jealous disposition being of such a nature, as to require a considerable length of time, and much patience and perseverance, before it will be overcome.

Sunday, 14th.—At half-past seven, A. M., I conducted divine service at my abode, and found it to be a time of spiritual refreshment. I continued in anxious expectation of a message from the King, until about eleven o'clock, when I found, on inquiry, that Apoko had not reminded His Majesty of seeing me to-day, because he thought I would not like to transact any kind of business on the Sabbath-day. (This idea was the result of a previous consultation with Apoko; during which, I explained to him the nature and claims of the Christian Sabbath.) I told him that my business with His Majesty was entirely of a religious nature, and that I had no objection to see him immediately. It was too late, however, to hope for an interview to-day.

Early this evening I held a prayer-meeting, which was no sooner concluded, than the rain, which had been threatening for several hours, commenced with awful violence. In a few minutes, the small yard in the centre of my residence was covered with water, to the depth of twelve or fifteen inches; and as the thatch of my sleeping-shed (I cannot call it a room) was in bad repair, the rain poured in, almost in a stream, upon my pillow. I soon began to feel the evil effects of the damps, and had some fears as to the consequences; which fears were heightened by the consideration, that my provisions were so nearly exhausted, that I could not make myself a cup of tea or coffee, having no sugar left; neither had I any flour, bread, or biscuit. Trusting, however, in the mercy of God, I partook of some native food, to satisfy the cravings of hunger, and slept in peace.

Monday, 15th.—I arose from my bed, determined to make an attempt to set out upon my journey back to the coast to-day, if possible; the commencement of the rains, of the violence of which a stranger to a tropical climate can form but a faint idea, together with the sickly state of several of my people, and the pressing claims of nearly seven hundred members of our society, rendering my speedy return imperative. I therefore began to pack up my things, while Apoko,* (whose attachment to me has daily increased,) true to the promise which he made me yesterday, repaired to His

* Apoko is the only person who is allowed to visit the King at *any* time he wishes. I therefore enjoyed many advantages, from being placed by the King under his care. I was informed that, had it not been so, I should have had much greater difficulties to contend with, in holding intercourse with His Majesty. Apoko is a fine-looking man, about thirty-six years of age, and seems to have great influence with him.

Majesty's residence, to remind him of the necessity of allowing me to leave.

In about two hours Apoko returned, accompanied by a host of attendants, linguists, and messengers, with a present from His Majesty, consisting of two ounces and four ackies of gold-dust, (£9 currency,) and a slave for myself;* also eight ackies (£2 currency) for my interpreter and other attendants. He also gave me the following message from the King:—"His Majesty knows that you cannot stop longer, on account of the rains; and as the thing which you have mentioned to him requires much consideration, he cannot answer you in so short a time: but if you will come up again, or send a messenger, after the rains are over, he will be prepared to answer you." With this message I was pleased, and said, that I would certainly either come again, or send a messenger at the time mentioned. I then repaired to His Majesty's residence, to take my leave, and found him seated in one of his apartments, surrounded by an immense number of attendants; when he requested me, with a courtesy which one could scarcely expect from a person in his circumstances, to present his compliments to His Excellency President Maclean, and take a message to him.

Having taken my leave, I commenced my journey at noon, preceded by an escort of troops. After I had proceeded a short distance along the street, Apoko came to testify his affection, by a hearty shake of the hand.

When I reached Franfraham, the troops left me, and I stopped a few minutes to emancipate the slave, whom His Majesty had given to me. This poor fellow is a native from the depth of the interior, and is now in the

* This slave, it will be seen in the sequel, Mr. Freeman had the pleasure of emancipating very soon.

prime of his life. On my informing him, that he was now a free man, he appeared overwhelmed with gratitude; and almost fell on the earth before me, in acknowledgment of the boon. He had not all the pleasure to himself, however; for while I enjoyed the luxury of doing good, many of my people looked on him with delight; and our satisfaction was heightened, when he told us, that he had twice been brought out for the purpose of sacrifice, during the recent "custom," and had twice been put in irons, and sent back alive; and, that when he was brought out this morning, he expected to be sacrificed in the course of the day. Happy change! instead of having his head cut off, and his body thrown to the fowls of the air, he now finds himself in the enjoyment of liberty, safely proceeding with us, far away from the scenes of his bondage.

I journeyed with speed, and reached the town of Eduabin about five, P. M., where I took my rest for the night.

Tuesday, 16th.—At six, A. M., I again proceeded. In the course of the morning a tornado, which had for a long time been grumbling in the distance, overtook us. We took shelter for a short time, and then ventured onward; as I chose rather to expose myself to the rains, however pernicious, than to the alternative of swimming across the rivers, which were swelling very fast.

The soil being clayey, the rain made the roads so very slippery, that nearly all my carriers, &c., were tumbling down with the boxes; and, while I was riding in my chair to rest myself a little, the hammock-men stumbled with me twice, notwithstanding great care on their part. During the whole of the day, I did not stop to take any food, but pushed onwards, like a man escaping for life.

Night closed in nearly an hour before I reached my resting-place; but we kept our path through the forest without much difficulty, and reached Fomunah at a quarter after seven o'clock, wet, weary, and hungry. I immediately repaired to Korinchi's residence. He seemed overjoyed to see me, gave me a hearty shake with both hands, put his arms around my neck in transport, and made me a present of palm-wine, and a mess of soup, made with the flesh of the monkey. I then retired to my lodgings, and thankfully partook of the Chief's monkey-soup, to satisfy the cravings of hunger, having little else to eat.

Wednesday, 17th.—Early this morning, Korinchi came to my quarters, shook me cordially by the hand, and testified his delight at seeing me safely returned from Kumási. On my telling him, that I should want him to assist me in holding farther intercourse with the King, by sending messengers, &c., and, perhaps, in returning to the capital in the course of the next dry season, he said, he would readily do any thing which I requested of him.

One of my attendants being so ill as to be unable to walk over the Adansi hills, I applied for assistance to Korinchi; who immediately supplied me with four strong men, to assist in carrying the invalid. About half-past eleven, A.M., I again proceeded, crossed the hills, and travelled through the forest until four, P.M.; when, finding the people weary, I was obliged to stop in a small croom, and take up my abode for the night.

Thursday, 18th.—At seven, A.M., I resumed my journey, under rather trying circumstances; being almost without food. About noon, I halted to rest the carriers, &c., and took some refreshment, consisting of a piece of boiled yam and a little butter, with heavy and sour pudding, made from Indian corn, having nothing better to eat.

About half-past four, P.M., I rested for the night, at a small croom, about seven miles from the river Prah. On my arrival at this place, I felt tired and hungry, and the God of Providence kindly "furnished me a table in the wilderness." A wild hog had been killed in the neighbourhood, a portion of which I purchased, and found it very delicious. "Thy bread shall be given thee; thy water shall be sure." My sleeping-place, it is true, was a very bad one, into which an Englishman would scarcely place a pig; but I laid me down with humble confidence, and slept in peace.

"How do thy mercies close me round!
For ever be thy name adored!
I blush in all things to abound:
The servant is above his Lord.

"Inured to poverty and pain,
A suffering life my Master led;
The Son of God, the Son of Man,
He had not where to lay his head.

"But lo! a place he hath prepared
For me, whom watchful angels keep;
Yea, He himself becomes my guard,
He smooths my bed, and gives me sleep."

Friday, 19th.—At six, A.M., I started for the Prah, which I reached in about two hours. I breakfasted at Prahsu, on the Fanti side of the river; and after resting the people, and allowing them time to refresh themselves, by bathing in the river, I again proceeded at one, P.M., and reached the small croom of Beraku about five o'clock, when I halted for the night.

Saturday, 20th.—At six, A.M., I set out for Fessu; which place I reached at noon; and as the day was excessively hot, and the people very weary, I determined on remaining here, and spending the Sabbath.

Sunday, 21st.—At half-past seven, A.M., I conducted

divine service, and preached from Mark viii. 36, 37. Many of the natives were present, and some of them paid deep attention. About five, P.M., we had a prayer-meeting.

Monday, 22d.—At a quarter before six, A.M., I started for Mansu. Arriving at a neat little croom on the way, I was pleased to find that a carrier, bearing provisions, whom I had been expecting several days, had just entered the place. Thus I was enabled to take a comfortable breakfast, consisting of suitable food; the want of which I had felt severely, during the last seven or eight days. My people, who had seen with regret the privations I suffered, sat at a distance, looking upon me while I was taking my breakfast, with countenances which told how happy they were in seeing my wants supplied.

After breakfast, I again proceeded, and reached Mansu at one, P.M. Gabri, the Chief, welcomed me back, and entreated me to stay with him until the morrow, as I had already travelled a fair day's journey; but, as I was extremely anxious to reach Cape Coast as early as possible, I told him I could not remain, but would pay him a visit at the earliest opportunity. On my inquiring whether he would like a Mission to be established at Mansu, he said, "Yes;" and he should feel very happy, if he had a Missionary residing with him. Gabri is one of the most respectable Chiefs in Fanti.

Mansu and the adjacent villages contain a population of at least ten thousand souls; and they are admirably situated for the establishment of a Mission.*

* Many important advantages would, in all probability, result from our having a School-house and Teacher at Mansu. It is two days' journey on the road to Kumási; and would, consequently, facilitate our operations in Ashánti. The situation also is open and healthy; and would, in due time, be a very eligible place for the residence of a Missionary.

Leaving Mansu, I proceeded to Wankwasu, a small croom, about nine miles from the last-mentioned place; where we rested for the night.

Tuesday, 23d.—At six, A.M., I again resumed my journey, and reached Yankumási at nine, where I stopped to breakfast. Asín Chibbu, the Chief, received me very kindly, and asked me to stay with him a day or two; but our societies on the coast acted as a powerful magnet, which seemed to draw me with almost irresistible force towards them. I therefore promised Chibbu a visit at some future opportunity, and hastened on my way with all speed. The road was so much overgrown with luxuriant vegetation, that I was literally dragged through the bushes, and was soon compelled to walk. The morning sun was also intensely hot, and the path so narrow, that an umbrella was of little use. Instead of passing through Domonási as I did on my journey up to Kumási, I left it on my left, and took a shorter road to Cape Coast.

About noon I reached Dunquah, ("Payntree's croom" of Bowdich,) where I rested my carriers, &c., a few minutes; after which I proceeded about four miles, took some refreshment, and then pushed forward to within about nine miles of Cape Coast. Finding that many of my people were unable to proceed any further, I left them in a little croom for the night, and urged on my way; taking with me only the hammock-men, (whom I had rested the greater part of the day by walking about twenty-five miles,) and also a soldier. As I approached nearer to Cape Coast, the roads were much better; and, having the advantage of a fine moonlight night, I reached the Mission-house in safety, about nine, P.M., and obtained a refreshing view of the "deep, deep sea," which unites Cape Coast with my native land, with feelings of humble gratitude to Almighty God who had mercifully preserved me in the midst of so many dangers, not imaginary but real, and brought me home in health, peace, and safety.

I trust, my dear Sirs, that these copious extracts from my Journal will convince you, that God, in his infinite mercy, is gently opening before us our way into the interior of this vast continent. Future difficulties will doubtless arise; but I am fully confident that they will not be of such a nature as to hinder the Christian Missionary from pressing on in the glorious conflict. It is true, that this spiritual Jericho at present stands strong, and that Satan, its monster king, still has the triumph of seeing thousands of helpless men, for whom Christ died, dashed into the dust in dishonour: but Israel shall surely triumph; the mystical rams' horns shall not be blown in vain; the enemy shall be taken in his stronghold, and the Redeemer shall have these "Heathen" for his "inheritance," and the "uttermost parts of the earth" for his "possession."

I believe that my long detention at Fomunah, on my way to Kumási, was the Lord's doing. The great length of time which I remained there, gave me an excellent opportunity of becoming acquainted with the people, and of gaining their affections. I also became accustomed, by gentle degrees, to those horrid and awful scenes, which are every-day occurrences in that place.

Fomunah is a much more desirable place for the establishment of a Mission, at the present time, than Kumási. The people are more prepared for the reception of the Gospel; and their Chief, Korinchi, is exceedingly well-disposed towards us. Nevertheless, I should have no hesitation in attempting the establishment of a Mission even in the capital itself.

To carry on this glorious work in Ashánti, and other parts of the interior, will require men of great nerve, patience, forbearance, and perseverance. I also deem it necessary to remind you of the importance of sending persons who are rather light than heavy in weight, as the hammock-men will not carry them, if they are very heavy. Yet, on the other hand, they must not be too small and weak: if so, they will never (humanly speaking) bear the heavy toils of travelling in this climate. If I were a little larger than I am, I should meet with almost insuperable difficulties in this respect. If I were not very strong, I could not have borne half the toils through which I have passed.

I have no doubt as to getting up to Ashánti for the future with much less expense than has been incurred in my first visit. The King would not make so much ado the second time, as I am no longer a stranger. I also think, that even with a stranger he would not adopt the same course as he did with me, inasmuch as the novelty is over.

While I was staying at Fomunah, the King sent a messenger to see what kind of a person I was. When the messenger returned, he asked him what he had seen, in language something like the following:—

THE KING.—You have seen the Fetishman?

MESSENGER.—Yes.

KING.—Had he plenty of drums with him?

MESSENGER.—I saw no drums.

KING.—Why! he is a Fetishman: he must have drums with him.

MESSENGER.—I saw no drums. He has plenty of boxes; but I cannot say what they contain.

KING.—Why did you not endeavour to learn whether the boxes contained drums or not?

I was informed that the King was exceedingly angry

with the man because he could not give him a satisfactory answer. At another time the King said, "Never since the world began, has there been an English Missionary in Ashánti. What can he want?" As I have been to Kumási, and not only so, but have visited him in his own residence; as well as having been a fortnight under the watchful care of his chief linguist, Apoko, who has his entire confidence; his jealousies are, doubtless, so far removed, that he will not be likely to detain a Missionary so long on the road again, while perplexing and puzzling himself with questions of the before-mentioned character.

It was manifest, that a great change had taken place respecting me in the mind of the King, after I had been a few days in Kumási; for he seemed very anxious to detain me, if possible; and I believe he would have kept me several weeks longer, thereby placing my life in the greatest danger from the rains, &c., but for the kindness of President Maclean, who, knowing the probable consequences of my being detained in that manner, wrote to the King, some time after I left Cape Coast, requesting him to allow me to leave Kumási whenever I thought proper.

I deeply regretted the necessity of leaving so early; but had I stayed longer, I must, in all probability, have remained until the rainy season was over, which I was not prepared to do.

Doubtless, there has been a great advantage gained by this enterprise; and I trust, my dear Sirs, you will, by the liberality of British Christians, and especially those of our own body, be enabled to follow up that advantage, by sending out, as early as possible, three or four Missionaries, at least, that more attention may be paid to Ashánti.

I intend sending up a messenger to the King, to

keep the communication open, as soon as the rains are over; and shall wait with great anxiety for an answer from you, as to what steps are to be taken. If it were practicable, a handsome present, of the description I mentioned in my last, [namely, a pony-phaeton, and harness, suitable to the country,] would be well received by the King, and be of much importance, in influencing his mind in our favour.

After I had prepared the preceding extracts from my Journal, I felt it my duty to hand them over to His Excellency, President Maclean; who, after he had perused them, returned them with the following letter, which he has kindly permitted me to annex to them:—

"My dear Sir,

"I herewith return your narrative of your journey to Ashânti, which I have perused with very great interest.

"I would fain hope that, from the manner in which you were received in your *avowed* character as a Missionary, throughout the whole of your arduous journey, there will not exist many obstacles to the accomplishment of the first object,—getting a *locus standi* in the country. Certainly I think there will be no *insuperable* obstacle.

"I hope and trust the Wesleyan Missionary Committee will be satisfied, that there is such an opening as will justify them, in pushing the advantage gained by your indefatigable zeal. I would almost go so far as to say, that if they *have the means*, a serious responsibility will rest upon them, and on Christian England, if so glorious an opening into interior Africa,—if so rich a harvest, be neglected. But I hope better things. And I do not despair of yet witnessing the peaceful triumph of the cross, even in that stronghold of Satan, Kumási.

"I expect considerable advantages will arise from the Christian education of the two Ashánti Princes, now in England. If well supported, for all depends upon that, their influence in Ashánti will aid the good cause much. I shall not fail to direct them to be introduced to the Wesleyan Missionary Committee.

"Believe me yours very truly,

"GEORGE MACLEAN.

"CAPE-COAST CASTLE,
"*July 9th*, 1839."

"The Rev. T. B. Freeman."

Thus, my dear Sirs, I have endeavoured to discharge what I feel to be a very important duty. And casting myself, as usual, on your kind indulgence, for having used so many words in support of a cause, which I know would strongly recommend itself to your hearts and affections without my saying anything,

I subscribe myself, &c.,

(Signed) T. B. FREEMAN.

MISSION-HOUSE, CAPE-COAST CASTLE,
July 10th, 1839.

APPENDICES TO THE FIRST JOURNAL.

APPENDIX, A.

Extract of a Letter from the Rev. T. B. Freeman to the Secretaries of the Wesleyan Missionary Society, dated Cape-Coast Castle, September 17*th*, 1839.

Your letter of July 23d is very encouraging. I feel thankful that the Committee has authorized me to purchase the house which I recommended. I will take care to proceed judiciously and cautiously, in making the purchase.

I am delighted to hear that you intend to send us two additional Missionaries, and one of them married. I need not tell you with what joy we shall receive them. May the God of Missions grant them a prosperous voyage!

I am very glad that you have received my letter of May 7th; and hope, ere this reaches you, you will have received my Journal and other papers. The results of my Mission to Ashánti are now beginning to be manifest. The King, I hear, from good authority, is becoming anxious respecting the establishment of a school in Kumási, and is expecting me to pay him another visit; and many of the Ashántis who became acquainted with me during my late visit, call at the Mission-house to see me, when they come down to Cape Coast. A brother of Korinchi has this morning paid me a visit, presenting his regards, and stating that they will be very happy to see me in Ashánti again. If the advantage already gained can be followed up, I have no doubt that, under the blessing of the God of Missions, we shall, in due time, meet with abundant success in Ashánti.

APPENDIX, B.

Letter from the same.

REV. AND DEAR SIRS,

I AM happy to inform you, that our new chapel at Anamabu is in a sufficient state of forwardness for constant use. The foundation was laid August 14th, 1838. It is built with stone, to the height of one foot above the ground: the remaining part of the walls are *swish*, and are two feet thick, very strong and durable, and carried to the height of sixteen feet. The roof is made with deal, purchased at a reasonable price in the neighbourhood, and thatched. The dimensions of the chapel are fifty-three feet by thirty, and it will seat from four to five hundred persons. The floor is of the same material as the greater part of the walls. A pulpit and communion-rails are erected, and the whole of the remaining part is fitted up with fixed benches. Had not the people exerted themselves exceedingly, it could not have been so forward; but I am glad to say, they assisted nobly, both in labour and contributions; and the happy consequence is, that it is placed out of all danger from the rains, which have been very destructive this season. A few days after my arrival from the interior, I went down to Anamabu, taking with me carpenters, bricklayers, &c., to prepare it for opening as early as possible. All things being ready, on Sunday, May 26th, 1839, I opened it for divine worship.

At seven, A. M., I read prayers, and preached to an attentive congregation, from, "Know ye that the Lord, he is God," &c. (Psalm c. 3, 4.) Many felt it to be a delightful service, and the tear of gratitude to Almighty God was shed. Our members at Cape Coast came down, though the distance is twelve miles and a half, to congratulate their Anamabu friends, and share with them in the solemn and sacred blessings of the day.

At three, P. M., I again preached to a large congregation, amounting to about one thousand persons, from Heb. iv. 9—13. The chapel would not hold the whole: several hundreds of Heathens crowded the windows.

At seven, P. M., I again preached from Heb. iv. 14—16. We had a large and serious congregation. Many present felt it "good to wait on the Lord." The collections amounted to £10. 3*s*. 9*d*., notwithstanding the previous exertions on the part of the people.

It affords me pleasure to state, that I called upon the gentlemen residing in Anamabu, a few days before the chapel was opened, to solicit their aid, and succeeded in every application. Several at Cape Coast also rendered us timely and friendly aid. The sum thus raised at Cape Coast and Anamabu amounts to £32 currency; for which we feel thankful.

Our cordial thanks are due especially to Henry Barnes, Esq.,—in whose house I always find a hearty welcome, and a comfortable home, whenever I visit Anamabu,—for his kind assistance, not only in liberally contributing, but also in superintending the work during my absence; and in sending his workmen (carpenters and bricklayers) to assist at various times, gratuitously.

During the building of the chapel, many of our people at Anamabu, not excepting some of the most respectable among them, were often seen busily engaged in carrying swish, &c., as early as two or three o'clock in the morning.

Since the chapel has been opened, our kind friend Mr. Barnes has, at his own expense, painted the pulpit and communion-rails, &c.; and as the inside of the chapel has had one coat of white-wash, it has a very neat appearance. Blessed be God, who thus prospers the work of our hands!

I have also the satisfaction of informing you, that our chapel at Winnebah is also opened for divine worship. The foundation-stone was laid July 5th, 1838. Our little society there exerted themselves to the utmost of their power; stimulated and led on by Mr. William De Graft, who is now residing with me in the Mission-house, as provisional Assistant. The walls are built with swish, on a stone foundation, and carried to a height of fourteen feet. The roof is made with native wood, and thatched. Its dimensions are thirty-four feet by nineteen.

After I had opened the Anamabu chapel, I proceeded to Winnebah, for the purpose of fitting up, and opening the chapel in that place. Finding, however, that it was scarcely ready, I sent up to Cape Coast for an extra carpenter; and then journeyed to British Akrah, (a distance of forty miles,) to visit our society, &c., recently established there.

During my short stay at Akrah, I received much kindness from the gentlemen and authorities; especially from J. W. Hanson, Esq., the Commandant, and from J. Bannerman, Esq., with whom I have always found a cordial welcome.

Having no convenient place for meeting the society while staying at Akrah, Mr. Hanson kindly lent me the large hall in the Fort for that purpose; and I am glad to say, that I found the society and schools in a flourishing condition. There are thirty-five members in society; and in the schools are sixty-five boys and twenty girls. The boys' school has been established six months, and the girls' two months. The local Government having undertaken to bear half of the expenses of the boys' school, the Commandant has kindly made comfortable arrangements for the Schoolmaster and Mistress to reside, and for both the schools to be kept in the Fort, until I can make some permanent provision concerning them.

The Government takes no part in the general management of the boys' school, that being entirely left to us. Several of the scholars, who knew not the alphabet when they entered the school, can now read lessons in the New Testament. God be praised, our prospects at British Akrah are of the most encouraging nature. Pray send a Missionary there without delay.

Having stayed at Akrah a few days, I returned to Winnebah, and proceeded to finish the chapel without delay. In eight days after my return, we had a neat pulpit erected, the floor fitted up with fixed benches, and every arrangement made for opening it on Sunday, June 23d, 1839.

At seven, A. M., we held a prayer-meeting in the chapel, and at eleven I read prayers and preached to an attentive and serious congregation, from, "For thy Maker is thine husband, the Lord of hosts is his name," &c. (Isaiah liv. 5—8.) God was in the midst of us, and blessed us. The Chief, and many of the most respectable Heathens in the town, were present; many of whom paid deep attention to the word spoken.

At three, P. M., I again preached to a large congregation, from, "It is appointed unto men once to die," &c. (Heb. ix. 27.) The Chief and his Captains, &c., again attended, and behaved well. The respectable conduct of these Heathens reminded me of the great change which has taken place in the character of the Winnebah people, during the last few years. Some time ago there was a small English fort in the centre of the town. Misunderstandings having arisen between the natives and the Commandant, the former rebelled against the latter, and slew him. The consequence was, that some British men-of-war fired on the town as they sailed past it, and battered the fort to the ground; causing the refractory inhabitants to retreat into the forest. *On the very spot* where the fort stood, and where these unhappy events took place, stands our chapel; and here also were collected together, peacefully listening to the words of eternal life, the descendants of those who had, in former days, been collected together to shed blood. This happy change has taken place, partly through the instrumentality of the local Government of Cape Coast; and partly by the introduction of that incomparable blessing, Christianity.

After the conclusion of the afternoon service, I spoke to the people concerning opening a school for the instruction of their children. They readily consented to send them, as soon as I could make arrangements for commencing.

The rains are now violent, and travelling is difficult; but as soon as they are over, (which will be, I hope, in a few days,) I intend sending down one of the youths whom I have had in training at the Mission-house, to commence the school. Winnebah is a place of great importance to us, being about midway between Cape Coast and British Akrah. While toiling along the coast for a distance of nearly one hundred miles, visiting our societies, I find Winnebah a delightful retreat from the heavy sandy beach, the burning rays of an almost vertical sun, and the strong breeze from the Atlantic. I hope to see much lasting good result from the erection of the chapel, and the establishment of a school at that place.

Our little chapel, or rather schoolroom, at Domonási, I am happy to say, is also fit for use.

I must here beg leave to insert a few extracts from my Journal for the *last* year, 1838.

November 22d, Thursday.—At five, A. M., I left Anamabu for Domonási. As I was passing through the glens, I saw a splendid production of nature: several large trees from thirty to forty feet high covered with blossoms nearly as large as a tulip, of a fine scarlet colour, ornamented round the lamina with a golden fringe, courted my attention. On examination, I found them to belong to the class "*Dydinamia*," of Linnæus. Amidst the various beauties of Flora, on which I have feasted my eyes, both in England and Africa, I have seen nothing comparable to this splendid tree: even the horse-chestnut, the glory of Mount Pindus, cannot vie with this production of the glen.

About half-past twelve I reached Domanási, and, to my great satisfaction, found our society increasing in divine knowledge, and in number.

Saturday, 24th.—I was engaged in levelling the floor of the little swish-chapel, which our people have built nearly at their own expense, intending to preach in it on the morrow, although it is in such an unfinished state.

Sunday, 25th.—At seven, A. M., a prayer-meeting was held in the new chapel. I felt greatly encouraged in seeing this African temple full of persons, joining in one general burst of praise to God. How applicable, spiritually, to this scene are the words of our hymn!—

"Hark! the wastes have found a voice,
Lonely deserts now rejoice,
Gladsome hallelujahs sing,
All around with praises ring.

"Lo! abundantly they bloom,
Lebanon is hither come;
Carmel's stores the heavens dispense,
Sharon's fertile excellence.

"See, these barren souls of ours
Bloom, and put forth fruits and flowers,
Flowers of Eden, fruits of grace,
Peace, and joy, and righteousness!"

At eleven, A. M., I preached to an attentive congregation on the "one thing needful."

Monday, 20th.—At half-past seven, A. M., I left Domonási for Abasang, and travelled through the glens until ten o'clock, when I halted in a small croom, and took breakfast.

Having swung my hammock to some trees, and rested awhile, I again proceeded on my way through a marshy country, where I found the heat from the sun to be almost insupportable.* After travelling a few miles in this burning heat, I felt sick and weary, and again swung my hammock, to rest under a large tree, from half-past one until a quarter after three. I then resumed my journey, and reached Abasang at a quarter past five, P. M. On my arrival I was directed to the Chief's residence, who met me in the yard with a hearty welcome, and offered me the best apartments in his house, during my stay. In the course of the evening, some of the Kabosirs, and our little society, came to visit me. I soon retired to rest, much fatigued with the toils of the day, in travelling through the worst road I ever saw.

Tuesday, 27th.—About seven, A. M., I walked into the yard, where I found the Chief and one of his Captains waiting to receive me. After the usual compliments, the Chief presented me with a sheep, a goat, and sixteen yams.

In the course of the day, the Chief privately informed me, that he felt very anxious to embrace Christianity, but found the Captains averse to it, and he could not do

* Although the heat of the sun is trying, the damps, early in the morning and late in the evening, are much more dangerous; so, by travelling during the heat of the day, I choose the less evil of the two.

as he wished in the matter: he therefore desired me to talk to them about it; which I promised to do. In the evening, I preached in the Chief's court-yard:* all the Captains, and many of the people of the town, attended.

Wednesday, 28th.—Sick. Two of the Captains came to make me a present of goats and yams.

Thursday, 29th.—Still very weak. Under medicine.

Friday, 30th.—I saw all the Captains, save one who is out of town, and had a long conversation with them in the presence of the Chief, respecting their opposition to Christianity. They acknowledged that they had opposed it; but said, that, since I had come to pay them a visit, and explained to them more fully the nature of Christianity, they believed it to be *palaver papa*, "a good palaver;" and that they freely withdrew their opposition.

Having, by the blessing of God, accomplished my object in visiting Abasang, I prepared for leaving it early the following morning.

Abasang is a native town of considerable importance, situated on a gently-rising hill, about twenty-four miles from the sea-coast. The number of its inhabitants is from fifteen hundred to two thousand. The chief article of trade is palm oil: the palm which bears the nut, from which the oil is extracted, growing in great abundance in the beautiful glens in its immediate neighbourhood. In the town, and about the skirts of it, there are many sheep and goats, and plenty of poultry.

December, Saturday, 1st.—At six, A. M., I started

* I sent a native Teacher to this place some months ago, who informed me that several of the townspeople would willingly attend divine worship, &c., but were afraid, as some of the Captains had opposed them; they had even gone so far, as to put some of them in irons, because they worshipped the true God.

for Domonási. Several of our members (now amounting to thirteen in number) accompanied me to the first croom on the road, where I took an affectionate leave of them.

During my journey I passed through a small village, where the people worship the devil, or bad spirit. I inquired after the Fetishman, but could not see him, being informed that it is his custom to go into the bush on Saturday mornings, where he conceals himself during the day.* I also crossed a small river, called the Amissah. It is about twenty yards wide at the ford, and four and a half feet deep. During the rainy season it may, in all probability, rise to seven or eight feet, or more.

At half-past two, P. M., I reached Domonási in safety.

Sunday, 2d.—At half-past ten, A. M., I preached from Isaiah lv. 6, 7. At three, P. M., I examined some candidates for baptism, At four, P. M., I preached from Colossians iv. 2; and, after the sermon, baptized six adults and seven children.

Monday, 3d.—At half-past seven, P. M., I held a Class-Leaders' meeting.

Tuesday, 4th.—At six, A. M., I started for Anamabu, which place I reached at half-past two, P. M.

It is with pleasure I also inform you, that we have a small society at a large croom called Salt-pond, (which takes its name from a salt-pond near it,) situated on the beach, about eight miles below Anamabu; and that they are very anxious to build a little chapel, which they will accomplish themselves; the laying of the foundation, the doors and window-shutters, excepted. Consequently,

---

* In every town or croom of importance, there is one of these Fetishmen to be found, whose employment is to delude these benighted people, and to keep them in a state of servile bondage, to answer their own base purposes. O Africa! Africa!

as soon as the rains are over, I intend to go down and commence the building for them, and then to have the doors and windows made at Cape Coast, and to send them down in a canoe. Without chapels very little can be done on this Station.

I trust, my dear Sirs, that you will not blame me for drawing upon you for £25 for the Anamabu chapel, £15 for the Winnebah chapel, and £5 for the Domonási chapel, as I have done so from pure necessity. A coat of plaster and white-wash, on the outside is nearly all that any of the above-mentioned buildings will require; and that I hope we shall be able to accomplish, without further assistance from you.

The heavy rains have done some damage to the vestry at Cape Coast, which will place me under the necessity of employing two or three bricklayers for some time in repairing it, after this season is over.

I had but just returned from Winnebah to Anamabu, and was resting myself a few days, when I received information that the vestry had suffered materially from the rains. This unpleasant news arrived as I was taking my dinner. I speedily packed up my things, and came to Cape Coast the same afternoon, fearing lest the chapel should sustain any injury. I am happy, however, to state, that it has taken no harm, neither is it in danger.

The two old native houses, which stood near the chapel at Cape Coast, I have purchased, and pulled down, to avoid any accident by fire. I have only drawn on you for the payment for one of them, as I am not prepared, at present, to give you a statement of the exact amount of the purchase, some trifling things in connexion therewith not being finally settled. I also hope to make some arrangements for removing the female school to the present Mission-house, as soon as I obtain your permission to purchase it for a permanent residence; and then there will be a year or two's rent of the house (the old Mission-house taken by Mr. Wrigley) in which the female school is now kept, which would nearly or quite pay for the purchase of the old house in question.

There will always be perplexities and expenses arising on this Station about houses, until a purchase is made, and the school kept on the same premises.

At Yankumási, a large native town in Fanti, about twenty-eight miles inland, is an excellent opening for the establishment of a school, &c. Asín Chibbu, the Chief, called on me at the Mission-house a few weeks after I passed through the town on my return from Ashánti; and on my asking him if he would assist us in erecting a chapel in his town, he answered, "Yes; if you will send a person or two to direct, I will find men to do the greater part of the work." For further remarks on the kindness of Asín Chibbu, and the character, &c., of his town, see my Ashánti Journal.

I verily believe, that, ere another rainy season arrives, there will be three or four new chapels erected in this neighbourhood by the Christian zeal of our native societies. The amount of good done here during the short time your Missionaries have visited the Station, is much greater in extent than that in Fanti country, though that is considerable.

The trading habits of many of our members cause them to travel hundreds of miles into the interior. To these parts they carry the word of life; and I am glad to say, that the Lord blesses their humble exertions in giving them "souls for their hire." Incredible as the following incident may appear, the fact is not the less certain. While I was in Kumási, one of the converts to Christianity *from the interior*, applied to me for Christian baptism. As I found, during his examination, every proof of a sincere desire and purpose to live as a true disciple of Christ, I granted his request; and publicly baptized him in the presence of many Ashánti s. Surely Ethiopia is stretching out her hands to God.

As I know that the bare statement of these facts will have more weight with you than any observations I can make, I need not cry, "Men of Israel, help!" I therefore humbly submit them to your serious consideration. Believe me,

Rev. and dear Sirs,
Your obedient Servant
In the Gospel of Christ,
THOMAS B. FREEMAN.

APPENDIX, C.

Visit of the Rev. Thomas B. Freeman to England; and preparations for the Ashánti Mission.

JUNE 18th, 1840.

WE have much pleasure in stating, that the Rev. Thomas Birch Freeman, the senior Wesleyan Missionary on the Gold Coast in Western Africa, whose Journal of his recent tour to Ashánti has justly excited so deep and universal interest, arrived in London on Thursday last. Mr. Freeman is accompanied in his temporary visit to this country by Mr. William De Graft, a native Local Preacher, and a valuable assistant in the African Mission. Their stay in England is expected to be very short; not exceeding, probably, four months, when Mr. Freeman hopes to return to the scene of his evangelical labours, accompanied by six other Missionaries. Four of these are intended to be his companions, in the glorious enterprise of attempting to establish a Mission among the four millions of men, who constitute the population of the powerful kingdom of Ashánti, and its dependencies; and thus to introduce Christianity, education, and civilization into one important portion of that great continent, to which Britain owes so vast a debt of reparation, for the wrongs and miseries of the accursed slave-trade. This Mission may now be considered as fully determined upon by the Wesleyan Missionary Society, in accordance with the resolution of the late Annual Meeting in London; and it will certainly be undertaken as soon as the Special Fund, now raising for that purpose, shall have reached the amount of, at least, Five Thousand Pounds; being the sum deemed requisite for outfits, passages, the expenses of introducing and establishing a new Mission in a heathen country, and the support of the agents to be employed for the first three years. The General Fund of the Society being already pledged for other existing and older Missions, to more than the extent of its present ordinary means, the Committee have been obliged to have recourse to the formation of a Special Fund for Ashánti and the Gold Coast, as the only plan at present available, for enabling them to meet this new and important opening in Western Africa. We earnestly commend it to the prompt and liberal support of the Christian public.

APPENDIX, D.

Ordination and Valedictory Services. Departure of the Rev. Thomas B. Freeman and party.

On Monday, the 1st of December, 1840, a special service was held at Great Queen-street chapel, London, connected with the departure of the Missionaries appointed to Ashánti and the coast of Guinea; and notwithstanding the limited extent to which previous notice of the Meeting had been circulated, the chapel was well filled with a very attentive and devout audience.

The service was conducted by the Rev. Drs. Bunting, Hannah, and Alder, and Messrs. Beecham and Hoole. The newly-appointed Missionaries, Messrs. Hesk, Watson, Shipman, Thackwray, and Walden, were introduced to the Meeting; and the three former gave a brief detail of the circumstances by which, under divine Providence, they had seen it their duty to offer themselves for the arduous services of a Mission to Africa. The five Missionaries were then solemnly ordained to the office and work of the Christian ministry. Dr. Bunting conducted the Ordination service; and the other Ministers above-mentioned assisted in the "laying on of hands." The Rev. John Beecham next addressed the Missionaries, on the peculiar circumstances and duties of the Mission to which they had been solemnly designated. He then introduced the Rev. Thomas B. Freeman, who, with deep feeling, acknowledged the kindness he had experienced during his visit to this country; and expressed his thankfulness for the success he had met with, in his endeavours to awaken a more lively interest and active exertion, in behalf of that part of Africa which it was his business to represent. Mr. De Graft, a native Fanti Assistant on the Mission, who had accompanied Mr. Freeman to this country, took his farewell of the Christian public, by a most appropriate and interesting address; at the close of which Dr. Bunting, in the name of the Committee, presented to him a Bible, as a token of their regard and affection, and expressed a hope, that he would still successfully study and publish those blessed and important truths which that holy book reveals.

The Rev. Dr. Hannah, Theological Tutor of the Wesleyan Institution, delivered to the Missionaries a very instructive and impressive charge; and, at the close of the service, the whole congregation appeared to unite most fervently in the prayer which was offered up in the behalf of the Missionaries, and for the success of the Mission, by the Rev. Dr. Bunting.

On Wednesday, the 2d of December, the Missionaries and Mr. De Graft took their formal leave of the General Committee of the Wesleyan Missionary Society, and of the Wesleyan Ministers of London and its vicinity, a great number of whom were present on the occasion in Hatton-Garden.

The sailing of the "Osborn," by which vessel the Missionaries were to proceed to Cape-Coast, was delayed until Thursday, the 10th of December: on that day the whole party embarked at Gravesend, and immediately set sail. They are, in all, eleven persons; namely, Mr. and Mrs. Freeman, and native boy; Mr. De Graft; Mr. and Mrs. Hesk; Mr. Watson; Mr. and Mrs. Shipman; Mr. Thackwray; and Mr. Walden. Never was a Missionary party dismissed from the shores of England with a more intense feeling of interest and sympathy. All acknowledge the very arduous and difficult character of the Mission, as well as its important bearings on the welfare of the human race, and one of the boldest efforts yet made by the Church, in modern times, to introduce Christianity and its attendant blessings to the independent Negro states of interior Africa. Thousands of prayers have been offered in behalf of these Missionaries and their undertaking; and we do not doubt that they will be constantly remembered at the throne of grace, by those who are concerned for the prosperity and extension of the kingdom of Christ.

[The party, having been favoured with a safe voyage, landed at Cape-Coast Castle, on Monday the 1st of February; all in the enjoyment of good health.]

APPENDIX, E.

Extract of a Letter from the Rev. Thomas B. Freeman, dated Anamabu, May 5th, 1841.

All the brethren, except Mr. Thackwray, have proceeded to occupy their different posts; and I have made arrangements for proceeding to Domonási with Mr. Thackwray early to-morrow morning. Mr. Brooking is now residing at Mansu, and making preparations for our enterprise in Ashánti. Mansu will be a place of great importance to us, while carrying on our operations in Ashánti; and I think we shall find it to be a very healthy situation. I have received an encouraging message from the King of Ashánti, from which I learn, that he entertains friendly feelings towards us, and will be very glad to see us in Kumási. On the 29th of March, we held our Missionary Meeting, which had been postponed for several weeks on account of our party not having arrived: President Maclean, with his usual kindness, occupied the chair. The Meeting was one of some interest; and the collection, including the subscriptions of our worthy chairman and other friends, and £14 from the societies in sheep, goats, &c., amounted to £51. 11*s.* 3*d.*

I trust that, ere this reaches you, an ample Special Fund for the support of the Gold Coast Mission will have been realized; and that you will send us out another Missionary without delay, as we shall very much need another brother to occupy Cape Coast, while Messrs. Brooking, Walden, and myself are in Ashánti.

APPENDIX, F.

Extract of a Letter from the late Rev. William Thackwray, Wesleyan Missionary, dated Anamabu, May 5th, 1841.

I AM just on the point of leaving for Domonási, most of my boxes and household requisites having arrived there already. I would not forget to mention to you with pleasure, that a native merchant here, Mr. Parker, has made me a present of a lathe, not of the first-rate kind, it is true, but still useful, which I immediately devoted to the Mission, and it has gone off to Domonási this morning, with other things. Mr. and also Mrs. Freeman are here at present; the former designing to accompany me to-morrow morning to Domonási. With respect to Ashánti we can say as yet but little or nothing. Mr. Freeman, as perhaps he will inform you, has had a very friendly and gratifying correspondence with the King of Ashánti; and we confidently hope, that, by the favour of an overruling Providence, the Gospel of our Lord Jesus Christ will be happily introduced, and established, among the barbarous and warlike Ashántis. Yes, I trust the blessing of heaven will descend upon them like showers upon the mown grass; that the moral wilderness may be glad for English Christian Missionaries, and that the intellectual and spiritual "desert" of Ashánti, will "blossom as the rose." True it is, that the national character of the Ashántis has been prominently distinguished by ferocity, and (perhaps sometimes not without cause) by political jealousy; and that, therefore, this great and critical enterprise should be undertaken with the utmost prudence, and managed with the utmost caution. Even at this moment, owing, I believe, to the death of one of the King's relatives, there is a great "custom" being made in Kumási, which is to last for several weeks, and in which perhaps one hundred and fifty, or two hundred, or perhaps more, will unhappily, by this blood-thirsty religion of the devil, lose their lives. Yet far be it from us to be discouraged. Other tribes and other people, as fierce as the fierce Ashántis, have been tamed and subdued, converted and evangelized, by the preaching of "the cross of our Lord Jesus Christ:" and does He still live? Yes, "He ever liveth." And are his will, and willingness, and power the same? Without controversy, "He changeth not;" and I delight, even on African ground, to remember, that it is declared, it is written in the volume of infallible inspiration, that the "Gospel of the kingdom shall be preached in all the world, for a witness unto all nations;" yea, and that another prophecy of the same volume is, "The kingdoms of this world shall become the kingdoms of our God and of his Christ." We will not, then, by the grace of God, be faint-hearted. Rather, we will be highly animated and encouraged in our blessed and soul-cheering work. The Lord has enabled me to introduce the Gospel into Egá, a croom on the beach about a mile from Anamabu. It was formerly visited by Mr. Wrigley, but it was afterwards relinquished, and in that sense neglected; and hence the partial success gained, had gradually vanished away. Mr. Hesk has been too ill to visit Egá, so that the interpreters and I have had it to ourselves. We did not hold regular service, (this would have been premature,) but catechetical conversations; and the effects are pleasing and promising.

APPENDIX, G.

Extract of a Letter from President Maclean, dated Cape-Coast Castle, September 11th, 1841.

Mr. Freeman's letters, and Mr. Hesk personally, will make you acquainted with the melancholy loss which your Mission in this quarter has sustained, by the late deaths of Mrs. Freeman and Mrs. Hesk. As Mr. Freeman will, doubtless, have detailed to you very fully the apparent causes which led to those lamented losses, I need not enter into them; but, as every death of a European, which occurs in this country, is invariably ascribed, in England, to the effects of climate, and as the late deaths, added to those of Messrs. Thackwray and Walden, will, I fear, cast a damp on the exertions of our Christian friends in England, I feel anxious to remove, in some measure, from your mind, the idea that these deaths have been caused *solely* by the climate. In point of fact, each of the lamented individuals in question had passed safely through the seasoning fever; and I do think, that, with sufficient prudence and care, their lives might have been preserved. I ought, indeed, to except Mrs. Freeman's case; for her death was occasioned by an hereditary and peculiar complaint. I am far, however, from taxing the others with positive imprudence or recklessness of life; but when persons have arrived at a certain age, their habits and opinions on the subject of health become generally fixed, and they will not readily forego those habits and opinions, however earnestly urged by those who are much better acquainted with the country and climate, than they can possibly be. While, then, I would fain hope that the friends of West African Missions will not be cast down by the late events, but will continue their generous exertions in a cause so sacred, I would, at the same time, take the liberty of suggesting that young persons should, if possible, be selected for the work of the Mission in this country. Their constitutions not being fully formed, they would become more readily and easily acclimated, than persons more advanced in life; and they would more willingly listen to, and adopt, the suggestions of persons more experienced than themselves.

In conclusion, I beg to assure you, that my poor services may be made at all times available, for the furtherance of the great cause, to which you and so many others have devoted their lives and means.

APPENDIX, H.

Extract of a Letter from the Rev. Thomas B. Freeman, dated British Akrah, September 10th, 1841.

WHILE the Expedition was staying at Akrah, we were visited by President Maclean, accompanied by Captain Tucker, Commander of Her Majesty's frigate "Iris," and the two Captains Allen, of the "Soudan" and "Wilberforce." Captain Tucker informed us of an opening for Missionary enterprise on the banks of the Gaboon, where some of the natives are very anxious for religious instruction; and have told him, that if a Teacher could be sent to them, they would furnish him with a house, and undertake to support him. Captain Tucker said he was so fully satisfied that the establishment of Missions, &c., in the slave-dealing states, would be the most effectual means of destroying the slave-trade, that he would embrace an early opportunity of taking one of us down in the "Iris" to visit these people, and see what can be done; after which he would bring him back again to the Station. This is a noble offer, of which, I trust, we shall be able to avail ourselves.*

With the Niger Expedition came the Ashánti Princes, and I am glad to find them promising young men. They will be exposed to many dangers on their arrival in Kumási. O God, preserve them! Mr. Brooking and I shall leave for Kumási in company with them. We start for that capital of Ashánti, God willing, early in October. Our prospects all around are cheering, and we are expecting much success and prosperity in our work. The mind of the King of Ashánti seems to be still favourably disposed towards us. May the Lord turn his heart as the "rivers of water!"

Though my opportunities of becoming acquainted, since my return, with the spiritual state of our societies, have been rather limited, yet I rejoice to say, that I find many things of a very encouraging character. There is a marked attention paid to the preaching of the word of life. Our seasons of grace at the Lord's table have been of the most hallowed description. The prayer-meetings are very exhilarating means of grace, and the congregations are generally good.

---

* Can you send us out a Missionary for this enterprise? Our party is now so small, that we could only spare one for a few months, or, at the longest, on a Mission of observation to the Gaboon. A man of great MORAL COURAGE, and PRUDENCE OF THE HIGHEST ORDER, would be required.

APPENDIX, I.

Extract of a Letter from the Rev. S. A. Shipman, dated Cape-Coast Castle, Nov. 9th, 1841.

HAVING but a very short notice of the sailing of the "New Times," I simply write to state, that Messrs. Freeman and Brooking left this for Kumási on Saturday last, the 6th instant, accompanied by the two Ashánti Princes. They were all in the enjoyment of good health and spirits, and are daily commended by us all to the blessing and protection of God our heavenly Father. As the suspicions and jealousies of the King appear greatly removed, no delay is expected from him, such as Mr. Freeman experienced before, but they hope to arrive in Kumási in a fortnight from the time of leaving Cape Coast.

You will be aware that the societies on the coast are now left under the care of Mr. Watson and myself. We have both, especially of late, been the subjects of much affliction, and are not yet able to undertake our work fully. Our health, however, is improving daily, as the latter rains have ceased, and the fine weather is setting in. Mrs. Shipman continues also to enjoy better health. We expect and are looking for a reinforcement soon.

APPENDIX, K.

Extract of a Letter from the Rev. John Watson, dated December 24th, 1841.

THE Rev. Messrs. Freeman and Brooking *entered Kumási*, the capital of Ashánti, on Monday, the 13th instant; though no letters have been received from them since their arrival. I saw an Ashánti at Elmina on the 21st instant, who was in Kumási when they arrived, and left it on the evening of the same day, for the coast. The "African Queen" sails this day at four o'clock; and it will probably be three weeks or a month before another vessel leaves the coast for England. Mr. and Mrs. Shipman, and myself, are all quite well, and enjoying excellent health and spirits. The former are intended to remain here, and the latter is expected to become the colleague of Mr. Brooking, when Mr. Freeman returns, which will probably be very shortly.

SECOND JOURNAL

OF THE

REV. THOMAS B. FREEMAN.

CHAPTER I.

DEPARTS FROM CAPE COAST FOR KUMASI—ASABU—AKROFUL—TUKWAH—YANKUMASI—CHIBBU—MANSU—BENEFICIAL EFFECTS OF THE MISSION IN MANSU—ERNEBIRIM—FASUWIA—CROSSES THE RIVER PRAH—ARRIVAL OF A MESSENGER WITH A LETTER FROM THE KING OF ASHANTI—ESIRIMAN—ANSAH—AKWANSIREM—PASSES THE ADANSI HILLS.

SATURDAY, Nov. 6th, 1841.—All things being ready, after great trouble in preparation, at half-past twelve, P. M., we started on our journey to Kumási. Our party consists of the two Princes,* Henry Smith, Esq., (who thinks of accompanying us to the River Prah,) the Rev. Robert Brooking, my interpreter, our servants, about one hundred and fifty carriers from the coast, with one hundred and sixty from Ashánti, and a Sergeant and six soldiers from the Fort. The party may altogether amount to three hundred and forty men.

The most difficult part of our work was that of conveying the carriage, which the Committee has sent out, as a present for the King. The narrowness of the road in many places impeded us much; and night coming on before we could reach a croom with the body of the

---

* William Quantamissah, and John Ansah, who had accompanied the Niger Expedition from England as far as Cape-Coast Castle.—ED.

carriage, we were obliged to leave it on the side of the road, with a few men in charge of it; after which we proceeded to the nearest village.

The men who carried our clothes, provisions, &c., not being aware of our having been detained with the carriage, had proceeded to a still more distant croom, where I had informed them we should probably stop for the night. In consequence of this, we were obliged to retire to rest, without any refreshment; and, as our mattresses were taken forward, nearly all of us had to sleep on the ground, in small huts. John Ansah slept in his basket, and I spread my cloak on the ground.

Sunday, 7th.—Early in the morning many of our carriers returned with some of the clothes, provisions, &c.

At about ten minutes before twelve, A. M., we held divine service: Mr. Brooking read prayers, and I preached from part of 2 Cor. v. It was an interesting service: many of our carriers were present. Lord, let thy blessing attend thy word!

About five-and-twenty minutes before three, P. M., we had a short but heavy shower of rain, with some thunder.

Last night the men who had the care of the carriage, saw a very large horned snake: they could not ascertain its length; in circumference it was about the size of a man's arm.

I have now spent another Sabbath in the wilderness. What a mercy it is that my lot was cast in a land of Bibles! How great are my privileges above those of the poor Pagans around me!

"I take the blessing from above,
And wonder at thy boundless love!"

8th.—We started from Inkubem at six, A. M. The

men travel much better with the carriage this morning. We reached Asabu at a quarter before eight, where we halted for breakfast. The morning was very fine, and the appearance of the country beautiful, with a balmy atmosphere. The plantations of plantains, &c., are in splendid condition; *Canna Indica* is in full bloom in every direction.

After breakfast we again resumed our journey. The heat was very oppressive. We were overtaken by heavy rain, which impeded our progress much. We rested to change our wet clothes for dry ones, and also to dine, at Akroful. We started from Akroful at a quarter past three, P. M., and reached Tukwah at half-past five, where we stopped for the night. The crooms we have passed through to-day are small; and the carriage has given us an immense deal of trouble, and very much impeded our progress. We are not more than one good day's journey from Cape-Coast, though we have been a day and a half actually travelling. To-morrow we intend to have the carriage drawn, instead of being carried; as such labour is too much for any men, even natives, to contend with, in a climate so hot and exhausting. I trust we shall succeed in forwarding the vehicle to Kumási, as it will be a most extraordinary sight, which, I trust, will operate favourably on the King's mind.

The fire-flies are numerous around us this evening; many of them flying about our little tent, and emitting their faint but beautiful rays.

O God, my God, how excellent is thy loving-kindness! In the midst of all my acute trials, thou cheerest my drooping spirits, and comfortest my heart. O let me daily see thee in thy splendid works around; let me feel thy love in my heart; let thy blessing attend me in this and every enterprise which may have thy glory, in the welfare of perishing men, for its object; and let me daily rejoice in thine abundant mercy, through my blessed Redeemer! Amen.

9th.—About eight, A. M., we started, having first put the carriage on the wheels. About noon we reached Dunquah, rested the people for half an hour, and then proceeded to Yankumási. On the way we were overtaken by a tornado: the rains and thunder were very heavy. Keeping behind with the carriage, I got wet, and did not reach Yankumási until half-past five, P. M.

Chibbu (the Asín Chief) was seated under his umbrella, with his Captains, &c., ready to receive us. Finding that I was on the way with the carriage, he had sent a party of men to remove the fallen trees, &c., out of the road. He received us very kindly, and seemed glad to see us.

10th.—We started, at half-past six, A. M., for Mansu, accompanied by Chibbu, and a party of his men; who assisted in removing the obstacles out of our way, in passing through the forest with the carriage. The day was very fine; and the beautiful scenery around us,—the appearance of so large a party of men, laden with packages, shouting as they wound their way among the gigantic forest-trees, over hill and vale,—the sound of Chibbu's rustic band, drums, &c., which were played nearly the whole day,—and the well-known sound of the axe and bill-hook, clearing some of the smaller trees out of the path, combined to form a scene of a very romantic and exciting description. At half-past six, P. M., we reached Akiási, having left the carriage about two miles behind us in the forest, on account of the darkness of the evening.

11th.—At half-past five, A. M., we went to bring up the carriage to Akiási, took breakfast, and proceeded to Mansu, where we arrived about noon. Gabri, the Chief, received us very kindly, and appeared very glad to see me. I had not seen him since my return from England.

12th.—We halted at Mansu to rest the men, and to make various preparations to facilitate our journey to Kumási, through the more thinly populated, and less cultivated parts of Fanti.

Mr. Brooking's few months' residence at Mansu has had a very salutary effect; and the people are much pleased at the idea of an European Missionary residing among them. Our little school, which has cost us some trouble to establish, on account of the prejudices of the people, contains eleven children, several of whom are beginning to make pleasing progress in their learning. When I passed through this place to Kumási in 1839, nothing had been done, and no Missionary had ever visited it; but now, my ears are saluted, and my heart gladdened, by the sweet melody of the children, who have learned to sing the praises of God. Small as the number of children may appear, this is a great change in so short a period.

Another source of encouragement is, that we hope soon to have a large and convenient Mission-house here, for the use of brethren passing up to Kumási, at which stores, &c., may be kept, and forwarded to Kumási whenever required. This will be a great advantage to us.*

---

* While preaching at Mansu, on my return from Kumási, I adverted to the wonderful change which had taken place in a few years, and reminded the people, that, formerly, no European would have thought of visiting Mansu, much less of residing there. I adverted to the scenes of bloodshed and desolation which had taken place in the neighbourhood, and the want of confidence among all parties, whether Europeans, Fantis, Ashántis, or Asins; and compared such a state, with our peaceful and quiet visits among them. They reflected on the fact, and were filled with astonishment.

13th.—At nine, A.M., we proceeded on our journey. In about two hours we were overtaken by a heavy rain, which continued, more or less, nearly the whole of the afternoon.

Gabri followed us to Inkwirasu, the first croom after leaving Mansu, and there bade us farewell, sending forward a company of men with a Captain, to clear the road more effectually, that we might pass with the carriage.

Though Chibbu had handsomely assisted us along from Dunquah to Mansu, he also sent a Captain with several men before, to assist Gabri's people in clearing the road to the river Prah.

The heavy rains, and the large stumps and roots of trees, made the road so bad, that we were obliged to leave the carriage about three miles behind us. We reached Ernebirim about five, P.M.

Sunday, 14th.—At eleven, A.M., I conducted divine service under the shade of some splendid Plantain-trees. Many of the people were present, and paid steady attention to the word of life.

Fifteen of our men had been left behind with the carriage, and we had decided on returning to them early to-morrow morning to bring it up to the croom, which work we hoped to accomplish by noon, or one, P.M., intending to take one hundred men with us, to assist in clearing the road. About one, just when we had finished our conversation about the carriage, to our great surprise, the men made their appearance with it in the croom. They were, I think stimulated to accomplish this extraordinary task, first, from a wish to please and astonish us, not considering the conscientious veneration in which we held the Sabbath; and, secondly, from an objection which they had to spend another cold damp night in the forest. Rain fell early in the afternoon, preceded by intense sultry heat.

15th.—At six, A.M., we proceeded on our journey. The roads were wet and heavy. We halted to breakfast at Kwatua-Kuma, a very small croom. After breakfast, the Princes, with Messrs. Smith and Brooking, left me behind at this place with the carriage, at my own particular request, and proceeded towards the Prah. I made this request, because it was necessary for me to travel as slowly as the carriage, which I feared would be irksome to my companions, as my attention to it was so much engaged, as not to admit of my having much intercourse with them. I stopped for the night at Bansu.

16th.—At half-past five, A.M., I renewed my journey. The roads were better, and we made greater progress. I reached Fasuwia at a quarter to five, P.M., and rested for the night. Very heavy rain in the evening, with thunder and lightning. I saw some splendid butterflies, with colours of the richest hue.

17th.—At half-past five, A.M., we proceeded on our way through a beautiful country, full of luxuriant vegetation. The heat was very intense. We halted for the night at Apunsi.

18th.—At five, A.M., we resumed the journey. The country is beautiful, but the heat was oppressive. There are splendid insects in great abundance. We saw a beautiful species of *Quercus*, heavily laden with acorns. We reached Dansamisu at six, P.M., and rested for the night.

19th.—At ten minutes to five, A.M., I started for the Prah, which splendid river I reached in safety about half-past eleven. I am truly thankful for journeying mercies. I found Mr. Brooking poorly; but my other travelling companions were in good health.

I feel it to be a cause of humble gratitude to Almighty God, that no serious accident has hitherto occurred during a journey of eighty or ninety miles through the Fanti country; while the carriage has been taken through the most rugged and difficult paths, over steep banks and rocks, down ravines, and over rivers.

My own good health is to me extraordinary, amidst so much labour, care, and anxiety, added to my many sorrows: but why do I speak of them?

> "'Tis magnanimity to hide the wound."

O my full heart!

> "Heaven gives us friends to bless the present life,
> Removes them to prepare us for the next."

Since we left Cape Coast, on Saturday, the 6th ult., I have not ridden more than ten miles; the journey I have generally performed on foot, in company with the men who are taking the carriage; and, on account of the incessant rain which we have had, the roads were so miry, that I was wet in my legs and feet nearly the whole of each succeeding day. The only inconvenience I have suffered from this exposure, has been constant and violent attacks of tooth-ache, a thorn in the flesh, to remind me, in the midst of my otherwise good health and arduous labours, that my deathless spirit is still inhabiting a frail tenement of clay.

On Thursday morning last, while busily engaged in starting the men with the carriage, in the twilight, about five o'clock, I met with an accident, which might have deprived me of the use of at least one of my fingers on my left hand, by the knuckle coming in contact with the edge of a sharp felling-axe, which cut some way into the bone.

20th.—The heat is very intense. In the afternoon I went up the river, for a short distance, in a canoe.

The weather was fine, and the scene indescribably beautiful.

From the great quantity of rain which has recently fallen, the river is higher than usual for this season of the year; and the increased depth of water adds greatly to its beauty. The foliage of the trees on its banks baffles all attempts at description. The gigantic *Bombax*, covered with climbers, *Epiphytical Orchidacea*, towering high above the other trees of the forest; the numerous varieties of *Mimosa*, growing from fifty to seventy feet high, and presenting to the admiring eye all the gracefulness and beauty of *Mimosa Sensitiva*. The Bamboo-palm, with its beautiful leaves, from eighteen to twenty-four feet in length; the *Elais Guineensis*, nearly equal in beauty to the former, and its interest heightened by its almost life-sufficing qualities; the Plantain-tree, with its splendid foliage, and beautiful nodding bunch of fruit; the gaudy plumage of the birds, which warble on banks or flit across the stream, and the ever-grateful, ever-pleasing sound of the rapidly-running waters,—all united to form a scene, of a most magnificent description.

Roll on, ye dark-brown waters, in obedience to the Almighty fiat! help to swell the proud waves of that ocean which bears the messengers of peace, and the glad tidings of salvation, to these dark and benighted regions; return again in rain to water the thirsty earth: beautiful emblem of those showers of heavenly grace, which will in due time water the moral desert of Africa, and cause it to rejoice and blossom as the rose, the droppings of which are already felt and seen. Yes; it is no wild enthusiasm to hope, and believe, that the day is coming when the waters of the Prah shall wander through Christian realms, while many shall admire its beauties, appreciate its worth, and adore the God of nature, and the God of grace, who causes its streams to flow.

Sunday, 21st.—Mr. Brooking is unwell. At eleven, A. M., I conducted divine service, and preached to a large congregation. Many of the Ashántis who are travelling with us were present, and great attention was paid to the word of life.

I intended to preach again in the cool of the evening, but was hindered by the threatening appearance of the clouds, which gave indications of a tornado.

22d.—At five, A. M., I collected the people together, lashed two large canoes alongside of each other, and took the carriage across the Prah. While engaged in preparations for crossing the river, a messenger appeared on the opposite bank, with a letter from the King of Ashánti, of which the following is a copy:—

"*Kumási, Nov. 19th*, 1841.

"REV. SIR,

"I AM now prepared to receive you and my nephews. I expected to see you here on the 22d of this month; but am now informed that you are detained on the road longer than I imagined: please, therefore, to let me know when you think you can reach Kumási; for I am anxious that you should proceed as quick as you can.

"Yours faithfully,

"QUAKO DUAH."

After breakfast I answered the King's letter, sent the soldiers back to Cape-Coast Castle with a letter for the President, and then crossed the river and proceeded with the whole party to Kikiwiri, where we remained for the night.

The croom being very small, and containing but few

CROSSING THE PRAH WITH THE CARRIAGE.

houses, many of the men were obliged to erect for themselves temporary sheds, covered with Plantain-leaves, to protect them from the rain which threatened to fall: fortunately, however, for the whole party, the night was dry and fine.

23d.—At half-past five, A. M., we pursued our journey, the weather still improving, with some indications of the approaching *harmattan* season; generally known by very cold nights, and a peculiarly dark and hazy atmosphere. We travelled through a part of the country thickly wooded, and gently undulating, and rested for the night at Esiriman.

24th.—At half-past five, A. M., we resumed our journey, and breakfasted in the forest. At ten, we passed through Ansah, formerly the residence of one of the great Asín Chiefs, now a small, diminutive croom. Its former extent may be ascertained pretty correctly, by some splendid Banyan-trees surrounding the present croom in different directions; which, doubtless, stood in the centre of some of the largest streets, when Ansah was in its prosperity.

I found a moss, of the most minute and beautiful description, growing on the leaves of a species of *Acrostichum*. The weather is still improving, the air is dry and pure, the roads are well cleansed, and travelling is both pleasant and interesting. We halted for the night at Akrofrum.

25th.—At half-past five, A. M., we went forward with an intention, if possible, to cross the Adansi hills before night. On our arrival at Akwansirem, where we took breakfast, we were met by another messenger from the King, accompanied by fifty men to assist us on our way. After we had travelled about two hours from this place, the dryness of the road, the peculiar state of the atmosphere, and the gradual ascent we made, all proved to us that we were attaining a considerable elevation. About noon we reached the small croom where I slept on my former visit to Ashánti, after my detection of poor Korinchi's deceit, and consequent determination to return to the Prah, if I could not immediately pass up to Kumási.

I rested at this little place under the influence of peculiar feelings. The old man, who is Chief of the croom, recognised me with a smiling countenance, and welcomed me with a present of a pot of palm-wine.

To heighten the interest of the scene, one of the messengers whom Korinchi sent after me on that trying occasion, was present, with several persons from Quisah. I trust I felt thankful to the God of all mercies, for favouring me with success in this work, amidst all my trials and conflicts, and bringing me again to gaze on these scenes which are rendered familiar by circumstances, connected with most interesting associations. Here memory, that invaluable blessing, seems over-officious; and, in spite of all my efforts to suppress them, my troubled thoughts fly back to those scenes of distress and anguish, through which I have been destined to pass during the last six months. O mystery of Providence! God of my life! thou art infinitely merciful, even in thy darkest and most mysterious dispensations!

> "What mighty troubles hast Thou shown
> Thy feeble, tempted followers here!
> We have through fire and water gone,
> But saw Thee on the floods appear,
> But felt Thee present in the flame,
> And shouted our Deliverer's name."

At half-past one, P. M., we arrived at the foot of the great Adansi hill: we stopped an hour to rest, and take refreshment, and then prepared to make the ascent.

Seventy men, part of them Ashántis, drew up the carriage to the summit, without halting. The sight was beautiful and interesting; from two to three hundred yards, the ascent approaches nearest to a perpendicular, of any I have ever seen; and, while we were making this ascent, the scene was almost terrific. The appearance of the carriage, winding up among the lofty forest-trees, surrounded by from one to two hundred native Fantis and Ashántis actually shouting for joy, as they beheld the carriage steadily ascending without accident, while all nature around looked gay; the lofty hills, rising in the distance on every hand; the fruitful valleys, winding to the right and left; the immense forest, stretching beyond, as far as the eye could reach; and all, as it were, laughing beneath the bright sun of a tropical sky; filled the reflecting mind with wonder and delight. But this was not all. For where is the Christian mind that is familiar with the past history of these once-hostile tribes—who were so long engaged in mortal conflict, producing all around a scene of almost unbroken desolation, both natural and moral—that does not behold in the conduct of the natives of both tribes,—in their harmony of meeting, and their unity of action,—a great moral change, a great moral triumph? Gazing on a sight like this, the beholder is reminded of those scenes, which the evangelical Isaiah's ardent and prophetic mind contemplated. He hears "the mountains and hills break forth into singing," and sees the trees of the fields "clap their hands."

CHAPTER II.

FOMUNAH—KORINCHI'S DISGRACE—SECOND LETTER OF WELCOME FROM THE KING—DUMPASI—INTERESTING CIRCUMSTANCE DURING DIVINE SERVICE—NATURAL SCENERY—LUDICROUS ADVENTURE ON LEAVING DUMPASI—AKWANKOWASI—SIGNS OF CIVILIZATION—A HUMAN SACRIFICE—EDUABIN—KARSI—PRINCE QUANTAMISSAH'S SISTER.

About a quarter before five, P.M., we reached Quisah, when we rested for half an hour, and then proceeded to Fomunah. On our arrival at Fomunah, I found the same quarters provided for me, which I occupied during my long detention, previous to my former visit to Kumási.

Strange, indeed, were my feelings on entering the simple dwelling, where I had before spent so many weeks of tedious and distressing anxiety, and experienced so large a measure of divine support and comfort!

Poor Korinchi, my old friend, and, I may almost say, companion, with whom I formerly spent so many interesting hours, is no longer Chief of Adansi. By some very turbulent conduct in the King's presence, during the investigations of a palaver between himself and one of his Captains, he incurred the displeasure of his Sovereign, has been dishonoured, and another Chief placed on the stool of Adansi in his stead. I understand he is now living at Bruman, a croom about twelve miles from Kumási: I therefore hope to see him again.

26th.—In the afternoon, the new Chief received us in due form, and according to the etiquette of the country.

We have determined to rest here for a few days: a repose which will be very grateful to my feelings, as I have walked nearly all the way from the Coast, a distance of nearly one hundred and fifteen miles, frequently over rough and heavy roads, with the daily care and anxiety of moving the carriage along unbeaten paths, and over rivers, &c., where no such thing had been before.

27th.—We were busily engaged in erecting a large, temporary shed for divine worship, &c. Mr. Brooking is still poorly. Lord of the harvest, give us, I entreat thee, strength to labour for the eternal welfare of our perishing fellow-men!

Many of my old friends have called to see me; others meet me occasionally in my walks through the town and neighbourhood, and, with smiling countenances, give me a hearty welcome.

The people, in every place where we rest, appear delighted to see the Princes, returning to their native home, so much improved, and under circumstances so pleasing. O that the great and important objects of their Christian education may be fully and entirely answered! May the God of all grace keep and preserve them from the dangers with which they are surrounded!

Sunday, 28th.—At half-past ten, A. M., divine service was performed. I read prayers, and Mr. Brooking preached. The congregation was large and attentive: many Ashántis were also present.

In the afternoon I again conducted the worship of God. The congregation was, as in the morning, attentive.

29th.—I was rather poorly. The heat was very intense during the middle of the day, with a strong *harmattan*.

My age has this day numbered thirty-two years; but how small a portion of my life have I spent in the service of God! and how very imperfect have been my best services, unprofitable servant that I am! May the God of grace strengthen me, and make use of one of the most unworthy of his children in carrying his eternal purposes of mercy to a guilty race!

"Much of my time hath run to waste,
And I, perhaps, am near my home;
O God, forgive my follies past,
And give me strength for days to come!"

30th.—I wrote letters, and sent off messengers and carriers to the coast.

Dec. 1st.—A person arrived from the King, informing us, that His Majesty will receive us in Kumási on Monday, the 13th instant.

2d.—Another messenger arrived, with a letter from the King, of which the following is a copy:—

"*Kumasi, Nov.* 30*th*, 1841.

"Rev. Sir,

"Yours of the 22d of this month I received on the 25th ultimo. I am very sorry that you could not reach Kumási on the 22d, as the *Adai* custom, which has now commenced, will not permit me to receive you until after the 10th of the next month.

"I am making arrangements for receiving you on Monday, the 13th; and give you this early information, that you may have plenty of time to make your arrangements also, for reaching Kumási at the time mentioned. Tell Mr. Henry Smith to come with you if he likes: it will afford me pleasure to see him. Salute my nephews with a kiss for me, and oblige

"Yours sincerely,

"Quako Duah."

3d.—Busily preparing to resume our journey.

4th.—At two, p. m., we started for Dumpási, where we arrived about a quarter before four. The road was well cleared, and prepared for the carriage: the natives were much surprised at seeing in their town a machine drawn upon four wheels. The weather was very hot and dry.

Sunday, 5th.—At half-past eleven, A. M., Mr. Brooking performed divine service under the shade of a large Banyan-tree. The King's messengers and many Ashántis attended. Mr. Brooking preached from Hebrews ii. At four, P. M., I conducted the worship of God in the same place. The King's messengers, with several of their people, and many of the inhabitants of the town attended. I preached from Acts viii. 34, 35. During the sermon, I asked them if they believed that I was speaking the truth; to which the chief messenger answered in the affirmative, saying they did not suppose I should come all the way from England to tell them lies; and that if they had thought so, they would not have come to hear me. They paid deep attention to the word of life. May the Lord seal the instruction on their hearts!

6th.—Remaining for a short time at Dumpási, I went into the forest, and saw a pretty variety of *Justicia:* the colour was pink and white, and the leaf large and deeply nerved, very much like *Justicia Nervosa.* I also saw a handsome species of *Hibiscus*, which I had never seen before; the leaf was large, and the flower pink and white.

The insects in the neighbourhood of Fomunah and Dumpási are very fine; many of the butterflies are large, double the size of the purple Emperor of England. Their colours are also rich. The wings of some are beautifully striated. One of my hammock-men caught a fine species of hawk-moth: unfortunately, the rich down was so much rubbed off from the wings, that I did not see it in perfection. Its principal colour was green.

In the evening many of our carriers, and a party of

the Ashántis, collected together at one end of the town, and danced for the space of an hour or more, to the sound of their rude music, which was played by the Ashántis. Though I could not, of course, admire the dance, yet the idea of the harmony which is now beginning to exist betwixt the two nations, produced in my mind the most thrilling sensation. Yes, the most bitter, the most determined, enemies are become friends; and thus is a gracious Providence, preparing the way for the introduction of the Gospel of peace among them.

The scenery about Dumpási, though not so bold as that of Quisah and Fomunah, is very beautiful. The town is skirted on one side by immense forest-trees, chiefly Silk-cotton, towering to an enormous height; (from one hundred and fifty to two hundred feet;) and, as the shades of evening approach, the appearance of the dark green foliage of the underwood, the huge grey trunks of the trees running perpendicularly to a height of eighty or one hundred feet entirely without branches, at which height the huge arms extend themselves almost horizontally to a great distance, presenting one of the most majestic objects on which the eye can rest; —and the empurpled heavens, appearing in the mighty distance beyond these sylvan shades, while the gentle zephyr is scarcely perceptible as it wafts over the way the balmy fragrance of some of Flora's richest beauties, —all combine to produce a scene bordering on enchantment. The peaceful shades of the interior of Guinea are peculiarly grateful to a reflecting mind. In walking through these splendid scenes, I felt the force of the following lines of an eminent poet:—

"'Tis the pure hour for poetry and thought,
When passions sink, and man surveys the heavens,
And feels himself immortal!"

7th.—At half-past four, A. M., I sent to call the people to prepare for resuming our journey. At five, nearly every thing was ready.

When travelling every day successively, there is but little trouble in managing the men; but if they are allowed to rest for a day or two, there is a danger of their unintentionally becoming almost unmanageable; or, at least, out of order. Of this I had a specimen this morning in the conduct of my hammock-men, who, though Pagans, are some of the most obedient and docile men in the country. They had been, as I have already observed, called up at half-past four; but five o'clock came, without any making their appearance, so that I stood waiting for them to take up my chair, and proceed with the rest of the party. I sent for them a second time, but they came not. I then thought it best to go after them myself; and, on entering their quarters, I found them all comfortably seated, taking an early breakfast. This was out of all order, as they were allowed plenty of time to take their meals whenever we rested during the day: they knew they were wrong, and took the alarm the moment they saw me. As I entered, they jumped up, and flew in every direction. They had been sitting round a large earthen pot of soup, out of which they were all feeding with their fingers. In their hurry they broke the pot to pieces, spilling the contents on the ground. The doors of the native dwellings are generally small; and as several of them tried to rush through at the same time, they knocked down a part of the wall near it. One of them ran into a small yard, where his progress was retarded by a wall about six feet high, plastered with swish or clay. Determined not to be foiled by the wall, though a pretty strong one of its kind, he, with astonishing activity, commenced pulling a part of it down, occasionally looking over one of his shoulders, to see if I was coming after him; and in a little time that seemed almost incredible, he was at his post with his companions. I need not say, that this fracas caused me no small amusement; and as these frail buildings are so easily repaired, the damages were not enough to cause much regret. When I pointed out to the men the inconsistency of their conduct in being so late at their posts, they acknowledged their error, and promised amendment.

At a quarter past five, A. M., we proceeded on our journey. The morning was very fine. We halted to breakfast at Sakwanta, and then proceeded to Akwankowási, where we arrived at ten; and as we had plenty of time before us, the King having arranged for receiving us in Kumási on Monday next, we took up our quarters for the night.

The scenery around this place is chaste and pretty. The croom is smaller than either Fomunah or Dumpási. It is situated on a rising ground, and surrounded by a belt of Plantains, beyond which rise, in majestic beauty, some large Silk-cotton trees, intermingled with some splendid specimens of *Acacia* and *Mimosa*, from thirty to fifty feet high. There are also several large trees, covered with papilionaceous climbers, with foliage of the most beautiful description. Walking out in the cool of the evening, I saw a species of *Acacia*, bearing a number of fine seed-vessels. I immediately had the tree cut down; and as I was watching it falling, I observed an immense moth, like some of the very large species brought to England from South America, fly from the top, and alight on a small shrub near the place where I stood. I had a small fly-net in my hand, but the handle was not long enough to reach it. I then tried to approach it by walking a few paces on the stem of a small tree near it, which grew in a slanting direction; but, before I could get at it, it flew away. I followed it through the forest for about one hundred yards without success. It was by far the largest insect of the kind which I have seen in Guinea, and was of a greyish colour, with large white circular spots on the wings.

These immense forests are full of objects of the highest interest to every lover of the book of nature. All around there is something on which to ponder and admire. The damp recesses produce the most splendid varieties of Ferns and Mosses, and other plants of the *Cryptogamia* family, which afford shelter and support for many kinds of moths and crustaceous insects, &c.; while the splendid vegetable productions of the higher grounds, with the beautiful insects flitting from tree to tree, fill the mind with pleasure.

In the course of the day, I saw in the town a white Negress. Her complexion was nearly as fair as that of a European: her hair, between an amber and a straw colour. She appeared to be about thirty years of age; but not so healthy as her jetty neighbours. It appeared to me as though her fair colour was the effect of some extraordinary family disease. It is not unusual to see the natives, and especially the men, with their arms and legs, hands and feet, covered with large white spots, from one to two inches broad, the effects of a disease called the *krankras*, and more frequently the effects of a kind of ring-worm, produced by an indiscriminate use of different species of *fungi*, indigenous to the soil of the country, which they use as mushrooms.

Many of the complaints of the natives appear to result from a careless selection of vegetable food; and there are instances in which vegetable matter, coming in contact with the skin, by some singular and extraordinary process causes a large swelling; which, on opening, contains a maggot about half an inch long.*

8th.—We stopped, as we intended, the whole day at Akwankowási: the heat was very intense. I cut down a species of *Mimosa*, to obtain some of its splendid seed-vessels, from twelve to fifteen inches in length: the foliage is exquisitely beautiful.

9th.—At half-past four, A. M., I sent round to call up the carriers, &c. At five, we started for Eduabin, and passed through a fine part of the country, more thickly populated and more extensively cultivated, than many parts of the interior through which I have passed since we left Mansu. We saw, a short distance from the path, a specimen of the Babab (*Adansonia Digitata*).

The roads are well cleared and prepared for us. We have to-day passed over several streams by means of temporary bridges, which have been thrown across by order of the King, to facilitate our journey with the carriage. These are the first attempts at making bridges which I have seen in the interior. They are constructed in the following manner: some stout, forked sticks or posts are driven in the centre of the stream, at convenient distances, across which are placed some strong beams, fastened to the posts with withes, from the numerous climbing-plants on every hand. On these bearers are placed long stout poles, which are covered with earth from four to six inches thick; and this completes the bridge. Great and important results are often produced by little things. And who knows to what this may lead? Our bringing the carriage, is the

* Probably a species of the *Filaria Medinensis*, or Guinea-worm, which is common in the southern parts of Asia, and in most parts of Africa.—ED.

cause of a better road being made through this part of Ashánti, than has ever been seen before; this is the unanimous testimony of all the people: good roads greatly promote civilization, and are an universal indication of national improvement.

At a quarter before three, P. M., we reached Eduabin, and halted for the night.

To-day I have heard of a repetition of those bloody scenes with which I became too familiar on my first visit to Ashánti. We rested and took breakfast at Amafuri, a pretty croom about a mile and a half from Bekwah, a large town, and the residence of Bekwah Osai, one of the most powerful of the Ashánti Chiefs. As the road to Kumási does not pass through Bekwah, we sent messengers to the Chief to present our respects, &c.; who, on their return, informed us, that a human sacrifice had been made in the town, and that the victim of this cruel superstition was lying exposed in the public street.

Merciful God, send down thy Spirit, enlighten these Pagans, and save the purchase of thy Son's atoning blood!

> "Assert thy worship and renown;
> O all-redeeming God, come down!"

Eduabin is beautifully situated on a small hill, surrounded by a splendid landscape. Its population is probably from seven to eight hundred, including the small crooms around. It is not now in that dilapidated state in which I found it on my first visit to Kumási: the houses are in better repair, and several new ones have been erected.

10th.—In the course of the forenoon, a misunderstanding took place between our Fanti carriers and the people of Eduabin, on account of the scanty supply of native food, with which the former were furnished. The Fanti complained, that himself and his companions could obtain no food; told some of the natives of the town that they ought to be ashamed of themselves, in allowing them to want food; and remarked, that when the Ashántis came down to Cape Coast, they always found a sufficient supply. One of the townspeople, piqued at the remark, took it up warmly, and said, "Well, if we do get plenty of food at Cape Coast, we pay for it." The Fanti, feeling at the time the cravings of hunger, and incensed at the insinuation of dishonest principle, into which he had construed the language of the Ashánti, answered, "We want nothing without paying for it; we are daily supplied with money to buy food; and do you think that our masters would allow us to take your things without paying for them?" These observations were followed by a scuffle between a few of the men of each nation; and the Ashánti who had been the principal talker in the affair, sustained some rough treatment. On hearing of this, I sent for the Fanti who had taken the leading part, and required him to remain on the spot, until I could investigate the matter. Shortly after, the King's messengers, and several of the Ashántis, came and entreated me to pardon the man. This I promised to do; but told them, that I must inquire strictly into the affair, and talk to the carriers, in order to prevent any thing of the kind in future.

Every preparation being made for our departure for Karsi, early in the afternoon we sat down to take refreshment, when I embraced the opportunity of investigating the above affair. On inquiry, I found that the Chief of Eduabin, to whom the greater number of the plantain plantations, &c., belonged, being at Kumási, the people were afraid to act in the absence of their master, and hence the scarcity of food that was in the town. This explanation, on the part of the Ashántis, was, of course, satisfactory; and ignorance thereof, on the part of the Fantis, was a sufficient excuse for their expressions of dissatisfaction. Things being thus comfortably settled, I then, in the presence of all the Ashántis, cautioned the Fantis against any unkind expressions or rash conduct; telling them, that we were now under the protection of the King of Ashánti, that I was responsible for their good conduct, and that if they had any complaints to make, they must bring them to me, and I would attend to them; but if they neglected to do this, and took the matter into their own hands, the first transgressor must expect just censure. Some of the men appeared affected, and all promised obedience. Gimahin, the chief of the King's messengers, said, "During our long and tedious journey of so many weeks, we have all been comfortable and happy; and it would be very foolish to fall out now, when we are nearly at the end of our journey."

We started from Eduabin at two, P. M., and reached Karsi about five. On our way we passed through Esargu, the little croom where I spent the last Sabbath on my first visit to Kumási. As we went along, the people recognised me with smiling countenances. The scenery of the forest near Karsi is peculiarly beautiful; the road, within a mile or two of the croom, leads through a splendid grove of *Acaciæ* and *Mimosæ*, many of them sixty or seventy feet high. O the majesty and splendour of these tropical forests! Hail, beautiful spots! may you soon resound with the name of Jesus!

11th.—At five, A. M., I called up the men to go into the forest and cut wood, &c., for a temporary cover; and by half-past twelve, P. M., we had a large, comfortable shed erected, thatched with grass and plantain-leaves.

In the course of the afternoon, messengers arrived from the King, with a present of three sheep and some palm-wine. Prince William Quantamissah's sister also came over from Kumási to see her brother. She is a fine young woman, about eighteen years of age. The chief messenger, who came from Kumási with the present, had in his hand a huge gold-handled sword, and a golden decanter: I presume they are the same which I saw on my first visit to the capital.

Sunday, 12th.—At half-past eleven, A. M., I conducted divine service under the large shed erected yesterday: the congregation was numerous and attentive. I preached from 2 Cor. viii. 9.

Mr. Brooking is poorly this morning. About half-past four, P. M., another party of messengers arrived from the King, with a present of palm-wine. The chief of the party rode on a strong Ashánti pony, with an Arabic or Moorish saddle and bridle.

CHAPTER III.

PREPARATIONS FOR ENTERING KUMASI—APOKO—FAVOURABLE RECEPTION BY THE KING—PRESENTATION OF THE CARRIAGE AND OTHER GIFTS—HUMAN SACRIFICES—A YOUNG EXECUTIONER—ASHANTIS ATTEND DIVINE WORSHIP—PRESENTS FROM THE KING—IMPORTANT CONVERSATION WITH HIM—SLAVERY—CHRISTMAS-DAY IN KUMASI—FAVOURABLE DISPOSITION OF APOKO AKIM—VALUE OF HIS SUPPORT—CURIOUS KIND OF FISH—COMMENCEMENT OF THE ADAI CUSTOM.

DECEMBER 13th.—We started from Karsi at five, A. M., and reached Kumási about seven. At the entrance of the town we halted, and had the carriage cleaned, and put in order for presentation. Afterwards we took breakfast, and waited for a messenger from the King. At half-past eight, my old friend Apoko arrived, with a countenance beaming with satisfaction and delight, on seeing me again. He was accompanied by a large train of attendants with gold-handled swords, and canes richly ornamented with gold. There were also several of the King's linguists in his train. They gave us a hearty welcome, telling us that the King would be ready to receive us soon. The carriage excited intense interest among a large crowd of the natives, who collected around while the men were preparing it.

Apoko left us for a time, and a servant from the King's household came to take charge of our luggage, and to see it safely lodged in our apartments.

About two, P. M., Apoko came to conduct us to the King. We found him seated in the same place where he sat to receive me on my first visit to Kumási. We paid our respects to him in the same manner as I had done previously, and then passed on, through an immense concourse of people, to take our seats at a distance, and there wait, to receive a return of the compliment from the King and his numerous Chiefs. His Majesty then sent us some palm-wine; and, after we had refreshed ourselves with a draught, the multitude was in motion, and the King and the Chiefs came round according to the usual custom. He stopped opposite us for some little time, and surveyed the Princes, Quantamissah and Ansah, from head to foot, (as they stood in their English military dresses, one on my right hand and the other on my left,) under the influence of considerable emotion. He appeared affected: it was indeed a noble scene. Yes; the King of Ashánti is capable of feeling some of those sensations which delight the heart, on a happy and auspicious meeting, after a long separation. If this be felt by the King of Ashánti, surrounded as he is by ignorance and gloom, O what must be the feeling of those happy spirits, who meet to part no more in the realms of glory! But whither am I wandering? I am still in the vale of tears!

I intended that the carriage should follow us in the procession, as we went round to pay our respects; but the crowd was so dense, that it was impossible; therefore I sent it to the place where we expected to take our seats. When the King came round, the carriage stood opposite to us, at a distance of six or eight yards; so that he came between us and the vehicle, and turning towards it, he surveyed it for some time with apparent satisfaction; after which he passed on, followed by many of his Captains. There was the same extraordinary display of barbaric gold, blood-stained stools, &c., as I witnessed on my former visit, with the exception of the horrible death-drum: this, I am glad to say, was not in the procession.

The gaudy pageant exhibited a hundred and twenty-five large Kabosirs' umbrellas, of various colours, some of which were very handsome. This was a larger number than I saw before. On my first visit I saw no female in the procession, strictly speaking; but on this occasion there was an elderly sister of the King, apparently occupying the position of Queen-mother,* who, with several of the King's wives, came round and shook us heartily by the hand.

Between the King's sister and his wives, there appeared about twenty-four girls, from eight to twelve years of age: their skins were marked with stripes of red ochre, pipe-clay, and charcoal, and each carried a small stick, covered with gold, about a foot long, one end of which was placed in their mouths.

14th.—At two, P. M., we visited the King. He was seated under his large umbrellas in front of his residence. I then formally introduced the Princes to him, and also Mr. Smith, (who had accompanied us from Cape Coast,) and also Mr. Brooking; and then, in the name of the Wesleyan Missionary Society, presented the carriage.

In doing this I told him, it was sent by the Society as a token of their good feeling towards himself and his people; and that they hoped he would use it, and that it would lead him to improve his country, by making good roads; which was one of the greatest means of promoting civilization, and also an indication of national advancement. He accepted the present, received the message in a very gracious manner, and begged me to present his thanks to the Society.

He further expressed his satisfaction at the return of the Princes; and his thanks to Her Majesty the Queen of England, and to Governor Maclean, for the kindness and attention which had been shown to them.

We then took our seats at a short distance, and the King and many of his Chiefs, &c., came and returned

* I find, on inquiry, that this person is the only sister the King has.

thanks according to the custom of the country. The carriage was then taken into one of the palace-yards, where the King met us to receive all the necessary information respecting the carriage, harness, &c. On my telling him, that Her Majesty the Queen of England, had seen it, he seemed much pleased, and said, "The Queen of England is Queen of Queens of the white people, and I am King of Kings of the black people; and now we have carriages alike: this is very good." After the necessary explanations were gone through, and the present was delivered up to the King, I felt thankful that so great a task, as that of conveying it for nearly two hundred miles through the forests of Guinea, where we had often been obliged to cut our way through the jungle, and to have recourse to various means, in order to transport it across the rivers and deep ravines, had been accomplished, and that so great a triumph of civilization over barbarism had been achieved. I felt it an ample reward, also, for an hundred and fifty miles journey on foot, and for the care and anxiety which I had felt during that journey. When we took our seats in the street where I introduced the Princes, &c., the King sent us some refreshment; consisting of Madeira wine, brandy, cherry-brandy, and liquors, with a supply of delicious water, all neatly served up in decanters on a tray, with tumblers and wine-glasses. The interview was altogether deeply interesting.

15th.—At half-past two, P. M., we went again to the royal residence, to deliver the presents which had been sent from Her Majesty the Queen of England, and the smaller presents from the Wesleyan Missionary Society. We took our own carpenters to open the packages. The first was a fine portrait of Her Majesty; with which the King was much pleased, and said, he should place it in his Stone-House, and often look at it, because it was very handsome, and because Her Majesty was his friend. The next box contained a view of Windsor Castle; and he was much pleased with the view of that noble residence.

After Her Majesty's presents followed several more from our Society; namely, cutlery from friends in Sheffield; a pair of boots, highly finished, from Macclesfield; a tin box from Mr. Chubb (japanned); some beautiful glass-ware, from Mr. Naylor, of London; and some handsome ladies' dresses, from friends at Keighley. All the presents were very graciously received, and the King seemed pleased with everything.

The King's sister (Queen-mother) was seated near him, and seemed much interested about the dresses. The King requested my interpreter to put on one of the ladies' cloaks, sent from Keighley; and he highly admired it. There were also some figured coloured muslin caps, from the same friends; with which the King was delighted, and said his Captains should wear them.

The beautiful chandelier, from Mr. Edge, of Westminster, brought out by Mr. Brooking, I am sorry to say, we could not present on this occasion; as the man who had charge of the glasses, had, we presume, fallen down with the box, during the journey from the coast, for we found three of the shades broken. We informed the King of it; and will try to make it complete, and present it as early as we can.

After these presents were delivered, the King returned his thanks to Her Majesty, and also to the Wesleyan Missionary Society; and placed before us refreshments of nearly the same description as those of yesterday.

16th.—I was busily engaged at my quarters: I had no interview with the King to-day.

17th.—I had no interview with the King. I was

glad to rest quietly at home, after so many days' excitement.

In the afternoon I heard that a Chief had died, and that three human sacrifices had been made in the town: the mangled victims were left in the public streets, as usual. O God, have mercy upon this benighted people! I saw a lad near my lodgings who is one of the King's executioners. He had decapitated a poor victim that morning. He appeared to be from sixteen to eighteen years of age. I asked him how many persons he had executed: he answered, "Eighty." O awful fact! eighty immortal spirits hurried into the eternal world, by the hands of a boy under eighteen years of age, and he only one of a large number engaged in the same dreadful employment! Surely, British Christians will not relax in their exertions, to send among the Ashántis the mild and peaceful Gospel!

18th.—Quiet at home. The heat is intense.

Sunday, 19th.—At half-past nine, A. M., I conducted divine service under a large shed, previously erected for that purpose. I read prayers, and preached from Isai. xlv. 22, 23. Many of the Ashántis were present, who paid serious attention to the word of life. The discourse was conversational; and many interesting and vital questions were answered by the people. They said at the close, that it was a "good palaver;" and that if all men would obey God, and keep his commandments, we should have a happy world. We then sung part of that beautiful hymn,—

"Come, thou Conqueror of the nations,
Now on thy white horse appear."

The singing seemed to fill them with delight. We closed the interesting service with prayer.

At four, P. M., Mr. Brooking preached from Isai. iii. 10. The congregation was even larger than in the morning. Many of the servants of the King's household were present, and one of the King's sons. This sermon was also conversational. Lord, hasten that happy day, when sanguinary Ashânti shall possess her sacred temples, erected for the worship of the living God, and her joyful myriads crowd the gates,

"Demanding life, impatient for the skies."

The King has sent us a bountiful supply of palm-wine every day in the week, except Tuesdays and Wednesdays, which are his fetish-days.

20th.—About three, P. M., Apoko came to inform us, that the King was sending us a present; and we took our seats to receive it, according to the usual practice. We had no sooner done so, than a long train of people made their appearance. Apoko and the other linguists took their seats opposite to us, surrounded by several messengers, with gold-handled swords. A number of persons then passed before us, each bearing on his head a block of fire-wood.* Then followed a beautiful cow and calf, several sheep, (some of them very large,) pigs, eggs, plantains, yams, and other vegetables, and fifteen ounces, twelve ackies, of gold-dust (equal to £63 currency, or £56 sterling). Mr. Brooking's share and mine amounted to £27 currency, which we gave for the benefit of the Mission. The King also sent us some palm-wine.

About half-past four, the King seated himself in one of the most elevated parts of the town, to drink palm-wine, and receive our thanks for the presents. We then left our habitation; and after passing through several streets, we came into one, from eighty to ninety

---

* "If we bring you mutton, beef, &c., we also bring you blocks of fire-wood to cook it." This is the idea conveyed in giving the fuel.

yards wide, where the King was seated on a rising ground, under his large umbrellas, surrounded by several hundreds of the people. Boys were standing on each side, cooling him with large fans; and a host of messengers, with gold-handled swords, glittering under the departing rays of the sun, formed a passage up to the place where he sat. We walked up, and thanked him, and then took our seats at a little distance. Shortly afterwards his servants arrived, with palm-wine, and a large calabash, partly overlaid with gold, for him to drink out of, and a large silver bowl, to hold under the calabash, to receive the palm-wine which might run down His Majesty's beard. While he was drinking, the large drums were played, and several arrows were shot from the bow, to let the people know that he was still holding the calabash to his mouth. He then sent us a supply of the wine, after which he returned to his residence.

The scenery around Kumási, as viewed from the high ground where the King was seated, is of the most splendid description. The noble forest, with its great trees of Silk-cotton, *Acaciæ*, *Mimosæ*, &c., stretching over a beautiful undulating country, as far as the eye could reach, filled us with admiration.

21st.—I prepared letters, &c., and sent messengers to the coast.

22d.—Busily engaged writing my journal.

23d.—In the afternoon we went to Bantama, and were much pleased with the beauty of the scenery around. On our return, we called at a house in an elevated, healthy part of the town, into which the King wishes us to remove early next week.

At seven, P.M., I retired to my apartments. At eight, Apoko came to say, the King wished to speak with us. We repaired to his residence, and found him seated, surrounded by his linguists, and a few messengers. The interview was quite private ; no Chiefs or Captains were present, all restraint was thrown off, and he conversed with us in a very open, free, and candid manner.

During this interview, I acquainted him with the motives which had actuated the British Government in taking the Princes to England, giving them a liberal education, and showing them the kindness which they experienced while in that country. I pointed out the great source from which England derived her wealth, power, and greatness ; and placed Christianity, that soul of all real happiness, in its proper position. I informed him of the kind feelings which England cherished towards him and his people, and of their anxiety to evangelize and civilize the African race.

The subject of slavery was touched upon, and he entered into it with great freedom. I told him of the antipathy which England felt to it, and of her perseverance in exertions to prevent traffic in slaves ; that she has ransomed the whole of the slave-population in her West Indian colonies, by paying to their owners twenty millions of money ; that no man could be a slave in England ; that a slave would become a free man the moment he placed his feet on British ground ; and that England had lately sent an expedition up the Niger, (of which river I found the Ashántis have some knowledge as the Kowara,) for the purpose of introducing among the numerous tribes on its banks, the comforts and blessings of civilization, that they may no longer have any pretext for selling slaves to obtain money and goods ; as by the introduction of agriculture and arts, they would obtain wealth from the abundant resources of their own native soil. The magnificent sacrifices and exertions which England has made, and is still making against slavery and the slave-trade, and to benefit Africa, filled his mind with astonishment ; and he appeared amazed at the idea of such noble disinterestedness. He said he allowed none of his people to sell natives of Ashánti into foreign slavery. "The small tribes in the interior," he said, "fight with each other, take prisoners and sell them for slaves; and as I know nothing about them, I allow my people to buy and sell them as they please: they are of no use for any thing else but slaves; they are stupid, and little better than beasts." I answered, "If the Dutch can take them to Elmina, and make valuable soldiers of them, it is a proof that you could make use of them in some way in Ashánti; which would be more beneficial to the country than selling them out of it." He evidently felt the force of the remark; and, with a smile on his countenance, dropped the subject.

I also embraced the opportunity of informing him, that our special object, as Missionaries, was the introduction of Christianity into his dominions; and, for that purpose, we begged his protection, and the favour of permission to build a Mission-House in Kumási: to which he answered, "I will protect you, and supply you with land, on which to build a house."

Part of the time was occupied in a lively and spirited conversation on England, and on the arts and sciences, in which Mr. H. Smith, and Mr. Brooking, William Quantamissah, and myself, all joined.

The rapidity with which travelling is performed by rail-roads and steam-packets, very much interested and astonished him. On some palm-wine being brought, he requested us to drink his health: we drank some out of tumblers, and the King used his calabash, partly overlaid with gold.

He asked me, if palm-wine could be obtained in England. I told him it could not; but the palm-tree was grown in England in large glass houses, heated by fire; and not only the palm-tree, but thousands of plants and trees from Africa, and all other tropical parts of the world. I farther observed, that the English made the nature and character of animals and plants, from all parts of the world, their study; and that is the reason why travellers in Africa notice them, and try to take them to England. I then referred to the suspicions of the Bantama people, when they saw me examining a tree on my former visit to Kumási; and told him, I was then looking after plants to take to England with me. He seemed highly amused, aud asked if the plants I took home lived throughout the journey. I told him, that several of them were growing when I left England.

The King smiled when I referred to the fears of the Bantama people, and appeared fully satisfied with the explanation.

This pleasing interview lasted two hours; when we closed the conversation, thanked the King for the favour, and retired.

25th.—I am spared to see another Christmas-day! spared amidst many troubles, severe conflicts, and poignant sufferings! O this frail bark,—

"Dash'd against the rocks and river,
In the midst of death it lives!"

O my Lord, my Friend, my Deliverer! thou hast indeed chosen me in the furnace of affliction; but whilst thou art my God, I can neither be "hopeless nor unblest." While I keenly feel the trials thou callest me to pass through, I cannot but rejoice in the success with which thou hast favoured my exertions in the work thou hast given me to do. While my dearest friends are taken from me, I am blest with seeing my most sanguine expectations more than realized, in the prosperity of our enterprise in Ashánti. I need trials, severe trials, to keep me humble. Lord, thou doest all things well!

At eleven, A. M., we held divine service. I read prayers, and Mr. Brooking preached on the nativity of Christ. There were but few Ashántis present, as no previous notice had been given. The little congregation was a very interesting one, and deep attention was paid.

At three, P. M., we dined under the large shed which had been decorated for the occasion, with some green boughs and flowers from the forest. The young men whom we had brought as Teachers, with other respectable young men from the coast, dined with us. We sat down, twelve in number, to a dinner of roast beef and plum-pudding, which reminded us forcibly of good old England; happy, sacred, and ever-fondly-cherished England! Several of the Ashántis collected around us. A Chief asked permission to sit near and see us dine: he said, he liked English manners and customs very much, and should try to follow them; asked if he were too old to learn to read, and seemed very much pleased when we told him he was not. He said, now that Missionaries were come to Kumási, he would avail himself of the opportunity of learning a thing so valuable. And who is this fine, handsome young man, surrounded by his attendants, sitting so humbly at a respectful distance from us, to take lessons on civilization? No less a personage than Apoko Akim, a nephew of the present King, on the sister's side, with only one person (Osai Kujoh) between himself and the throne of Ashánti. This fact speaks volumes.

About one, P. M., Prince John Ansah's aunt sent us a present of yams, fruit, and a little gold-dust. At two, the King sent us a present, consisting of two fat sheep; one for the Princes, and the other for Mr. Brooking and myself. Apoko stated, that His Majesty had heard that this was Christmas-day, and that he sent the sheep by way of congratulation. I presume the King received this information from Apoko; for I had conversed with him early in the morning, and told him the reason why we kept Christmas-day.

About half-past three o'clock, the King sent us some palm-wine.

This, I presume, is the first Christmas-day on which the Gospel has ever been preached in Ashánti. May the day soon come, when thousands of enlightened and evangelized Ashántis will hail the annual return of this festival, with the satisfaction and delight with which we regard it!

After dinner we sung some hymns, and then went out for a walk. On our way home, I saw the corpse of a young slave, about twelve years of age, slung to a pole, and carried by two men. This led to the disclosure of a fact, of which I had hitherto been ignorant; namely, that all slaves, except a few favoured ones, are considered not worth the trouble of a decent burial, and are consequently taken, and thrown into the water which runs round the town, where they are eaten by the thousands of fishes which this small river contains. No persons are allowed to touch these fishes. They are nearly the colour of an English eel, from twelve to eighteen inches long, about the thickness of a large English trout, and the head much more flat than that of a dolphin. They are so tame, that if a person stand near the water where the descent is very gradual and flat, and throw a few crumbs of bread into the water, and then drop some on the dry land close to the water's edge, they will actually come several inches out of the water to take them. I had often heard of these fishes, but was incredulous until the other day, when I saw at least fifty of them in the water, not more than three or four inches below the surface, tumbling one over the other to obtain the crumbs thrown in, like so many boys scrambling for an orange;

some of them, by a powerful motion of the head and tail, managed to move several inches out of the water, to obtain the crumbs, and then returned to their natural element.

Sunday, 26th.—At the commencement of the Adai custom, all strangers are expected to go and pay their respects to the King, by way of congratulation on his continued good health, &c. After passing through part of the town, the King came back, and took his seat in the street opposite his residence, where he received the accustomed salutations, and then retired to his house.

At a quarter to four, P. M., we conducted divine service. Mr. Brooking read prayers, and I preached from 1 Tim. iii. 16. The congregation was very large and attentive. One of the King's sons, and several Chiefs and members of the King's household, were present. The discourse was, as usual, in a conversational form. It was a delightful afternoon. How mysterious are the works of Providence! The Lord calls us to pass through heavy and sore troubles; but with reference to our work, every obstacle seems to be removed out of the way. The people appear under no restraint: they come and hear for themselves, and pay deep attention. Even those who may at some future day fill the throne, come to hear of the salvation of God. My most sanguine expectations never presented to my mind scenes like this at Kumási in 1841. God be praised for these tokens of his presence.

27th.—Early this morning the King went down to Bantama, to visit the tombs of his ancestors. He returned about half-past ten, A. M. About eleven, Apoko went to speak to the King about our removal into a larger and more airy house, which His Majesty had provided for us in an open and healthy part of the town. He soon returned to say, that the house was ready for us, and that we could remove as early as we pleased: consequently, after taking some refreshment, we commenced our removal without delay. We succeeded in taking away a sufficient quantity of our things, to admit of our sleeping in our new quarters.

We were glad to remove, as the part of the town in which we have been residing is low, damp, and unhealthy, and has been the cause of some sickness among our party. John Ansah has been ill for several days, with a seasoning fever; which, I am happy to say, by the blessing of God, I have been enabled to check.

Mr. Smith, and Mr. Brooking, and several of the servants, have been unwell; and I have suffered, for many days and nights, from violent pains throughout my whole frame, the effects of sleeping so many nights in a damp room, the walls of which, being made of clay, and having been recently built, were far from dry. These, however, are but trifling difficulties, when compared with the success with which the Lord is blessing our exertions.

CHAPTER IV.

ENTERTAINMENT GIVEN BY THE KING OF ASHANTI TO THE STRANGERS—VISIT TO THE "STONE-HOUSE"—IMPORTANT DECLARATION OF THE KING IN REGARD TO THE MISSION—AFFECTING REMINISCENCES—THE NEW YEAR—DEVOTIONAL SERVICES OF THE NEW-YEAR'S DAY—SINGULAR DOMESTIC SCENE IN THE PALACE—MEMBER OF THE ROYAL FAMILY SICK—THE KING PROMISES LAND FOR THE PURPOSES OF THE MISSION—CONVERSATION ON THE SUBJECT OF EDUCATION—MAGIC LANTERN—CUSTOM.

December 28th.—About seven, A. M., the King sent us an invitation to dine with him to-day; and requested me to send my cook to assist in preparing the dinner.

About a quarter before three, we were ushered into a large, open, oblong, square yard, about eighty feet by forty-five; (the same place in which the King was seated to receive the presents;) where, under the shade of several large umbrellas, a long table was placed before us. Our dinner consisted of soup, fish, roast mutton, roast fowls, boiled yams and plantains, kidney-beans, &c., which was very well served up in the European style. At the end of our table were placed two others, with very short legs, (about twelve or fourteen inches long,) on which were plates and dishes for the King and the principal members of the royal family; on one of which were displayed several pieces of silver plate, of Portuguese manufacture.

Before we sat down, we informed the King, that all these good things were the gifts of God, and that we felt it our duty to ask His blessing in the use of them; to which he readily consented; and my interpreter asked a blessing aloud in the vernacular tongue of Ashánti. We then took our seats. I was requested to take the head of the table, the Princes, William Quantamissah and John Ansah, supporting me on my right hand and on my left. The other guests at our table were Mr. Smith, the Rev. Mr. Brooking, Mr. Huydecoper, (the Dutch Agent,) and my interpreter. At the head of the low table, directly opposite to me, sat the King, in an European dress. His coat was of brown velvet, covered with silver lace, such as might have been fashionable in England, in the latter end of the reign of George II. His trousers were of white satin; his shirt was made of white linen; and his hat, (which he took off when he sat down,) of black beaver, with three bands of silver lace round it, the under side of the brim being covered with silver lace. His sandals were highly ornamented with gold and silver. He also wore a spotted silk-muslin sash. A pair of golden knives, with mother-of-pearl handles, in golden sheaths, were suspended from his neck by a gold chain; and another, of a more massive character, coiled six or eight times round his neck, and hanging loosely down the breast, nearly to the waist, completed the dress of the Monarch of Ashánti. On his left hand, a short distance from the table, sat Osai Kujoh, the successor to the throne, in a fantastic, military dress, of red velvet, with yellow stripes, and a square-cornered cap, with tassels of the same description. Near to him sat another Prince, clothed in one of the large loose ladies' cloaks, sent out as presents from friends at Keighley.

Behind these Princes, were seated several Captains, belonging to the King's household; and on the King's right hand, at a short distance from the table, sat Apoko with other linguists.

Behind us, at the farther end of the yard, a band, consisting of several native musicians, with flutes, clarionets, drums, and a French horn, was stationed. The instruments were European, and the men had been sent down to Elmina Castle, to receive instructions in playing them.

The King inquired whether a band of music during dinner was customary in England; and on our answering in the affirmative, the men were directed to play.

On sending the soup round, I asked, whether the King would take any, to which he answered, "Yes;" and when it was placed before him, he tasted it, and then, according to Ashánti custom, gave the remainder to some of his attendants who were near him. Osai Kujoh also tasted it. While we were taking our portion, a bountiful supply of native soup was placed before the King, which he sent round to his Captains and people.

During dinner, a fine sheep, roasted, was placed before the King in a large polished brass pan: he asked me, whether sheep were ever roasted whole in England? I told him there were instances of it; and that deer, and sometimes bullocks, were roasted entire. He appeared pleased with the answer, and then, with the assistance of some of his servants, proceeded to cut up the sheep, and to send part of it round to the Chiefs and Captains. To us he sent a leg, begging that we would taste it: we found it to be delicious meat.

After the dishes of meat were removed, the table was laden with sweetmeats; namely, an excellent plum-pudding, the materials for which had been supplied from my small travelling store; a pine-apple, papaws, preserved ginger, slices of sugar-cane, &c. We informed the King, that plum-pudding was a favourite dish in England, and begged him to take some, to which he readily consented; and on a slice being placed before him, he tasted it, said it was very good, and then gave the remainder to his attendants.

After the pudding, &c., were removed, we rose and drank His Majesty's health; in proposing which, I embraced the opportunity of congratulating him, on the pleasing and interesting circumstances under which we were assembled, adverting to the auspicious return of the Princes, and expressing our earnest hopes and prayers, that the English and the Ashântis might become one in spirit, and that the blessings of Christianity and civilization, which England enjoys, might in due time, be experienced in Ashânti. He seemed much pleased, and nodded his assent and thanks.

We then proposed and drank the health of Her Majesty Queen Victoria; after which, Quantamissah proposed the health of President Maclean, and spoke of the kindness which he and his cousin had received, both in England, and at Cape-Coast Castle.

The King then requested us to go and see the Stone-House, built by Osai Tutu Quamina. We kept our seats a few minutes, until the King had arrived there, and had taken his seat to receive us. We were soon summoned by a messenger, and proceeded to the house. It is built with stone, has a flat roof, and is about the size of many of the small villas in the vicinity of London. We entered a court yard, ascended a flight of stone steps, and passed through an ante-room into a small hall, in which were tastefully arranged on tables thirty-one gold-handled swords. In the same room were several of the King's calabashes, overlaid with gold, out of which he drinks palm-wine. Passing into another room, we found the King seated in company with Osai Kujoh, and attended by Apoko, and other linguists. On tables in different parts of the room various articles manufactured in glass were arranged, such as candle-shades, beautifully cut glass tumblers, wine-glasses, &c., time-pieces, covered with glass-shades, &c.; and almost every piece was decorated with golden ornaments of various descriptions; large pieces of rock gold, weighing several ounces each, and a great number of gold chains. The weight of pure barbaric gold which we saw, would probably be from eight hundred to one thousand ounces.

Two small boxes, about sixteen inches deep, were shown as specimens of native workmanship. They were covered with green velvet, and ornamented with large round-headed tacks, like an English trunk. The tacks on one were of solid silver, and on the other of solid gold. While I stood admiring them, the King came to me, and corroborated the statement which was made respecting them.

Whilst examining some of the articles in another part of the room, the King again came up, and accosted me in the following manner:—"In days that are past, I could hardly believe that the English were so disinterested, as to take so much trouble in teaching the natives of Africa; and when you were here before, I could hardly feel satisfied respecting it; but I have no fears now. You paid me a visit some time ago; since that period you have been to England, and have returned to Kumási to see me again, bringing my two nephews with you. I thank you for your kindness; and I am fully satisfied, that your object in coming here is to do good."

I answered, "I am very glad your Majesty is satisfied respecting the motives which lead us to come to Kumási; and I trust, that the more you know of us, the more will you be convinced that the welfare of Ashánti is our object."

After we had gone through the principal rooms in the house, we returned to the dining-table, and partook of some fruit. The King again took his seat at the head of it, and conversed with us very freely on various topics for about half an hour, when we thanked him for his kindness, and took our leave. After we left, he sent the band and some of his people, to conduct us to our quarters. The men played several English tunes during the afternoon, with more correctness and ease than a stranger would have expected.

When we reached our lodgings, I endeavoured to collect my thoughts, and reflect on the extraordinary scene which I had that day witnessed; and the more I thought on it, the more did my astonishment increase. I had seen the proud sanguinary Monarch of Ashânti, whose smile is life, and whose frown is death, among his people, dressed in European clothes, surrounded by his warlike Chieftains, sitting at table, and eating in public, with several Englishmen, some of whom were Christian Missionaries,—persons of whom he had no knowledge until the year 1839, and then whom superstition would naturally have led him to fear and avoid; and whom they were disposed to pronounce, as the greatest enemies of their country. The finishing stroke was given to the splendid picture, by the presence of two native Princes, enjoying all the advantages of a liberal and religious education, and under the influence of feelings favourable to the introduction of Christianity into their country.

29th.—Busy writing, &c. Mr. Smith, Mr. Brooking, and the Princes, visited the King. He was very familiar. Mr. Brooking directed the carpenter in hanging some of the King's pictures. Mr. Smith started for Cape Coast.

31st.—The last day of an eventful year, during which I have enjoyed greater happiness, and have had greater trials, than at any former period of my chequered life. At the commencement of the year, I was in possession of one of the most amiable and best of wives. At the end of the year, I mourn her early death, and am left a widower in a foreign land. How powerfully does she, being dead, yet speak, reminding me to be "also ready" to meet my Judge! Amidst all these poignant sufferings,—the loss of my wife, and that of some of my brethren who had laboured with me in the same field,—I rejoice that I can say, "Bless the Lord, O my soul, and all that is within me, bless his holy name. Bless the Lord, O my soul, and forget not all his benefits."

January 1st, 1842.—I am spared to see the commencement of a new year. O my God, thy mercies are boundless! I bless thy name for the numerous manifestations of thy love which I have experienced during the year that is past; and humbly believe, that the severe trials I have had, were sent in mercy both to myself and my wife. Lord, help me to trust thee where I cannot trace thee, and to confide in thy infinite and eternal goodness! Graciously comfort and support, preserve and direct me, so long as I may continue in this vale of tears: make me a blessing to my Christian and Pagan fellow-creatures! Pardon the sins of the past, and grant me grace to live more fully devoted to thee, than I have ever yet done. Grant that in my experience this year, should my life be spared, I may realize more abundant spiritual joys; and that my spiritual progress may be marked by more self-denial, more holy zeal in my Master's work, and more of that "unconquerable mind that was in Christ my Head." Be with me, O Lord, in my pursuits, studies, duties, and engagements. Strengthen my mind in the walks of science and useful learning; and, above all, illuminate it on the sublime subject of Christian theology; let its great and glorious doctrines be better understood, and more deeply felt and enjoyed by me; and let this year be one of more extended usefulness on my part, than any I have yet lived. Lord, hear my prayer, and grant my request, for thy name's sake! Amen.

Sunday, 2d.—The first Sabbath in the new year.

Blessed be God, I feel under the influence of solemn and hallowed feelings.

At half-past six, A. M., I read prayers, and preached from John xi. 40. Several Ashântis were present, and very attentive. At twenty minutes past four, P. M., I again preached, (Mr. Brooking was poorly,) from Isaiah lv. 3: we had an interesting congregation. Deep attention was paid to the word of truth. O that thousands of the Ashântis may come to these living waters!

At a quarter past seven, we met to commemorate our Saviour's dying love, and to renew our covenant with God. Our party was small, consisting chiefly of the Mission-family, including the Princes, and a few pious friends from the coast, and other places. The Lord was indeed with us, and we felt it to be a hallowed season. I was powerfully reminded of our delightful and happy Covenant-Service, last year, on board the brig "Osborn." Several of those who were then with me, are now in the regions of glory. All hail, ye happy spirits! Drink from the vivifying stream, "pluck the ambrosial fruit,"

> "Walk with God,
> High in salvation, and the climes of bliss!"

By faith we hear your triumphant shouts, which, for our encouragement, seem to be wafted down on the wings of mercy. We are only divided by a "narrow stream;" and, taking into consideration our longest possible period in this life, we shall soon, very soon, join your illustrious society, and share your happiness and glory. Lord, keep us to that day!

3d.—Early this afternoon we received intelligence, that the King wished to see us in the course of the afternoon; and about four o'clock, messengers came to our quarters, stating, that the King was waiting for us at his residence. On our arrival, we were ushered into the spacious area where we dined last Tuesday, and found the King seated in an elevated room, having an open front at the end of the yard, under a large and splendid silk umbrella, surrounded by his family, many of the Princesses, children of the two former Kings, his sister, and several of his wives. One side of the yard was occupied by numerous females, part of whom were wives of the King, and the others, attendants and children. On the opposite side, in another elevated room with an open front, a number of native musicians were placed; and down in the yard, in front of the band, sat the King's chief eunuch, and several little boys who attended upon him.

The Princes, Mr. Brooking, my interpreter, and myself, took our seats at the lower end of the yard; on our right, stood twenty little boys, each bearing a gold-handled sword, several of whom were covered with golden ornaments. One wore a cap decorated with eagles' feathers, and a pair of golden rams' horns. Many of the royal family, were dressed in rich silk cloths, their ankles, wrists, breasts, shoulders, and necks being decorated with golden ornaments. The King was dressed in a very handsome cloth of native manufacture, and a leopard's-skin cap, richly ornamented with gold; he had also similiar ornaments upon his arms and legs. His sandals were heavily laden with gold and silver.

No adult males of the royal family were present, save Quantamissah and Ansah. Not even Osai Kujoh was permitted to witness the scene about to take place. The only men besides ourselves who were suffered to attend, were the eunuchs, their attendants, and the men composing the band. Apoko and the principal Chiefs, linguists, &c., were all excluded, on account of the

King's wives; no male Ashánti being permitted to see them. If any of them are walking in the streets, every man is obliged to avoid them, either by turning into another street, or by retiring into a house out of the way, or by retracing his steps; and if he have not time to avoid them in this manner, he must turn his face to the wall, and wait until they have passed by.

Shortly after we had taken our seats, the King rose from his chair, descended into the yard, and came and spoke to us in a very cordial and affectionate manner. He said, no Ashánti Chief or Captain was ever allowed to be present on occasions like these. He never allowed them the honour of meeting him with his wives; but that he had made arrangements to meet us under such circumstances, as the best means he had of testifying his satisfaction, in the safe and happy return of the Princes, and in the kindness which had been shown both to them and to himself.

The band then played, when several of the King's wives, and some young women, from fifteen to twenty years of age, members of the royal family, laden with golden ornaments, engaged in a sort of dance, by moving round the yard one after the other, in rapid but graceful succession. There was nothing in their appearance offensive to the eye, or disgusting to the mind. They were handsomely dressed, and behaved with the greatest decorum. While they were dancing, the King kept his seat. When they ceased, he descended into the yard, and began to dance himself. When he passed us, he said, it was not usual for the Kings of Ashánti to dance before their wives in the presence of any one; but he did so before me, in honour of the Queen of England. He then danced away, and took his seat; then several of the females, among whom was the Queen-mother, followed, singing at the same time war-songs in honour of the King and his ancestors, and proclaiming their "strong names." *

Once more the King came down, and joined in the dance with the females, they continuing to sing his 'strong names," &c., some of which were, "The King of Ashánti is the only King in Africa who has fought with the great guns;" (alluding to the cannon in the forts on the coast;)—"The King of Ashánti fought with, and killed, the King of Buntuku." The latter, the King himself came up to explain as follows: "Osai Tutu Quamina, at the commencement of the Buntuku war, danced with his wives on the eve of his departure for the battle; and, while dancing, he declared that he would conquer and kill the King of Buntuku, and give his body for food to the beasts, and the eagles should eat out his eyes. He went, he fought, he conquered;

---

* In singing the praises of their Kings and principal Chiefs, the Ashántis extol the qualities and martial deeds, which have acquired for them the characteristic appellations by which they are severally known; and this is termed, "proclaiming their strong names." Dupuis, in describing a public procession which he witnessed in Kumási, states, that all the Chiefs of the first class were "followed by a group of parasites, whose business it was to proclaim, in boisterous songs, the strong names of their masters." One of the songs commenced, "Where shall we find such a warrior as the strong and beautiful Apaku Kujoh, whose eyes are like the panther in fight?....Who fought the Gamans, and killed their Kabosir Adouai? Apaku Kujoh!" &c., &c. The "strong names" of the Ashánti Monarch were, on this occasion, "proclaimed" by the tributary King of Banna, who, silencing his own band and sycophants, by an authoritative wave of the hand, snatched a scimitar from a youth in attendance, and, with violent gestures, and flourishing of the weapon, sung, "Ashántis, who is there so great, so good as Sai? Nowhere can you see such a King. He says, 'Destroy this country,' and it is a desert: the people are killed with his shot and powder. When he makes war, he is like the tiger. Can any one fight the tiger?" &c., &c.—EDIT.

slew the King, as he said he would; and gave his body to the beasts, and the eagles ate out his eyes." *

The King then took from one of the little boys, who was standing near us, his gold-handled sword, and having fastened it to his waist, danced a little; he then took from another boy a musket, highly ornamented with gold and silver, and danced again. Afterwards he came up to me, shook me by the hand, turned, and danced away among his wives, &c. Taking the sword and musket into his hand, was to show us, that when they went to war, he himself fought personally.

The women then sang,—

> "The Englishman lives in Sebu Seki.
> To-day he has come to visit the King.
> The King has danced before him
> In the presence of his wives,
> And done what he has never done to
> An European before. He has walked
> Up, and shaken hands with him."

Several of the King's wives, with other female branches of the family, were very fine young women.

During the time we were there, the King sent us palm-wine, and appeared highly pleased. About seven, P. M., we retired to our residence.

---

* In this scene, the reader will recognise the perpetuation of an ancient custom. The women of Israel also celebrated the triumph over the Philistines with singing and dancing, and "answered, as they played, and said, Saul hath slain his thousands, and David his ten thousands." (1 Sam. xviii. 6, 7.) Dancing is likewise practised by the Africans on sacred as well as other occasions. As David, on the removal of the ark, "danced before the Lord with all his might," (2 Sam. vi. 14,) so, among the Ashántis, dancing is connected with the most solemn ceremonies of their religion.—Edit.

As the night approached, the King, his wives, &c., in their rich silk dresses, formed a group in the centre of the yard: the scene was certainly one of the most extraordinary I ever witnessed. The display of gold was immense.

4th.—In the morning I sent for Apoko, to inform him that I wanted to see the King, respecting land for building. Shortly afterwards a messenger came from the palace, stating, that a female member of the family was sick at Jabin, and that the King wished to know, if I could send her medicine. I answered, that I could not prescribe remedies unless I saw her, and ascertained the nature of the malady under which she was suffering; that to give a person medicine without seeing the patient, was like walking a dangerous road in the dark. The messenger said, she was unable to come to Kumási: I therefore offered to go over and see her.

The messenger repaired to the King, and soon returned to say, that he would be thankful if I would go and see her. About a quarter before four, P. M., Apoko sent to say, that the King would see me respecting the land, and that we were to go to him directly. We found him seated in one of the rooms in the Stone-House. He received us very kindly, and told us, that we should have land near the spot where we are residing.

We had a long conversation on Christianity, and civilization: I pointed out the advantages resulting therefrom, and answered several important questions on these subjects. One objection which had been raised in his mind respecting education was, the danger of it making the people rebellious; in which, I found, he was encouraged by Apoko, and other Chiefs. I told him, that in education, as well as in all other good things, there was a possibility of abuse; and that there would, doubtless, be a few unfavourable exceptions; but that, in general, it had a tendency to make the people more dutiful, and more obedient. He saw the propriety of my remarks, and said he would consult the Chiefs on the subject of sending their children to school. Thus far, all our negotiations are promising. O thou God of Missions! give thine own work success in this benighted land!

> "Let the Heathen fall before thee,
> Let the isles thy power declare!"

5th.—About half-past eight, the King sent to inquire if I would accompany Mr. Brooking and the Princes to his residence, and teach him the use of the magic-lantern. On our arrival, he was seated in the court-yard of the Stone-House, with very few attendants. We fixed the lantern in a kind of pent-house on one side of the yard, and the King took his seat on the opposite side. All our preparations, however, were useless for the present; as we could only obtain palm-oil for the lamp, which would not answer. When obliged to desist for want of the oil, the King came into the pent-house, and sat down on a couch. He directed my attention to that article of furniture, and said, it was made in Kumási. At this I was surprised. The frame-work was a kind of ebony, and very neatly made. The covering was of striped silk.

6th.—I started the Governor's messenger with letters.

Yesterday, preparations were made for a "custom," on account of the death of one of the King's daughters, recently deceased: early this morning, muskets were fired, and three human victims were sacrificed!

7th.—I took a rough sketch of a species of *Ficus*, growing in a street near our quarters. This is one of the most splendid specimens of that plant I have ever seen. It is about sixty feet high; the branches covering a considerable space of ground, and its leaves are small. Its greatest peculiarity is, that of throwing out roots from the trunk of the tree and the large branches, at a height of from twenty to thirty feet from the ground; something like the true Banyan, or *Ficus Religiosa* of India.

About four, P. M., the King came to our residence to pay us a visit. He went into all our rooms, and examined every thing they contained with much interest. He was accompanied by Osai Kujoh, Apoko, his chief eunuch, and numerous messengers.

CHAPTER V.

VISIT TO JABIN—SEIWA, THE QUEEN OF JABIN—HISTORY AND DESCRIPTION OF THE TOWN—LETTER FROM MR. BROOKING—EXECUTION OF TWO CHIEFS AT KUMASI—ANNOYED WITH ANTS—IS VISITED BY THE DAUGHTER OF SEIWA—RETURNS TO KUMASI—MEDICAL ADVICE SOUGHT BY THE NATIVES—SINGULAR PRACTICE AT EXECUTIONS AND SACRIFICES—CONVERSATION ON THE POLICY OF PUBLIC EXECUTIONS—FAVOURABLE IMPRESSION PRODUCED BY THE SUCCESSFUL MEDICAL TREATMENT OF A SICK CHIEF—LAND GIVEN BY THE KING UPON WHICH TO ERECT A MISSION-HOUSE.

JANUARY 8th.—At a quarter past ten, A. M., I started for Jabin,* accompanied by my interpreter, two messengers from the King, my hammock-men, carriers, and servants.† We went from Kumási in a north-easterly direction, and passed through a country by no means striking in its appearance, for several miles. The soil is poor, when compared with that in the vicinity of Kumási, and does not produce such splendid forest-trees. We passed through several small crooms, and stopped to take refreshment at Mampon, a small but neat croom nearly due north from Kumási, about eight miles.

At one, P. M., we resumed our journey, and travelled at the rate of about four miles an hour, until a quarter to seven, when we reached Jabin. As night had already closed in, I had no opportunity of seeing the town this

* A place of considerable importance in the history of former negotiations between the British and the King of Ashánti; called by Bowdich, Dwabin, and Juabin by Dupuis. As the vowel signs of the Ashánti alphabet have the same sounds as in Italian, the *a* in Jabin must be articulated like *a* in father.—EDIT.

† The occasion of this journey to Jabin is stated in the entry under date of Jan. 4th, of this Journal.—EDIT.

evening: having walked the greater part of the journey, and when it became dark, striking my feet severely against the roots of the trees which crossed the path, I felt tired, and little disposed to perambulate.

Shortly after my arrival, I went to see Seiwa, the Queen of Jabin. We passed through several court-yards, and found her sitting in a small room, surrounded by her attendants. She received me very kindly, and bade me welcome to Jabin.

On my return to my quarters, I found that the men who carried my bed, &c., with the canteen, containing food, had not arrived; the men whom I had sent into the forest with torches to look after them, could not find them; so that I began to suspect, I should neither have food to eat, nor a bed to lie on. While making up my mind to this, Seiwa sent me a large dish of savoury soup made with venison, fresh-water fish, and yams. Thus, when I little expected it, I found my wants supplied, and a table mercifully furnished in the wilderness, of which I partook under the influence of grateful feelings. Our little family then collected together, and a very strange and extraordinary thing took place in Jabin: an altar was, for the first time, erected to the Lord God of hosts, and the whole of that beautiful hymn, "Jesus, the name high over all," &c., ascended to heaven from grateful hearts.

There is a beauty in the fourth verse,

> "O that the world might taste and see
> The riches of his grace!
> The arms of love that compass me,
> Would all mankind embrace;"—

which, when it is sung by the Christian in barbarous regions, surrounded by all the horrors of superstition and Paganism, fills the mind with an overwhelming influence. O the blessedness of feeling that happy consciousness of being compassed by the arms of almighty, redeeming, sanctifying, preserving Love! How it cheers the Missionary, while a solitary and bereaved wanderer, thousands of miles from his native land! Though he may be no stoic, and may possess the feelings of other men, which often require a mighty effort to keep the mind in a proper state of equilibrium; though his thoughts often fly back to his native land, with all her precious advantages, her hallowed privileges, her beautiful temples, her guarded hearths, and happy families; while the breast heaves, and the silent tear steals down the cheek; yet it is not at such times as these. No; he rather feels that to be engaged in spreading the savour of a Saviour's name in barbarous regions, is indeed worth living for: however much his hardships and privations may be the means of shortening his earthly career, yet

> "That life is long, which answers life's great end."

I lay down to rest on my travelling-table; the man, however, arriving with my bed before I had fallen asleep.

Sunday, 9th.—I was fatigued from the long journey of yesterday, and was obliged to remove into better apartments.

Expecting to see Seiwa concerning the malady under which she is suffering, we had no opportunity of holding divine service this morning.

In the afternoon she sent for me. She is suffering under a severe nervous affection, which has deprived her of the use of her left arm, the large muscle being constantly in violent action, accompanied with intense pain. Numerous remedies had been applied, during her residence in Akim, together with other medicines, which, I fear, have made it far worse than it otherwise would have been. I found her exceedingly ignorant respecting the complaint. She imagines that she has been poisoned, and that the violent action of the large muscle, is that of a worm. I endeavoured, with but little effect, to convince her to the contrary. I hope, however, to be more successful in a day or two; and that I shall prevail upon her to consent to take those medicines, which may at least afford her relief, if they do not effect a cure.

In the evening we held a prayer-meeting, and I gave an exhortation. Some of the natives were present, and very attentive. O God, grant that this "bread, cast upon the waters" with a trembling hand, may "be seen after many days!"

10th.—I had an opportunity of seeing the town. It has been in ruins for several years, on account of the absence of its rightful owners. Some of these have returned, and are busy in rebuilding the place.

Shortly after the battle of Dudua, and the consequent peace between the Ashántis and the Coast, Boitin, the Chief or King of Jabin, incurred the displeasure of Osai Akoto, the then reigning King of Ashánti; and a very serious quarrel took place between Akoto and the Jabin Chieftain, who was a member of his own family. In consequence of this quarrel, Osai Akoto sent an army to advance upon Jabin, to bring the refractory Chief to obedience. Boitin collected his people together, and prepared for a desperate struggle. His brother, Kŏfi Boitin, took command of the little army, and occupied a position at the entrance of the town. A Captain was left at Boitin's residence, in charge of the principal members of the family, with express orders to put them all to death, rather than allow them, in the event of a defeat, to fall into the hands of the enemy; while Boitin stationed himself in the rear of his people, to encourage them to persevere in the combat. Though Boitin's army must have been far inferior to the King's in numerical strength, yet a conviction of their extreme danger, the probability of the destruction of their families, and their native town, in case of failure, inspired them with unwonted courage; and though they could not gain the victory, they withstood the charges of the enemy for several hours, during which time, preparations were made in the town for a retreat. Much of Boitin's property had been already destroyed, to prevent the possibility of its falling into the hands of the victor; a quantity of gold-dust had been mixed with copper, and thus rendered comparatively useless; and when the troops were unable any longer to maintain their position, Boitin effected a retreat with his army and remaining property, together with the principal part of the population of the town.

With the bravery of his troops, and the result of the battle, Boitin could not but feel highly satisfied. During the battle, however, an event took place which must have been to him a source of great grief. The Captain left in charge of his family, finding the battle waxing hotter every moment, and concluding, that the troops could not stand their ground, rashly put the family to death, and then destroyed himself and the habitation with gunpowder. Boitin's mother, however, who is aunt to the present King of Ashánti, by some means escaped destruction, and fled, with her two sons, a daughter, the army, and part of the population of the town, into Akim; where they took refuge under the protection of the British authorities, at Cape-Coast Castle.

When the present King ascended the throne of Ashánti, he used every means in his power to induce

Boitin to return to his native country; but failed of success.

In 1839, Boitin died in Akim, and his brother succeeded him.

In 1840, Boitin's brother also died in Akim, leaving every thing in the hands of their aged mother, Seiwa, the present King's aunt. Having lost her sons, and finding herself solitary, Seiwa, by the permission of the local Government of Cape-Coast, has returned to Jabin, with many of the people. About a thousand of the people are still in Akim, having refused to accompany their aged Chief to Jabin.

Jabin, when in a state of prosperity, from the time Mr. Bowdich speaks of seeing the young Chief at Kumási, at the great Adai custom, down to the retreat of Boitin, must have been a very interesting place. Then the town was destroyed by the Ashántis; and, from the extent of the ruins, I should think, it must have been half as large as Kumási. The population, including that of the surrounding crooms, may have been from ten to fifteen thousand.

Though there are many houses remaining, and some of the streets are re-formed, the town is full of mounds of earth, the sites of former houses and establishments, where many of Boitin's Captains resided, with their numerous followers. I am at this moment sitting under the shade of a beautiful tree, with the ruins of Boitin's premises before me, at a distance of about eighty or ninety yards. They must have been almost as large as those of the present King of Ashánti, in Kumási. I am informed, that Boitin was, in the time of his prosperity, very rich, and vied with Osai Akoto, in his display of barbaric gold on every public occasion.

This morning I walked over part of the ruins of

Boitin's habitation. In a shed, which with three others surrounds a court-yard, I saw some of his large drums: two of them were what the natives would call "decorated," with several human skulls on each, and another had appended to it from fifteen to twenty-five human jaw-bones.

Fifty yards from Boitin's premises stands the most magnificent specimen of *Ficus* that I ever saw. Its height is about sixty feet, the girth of the trunk thirty-nine feet, the roots branching off from the trunk at about two feet from the ground in every direction, with part of them rising a foot above the earth, at a distance of eight feet and a half from the trunk: the space covered by the branches is one thousand five hundred and twenty square yards. It is now crowded with leaf-buds, just beginning to open. A young Silk-cotton tree has grown out from among its roots, and shows its head out of the centre of the branches. Beneath this tree is a small mound, which was kept in proper form, and polished with red ochre, on which Boitin sat under his large umbrellas, to keep the Adai custom. In front of it, doubtless, the head of many a human victim has tumbled to the ground, before the knife of the executioner.

The soil of Jabin is rather light and sandy; not so rich as that nearer to Kumási. The general character of the vegetation is also different. The Silk-cotton and other forest-trees are, generally speaking, not so fine as they are near to Kumási, and Mansu in Fanti. There is a greater tendency to produce grass; and I am informed, that the forests become less dense, and high grass becomes more the prevailing vegetation, every succeeding day's journey from Jabin into the interior.

11th.—The heat was very oppressive. Seiwa was more tractable and very kind, sending me soup, &c.,

ready cooked, every day. I was busy finishing a sketch of part of the town.

Yesterday I despatched a messenger to Mr. Brooking at Kumási, acquainting him with the nature of Seiwa's malady, and of my intention of stopping at Jabin until Thursday. This afternoon I obtained from him the following letter:—

"I RECEIVED yours about three o'clock yesterday, and, according to your request, I went and informed the King of your hopes of, at least, alleviating the pains from which his aunt has been suffering. We went down last evening about seven o'clock, and remained with him until nine. We should have stayed longer, but I had an attack of fever, and was obliged to ask leave to retire.

"He still retains all the good humour which has characterized his conduct ever since we arrived, and is willing that you should stay until Thursday.

"There have been two Chiefs executed since you left,—one on Saturday evening, and another on Sunday evening,—for various crimes of which they have been found guilty. I unexpectedly saw the one who was decapitated on Sunday evening. He was killed at the head of the street in which we live, just before the conclusion of the service. Immediately after, I went out a few minutes to enjoy the evening air; and when I arrived at the head of the street, I saw the poor creature just bound to a pole with both his hands struck off. The executioner then cut away a part of the chin with the beard, after which he was removed.

"Judge of the feelings which it produced on me! We are all, by the blessing of God, in good health. The Princes desire their love to you.

"Believe me, &c.,

"ROBERT BROOKING.

"P. S. We are going this evening to exhibit the phantasmagoria. The King has heard that our oil has arrived, and is anxious to see the exhibition."

12th.—This morning Seiwa sent to beg that, instead of leaving for Kumási to-morrow, I would remain at least until Monday next. As I am now very anxious to return to the coast, I consented to stop until Saturday morning, with which she is satisfied.

In the afternoon Seiwa sent me a present, consisting of nine ackies of gold-dust, a sheep, yams, plantains, bananas, palm-nuts, tiger-nuts, ground-nuts, rice, papaws, and a little gold for my interpreter and servant. I went and returned thanks.

Last night the ants invaded my dwelling, and came even upon my pillow. While I was sleeping, one or more of them found the way into my ears, and the noise they made there, together with their running over my face, (for they did not bite me,) aroused me from my slumbers. I brushed them from my pillow, took some cotton-wool, which I dipped in spirits of hartshorn, and put it into my ears, and was soon again locked in the arms of sleep. Early in the morning, on awaking, I found about me more ants than before; and was obliged to comb and brush them out of my hair.

Some may ask, "How could you sleep under such circumstances?" I reply:—It is astonishing, how soon a person can, if he try, become inured to numerous inconveniences. I have often slept on the ground, in places no better than an open shed, with little protection from snakes, scorpions, centipedes, &c., without any fear, or even annoyance. Confidence in the divine protection will ever compose the mind, amidst all the dangers and privations, to which travellers may be exposed in these barbarous regions.

13th.—Busy writing part of the day. As Seiwa is anxious to detain me, I have consented to remain until Saturday.

14th.—Preparing letters for England the greater part of the day, and in the evening made arrangements for returning to Kumási to-morrow. Seiwa's daughter came and sat by me for half an hour, while I was sitting at my writing-desk. She is an interesting person, about twenty-eight years of age. She said, she did not often come out into the town, because its dilapidated condition painfully reminded her of the loss of her relations, and the prosperity of bygone days. I sympathized with her, and directed her attention to the comfort which Christianity affords, in seasons of severe trial, by displaying the future, and intimating a higher and more exalted state of being. She seemed to feel the truth of my remarks. Merciful God, save these poor Pagans!

> "Awake them by the Gospel call;
> Light of the world, illumine all!"

Late in the evening I saw Seiwa. She said, she was very sorry I was leaving the town so soon, and asked, whether I could not, by sending an excuse or an apology to England, take up my permanent abode in Ashánti. I told her, I should have pleasure in remaining longer; but that my duties imperatively demanded a speedy return to the coast; but when I came to Kumási again, I should endeavour to pay her a visit.

15th.—I took an early breakfast, and called on Seiwa to take leave. Though far advanced in years, (for she must be, at least, from sixty to sixty-five years of age,) she walked with me, accompanied by her daughter and several of her people, to the entrance of the town, and there bade me farewell. At a quarter past eight, A. M., we commenced our journey, and travelled until twenty minutes past one. We then halted to dine at Mampon, a small croom, about eight miles from Kumási. Here we remained until the arrival of the King's messengers, who were sent to accompany me; they having dined on the path earlier in the day, and promised to overtake us at Mampon. At twenty minutes past three we resumed our journey, and reached Kumási at five. Though I had walked all the way, a distance of about thirty miles, I did not feel very weary. The country through which I travelled is not so interesting in appearance as some places between Kumási and the coast: there is still, however, much to arrest the attention of a lover of the book of nature.

The Silk-cotton trees on every hand are laden with blossoms, beginning to fall. Pine-apple plants are growing by thousands on each side of the path, presenting their scarlet fruits, about one-third of their full size. The species is very much like the black Jamaica Pine; leaves rather long, slender, and slightly tinged with purple near the centre.

In the low lands, on the banks of some of the small rivers, a fine large white variety of *Pancratium* is luxuriating, producing an immense profusion of flowers. Though the soil is inferior, yet the grass on the side of the path is in some places from sixteen to eighteen feet high, and now in full bloom. The spikelets are from nine to twelve inches long.

Sunday, 16th.—At half-past six, A. M., Mr. Brooking read prayers, and preached from John iii. 14. Several of the Ashántis were present; among whom was Dagawa, one of the messengers who accompanied me to Jabin. In the course of the day several of the natives came to ask for medicine. Nothing seems to have so great an influence in gaining their affections, as an affectionate attention to their bodily ailments.

At four, P. M., I conducted divine service, and preached from 1 Tim. ii. 1—5. The Lord has been with us to-day in our devotions. Blessed be his holy name!

17th.—The Ashánti are evidently under an impression, that because the English have such a horror of human sacrifices, they do not make public examples of the greatest violators of the laws: hence the King on one occasion remarked,—"If I were to abolish human sacrifices, I should deprive myself of one of the most effectual means of keeping the people in subjection;" and, under the influence of this feeling, he has confounded the sacrificing of hundreds and thousands of innocent victims, with the punishment of those who may have forfeited their lives on account of flagrant transgressions of their country's law. Hearing of the case of two criminals, I thought this an excellent opportunity of making our ideas on this subject known, that we might have a still greater influence over the public mind, in our opposition to human sacrifices. Consequently, I walked into the town, accompanied by the Princes, Mr. Brooking, and my interpreter. We found the criminals seated on blocks of wood, in a street near the King's residence, each accompanied by an executioner. One of the executioners was the lad who told me, on the 17th of December, that he had himself decapitated eighty persons. Two knives were forced through the cheeks of each criminal, one on each side, which deprived them of speech.* This is done, it is said, to prevent them cursing the King. We did not

* For an explanation of the reasons for this practice at executions and sacrifices, see Beecham's "Ashánti and the Gold-Coast," pp. 215—222.—EDIT.

stop to gaze on the horrid spectacle; but proceeded to Apoko's residence, to pay him a visit. While we were conversing with him, the two criminals were mentioned; and, without making any allusion to human sacrifices, I remarked, that those who were guilty of treason in England, were generally made public examples of, and that it was a sad thing to see men so rebellious. Apoko appeared much pleased with the remark, and accompanied us, on our departure, a short distance from his house. Our principal object in calling on Apoko, was, to avoid giving the people an idea, that we had walked out on purpose to see the execution: especially as I had a good excuse for calling upon him, having not seen him since my return from Jabin.

On our way from Apoko's house, we again passed the place of execution. Before we arrived, the drum played, and one criminal was decapitated. The head was off in an instant; and, before we were aware of what was then to take place, a man came running past us with the head of the criminal in his hand, followed by the executioner, with his large blood-stained knife; and just as we went by the place, the other criminal was beheaded.

In taking such a step this morning, we, of course, did violence to our feelings; but our peculiar position seemed to demand it.

18th.—Early this morning Apoko came, to request that I would accompany him to visit a friend, who was very ill. I went with him, and found the sick man, who is one of the greatest Chiefs in Kumási, labouring under a severe attack of bilious fever; which had been increasing in strength for the last three days, and now assumed a very threatening aspect. I returned home, and prepared a strong dose of medicine, which I gave him. I watched him during the day, and found him more quiet, but the fever very obstinate. At length, he obtained considerable relief; and the strength of the fever appeared to be breaking.

When this favourable change became apparent, his friends, wives, and attendants endeavoured, by every means in their power, to testify their gratitude. I shall never forget the countenances of his slaves when I first saw him; they watched my features with most intense interest, to ascertain, if possible, whether I thought he would recover; and when I told them there were hopes respecting him, their joy was very great. They appeared to love their master; and, I believe, sincerely wished him to live, from motives quite disinterested: but at the same time they knew, that, if he died, they would all be sacrificed, to accompany their master into another world; and hence, doubtless, for their own sake, they wished that he might be raised to health and strength.

In the course of the afternoon the King sent, expressing a wish to see me. We walked down to his residence, and found him in the Stone-House, surrounded by a few of his attendants. He welcomed me back to Kumási, and asked several questions respecting his aunt, the Chief of Jabin. He expressed his thanks for my kindness in paying her the visit; and then conversed with us on various subjects. Before we left, he ordered a small portable medicine-chest, of English manufacture, to be brought to me, requesting that I would examine its contents. It is of neat workmanship, and, in England, when new, and full of good medicine, might have cost from eight to ten pounds. I could not, consistently with proper delicacy and prudence, inquire how he came in possession of it; but, from all I could learn, I think there is not a doubt, that it was part of the spoils of the war in which Sir Charles Macarthy fell; for I think no European would run the risk of presenting, to any King of Ashânti, a chest containing laudanum, calomel, and other powerful and dangerous medicines: but this was a question which I, of course, hesitated to ask. During this interview, he promised to send men with our carpenters and sawyers, to receive instruction.

19th.—I visited the sick Chief, and found him easier; but the fever was returning, and he complained of violent head-ache. I told him he must be cupped; to which he objected, saying, "This is an unlucky day." I, however, insisted upon it; telling him, that it might be to him a much more unlucky day, if the fever were allowed to return in its full strength. He then quietly submitted, and soon obtained relief. By the use of calomel, refrigerant and tonic draughts, by the blessing of God, I succeeded in subduing the fever in the course of two days and one night.

Several of the King's messengers were continually coming to see the Chief, and to watch the result of my exertions. One of them remarked, while I was standing over him, and attending to him, that I loved the Ashântis.

20th.—The sick Chief is still better. I am busy writing, having received letters from England.

At six, A. M., the King came to our abode, and gave us land on which to build our Mission-house. It being the time of the little Adai custom, he went to Bantama, to visit the tombs of his ancestors.

21st.—The Chief is recovering fast, telling his friends, that I have succeeded in saving his life.

CHAPTER VI.

CONVERSATION RESPECTING THE ESTABLISHMENT OF A SCHOOL AT KUMASI —OBJECTIONS OF THE NATIVES STATED—DREADFUL FIRE IN THE CAPITAL—HALF THE TOWN CONSUMED—PROVIDENTIAL PRESERVATION OF THE MISSION PARTY AND PROPERTY—GREAT DISTRESS AMONG THE INHABITANTS—CONDUCT OF THE MOORS DURING THE FIRE—ENLIGHTENED VIEWS OF OSAI KUJOH, THE HEIR-APPARENT TO THE THRONE OF ASHANTI—DEPARTURE FROM KUMASI AND ARRIVAL AT CAPE COAST.

January 22d.—An eventful day, replete with manifestations of the kind regard of a gracious Providence. About nine, A. M., Apoko came to have some conversation with me on the subject of schools; and mentioned, that several of the Chiefs had said, their King could neither read nor write, nor could they, and therefore they thought, it would not be proper for their children to be educated. I saw at once the ground of their objection,—a fear, that if their boys were educated, they would be disobedient and troublesome, and perhaps despise them on account of their ignorance. At this I wondered not, knowing such an objection to be quite natural, and that there were many even in enlightened England, who had fears on this point; or, at least, there were those who were not strangers to these apprehensions twenty-five years ago. Finding, however, that Apoko seemed to speak rather lightly of schools in the abstract, I thought it necessary to reply to him somewhat strongly on the subject, as far as I could, without my remarks being possibly construed into unkindness. Fully aware, that if I allowed these objections to pass unnoticed, they would say, "If schools are important, he would vindicate them, and press their claims;" and then if I spoke too strongly, they would say, "This man is so earnest, and speaks so much, that he has probably some political object in view;" I endeavoured therefore to take the middle course, stating, that I felt too much interested in their welfare, not to speak at such a time, and was determined that they should not have occasion, on some future day, to accuse me of unfaithfulness, when the welfare of the nation depended so much upon the line of conduct which they might now pursue. These remarks, with many others, had a powerful but favourable effect on Apoko's mind; and I could perceive that an impression was made which would not be speedily removed. The Princes and Mr. Brooking took part in the conversation.*

During the conversation with Apoko, news was brought to us, that the town was on fire. We immediately went out, and found that a quantity of high grass, which covers several acres of land on the outside of the town, behind our quarters, was on fire. Much of the grass being very dry, it being the *harmattan* season, and its average height from twelve to fifteen feet, the flames were making rapid progress, and threatened our dwelling with destruction. The King came out, sum-

* Notwithstanding the excitement produced by the fire, which immediately followed this interview, Apoko went and told the King all that I had said, and the earnestness with which I had spoken. The King remarked, "Did he indeed say so? Well, he has come to Kumási, bringing no trade palaver. He is not come to make arrangements for sending slaves down to the coast. It is evident that he is come here to do us good; and, therefore, that which he recommends so strongly, and with such earnestness, must be of importance to us."

Having so far gained the point, I thought it best to say nothing further respecting it at present; resting assured that, with such a footing already secured, and with so large a share of the King's confidence, every thing connected with Christianity would, in due time, by the blessing of God, follow in train, "*first the blade, then the ear, after that the full corn in the ear.*"

moned the Captains and people to try to check the progress of the fire; and sent to us, that we might be on our guard. We mustered all the strength we could, and began to cut down the grass near our abode, that the flames might not invade us; and the Lord mercifully interposed, by causing the wind to blow in such a direction, as to arrest the conflagration in its approach. Though the fire came within two yards of our dwelling, which is covered with a light thatch of Bamboo-leaves, and would ignite like tinder, yet we sustained no damage.

While we were anxiously watching the progress of the fire among the grass, information was brought that a house, in an opposite part of the town, about a quarter of a mile from us, was in flames. This placed us in more danger than from the fire among the grass, as the wind was blowing from that direction. Several of us ran to the spot, and found a number of houses on fire, which was rapidly advancing towards us, and now the destruction of our quarters seemed almost certain.

I had, soon after the commencement of the flames among the grass, taken the precaution to remove my books and other valuables into my travelling-boxes, ready for taking away, and the Princes and Mr. Brooking now followed my example, and we immediately commenced removing all our things into the street. While thus engaged, one of our men came running to say, that the fire must be at our dwelling in a very few minutes: and it certainly would, had not a gracious Providence again interposed; for just as the flames came near to the line of houses connected with our lodgings, the wind changed, and blew in a direction sufficiently oblique to screen us from harm. Had not this alteration taken place, our dwelling must have been destroyed, and, in all probability, much of our little property. We felt thankful to God, and adored his holy name. The fire continued to rage for several hours, until more than half the town was in ruins. When all danger respecting our dwelling and property was past, we went to the King's residence, near to which the fire was still raging. We found the King in the street anxiously watching its progress, and trying to check its approach to his premises. Thatch had been torn off from many of the houses near; but it was thrown into a deep ravine near the King's house, at the end of a street, toward which the fire was approaching. We immediately saw the danger; and while the King was busily engaged at a distance, we removed the greater part of the thatch out of the way of the flames. I was down in the ravine assisting in throwing it out of the way, when Osai Kujoh, the heir-apparent to the throne, passed by, and expressed his thanks.

Shortly after, we saw the fire raging in another place nearer to the royal residence: a quantity of thatch had been torn off and thrown on the ground, and the fire had already caught one end of it, which we succeeded in quenching, and thereby saved the King's house from almost certain destruction. It seemed that the people apprehended no danger from this quarter, after the thatch had been torn off; and therefore had left it without any one to watch it. At length the progress of the flames was arrested; but the destruction has been immense. The space of ground over which the fire passed, is about half a mile in length, and seven hundred and fifty yards in breadth, containing the most populous part of the town.

Mr. Ruydecoper, the Dutch Resident, has saved his property; but his residence is destroyed. All the houses near the market-place are destroyed. I hear also that many of the Fanti traders have only succeeded in saving a very small portion of their property.

The beautiful Banyan-trees, in those streets where the fire raged, are shorn of all their verdant splendour. The King's fetish-tree, in the market-place, has been much injured; and a large Silk-cotton tree, near it, about one hundred and fifty feet high, has its leaves burnt to the very summit.

My patient, the Chief, who had so severe an attack of fever, has lost his house and much of his property, and was obliged to escape for his life on the shoulders of one of his attendants. One of the messengers, who came down to Cape Coast to conduct us to Kumási, lost his house, wives, children, and all his property; and, I am sorry to say, these are not the only victims.

As I passed the market-place in the evening, I saw a poor woman running about and beating herself, while her cries resounded through the place. I asked her the cause of her grief. She stated, that she had a child in the bush sick with the small-pox, and had gone to nurse it, leaving her sister at home with an aged mother. On her return this evening, she found the house and property destroyed, and her aged mother burned to death. I listened to this mournful tale with an aching heart. The corpse, covered with a cloth, was placed on a little mound of earth, and the two sisters were weeping over it, having nothing to comfort them.

O Christianity, "thou soul of happiness," had they in possession thy sacred comforts, their griefs would be comparatively light! Could they, through thy medium, behold the happy spirit of a sainted friend in glory, though the tears might still flow, yet they would fall without bitterness. O when will the happy day arrive, when this sovereign remedy for the miseries of the world will be known in these barbarous regions?

An aged Moor perished also in the flames. One of his hands was the only part of him that could be found. The Moors acted very foolishly during the fire, and exposed themselves to much ridicule. The poor man who perished had been requested to make his escape before his house took fire; but he obstinately refused, saying, God would preserve his house. They manifested no activity in attempting to check the progress of the flames even when near the royal residence. While we were busy, labouring with our hands, three of them stood praying; one held up his fingers, and kept moving his hand steadily backward and forward; another counted a string of black beads. Several fetish-women stood before the King's house using their incantations; and the people as they passed, being busily engaged in checking the progress of the enemy, told them to get out of the way with their nonsense. When it was nearly dark, the King walked round to a street near our residence, and sat down, attended only by a few of his domestics. William Quantamissah, John Ansah, and I, were walking near him; and when we found that he recognised us, we went and spoke to him, in terms of condolence. He expressed his thankfulness for our exertions, and was evidently in an humbled frame of mind. I pointed out to him the importance of securing property by building more substantial houses. He answered, "By God's help, I will try and do so, by and by." The ruins continued to burn during the night, falling into the streets at different intervals with a heavy crash.

Sunday, 23d.—On account of the confusion from the effects of the fire of yesterday, we could not secure our regular service this morning. I felt indisposed from want of rest, and the extreme excitement of yesterday, which kept me up until early this morning. At four,

P. M., however, I conducted divine service, and preached from Isai. xl. 5. The Lord was with us.

24th.—The town wears a melancholy aspect. Thousands of persons are burnt out of house and home. I learn that a considerable quantity of gold-dust and ivory have been lost by the fire, and also that ten persons have perished.

The King sent a messenger, to thank us for our exertions on Saturday.

Early in the morning, the King was out in the town surveying the ruins.

In the afternoon, Osai Kujoh came to our lodgings, sat and talked with us about the fire, and then requested me to show him my insects. He also thanked us for our exertions during the fire on Saturday; and on expressing our regret at the catastrophe, he said, it was cause of thankfulness to God, that we have any houses left. Such an expression as this may sound strange to an English ear from the lips of such a person; but it is no more strange than true. The King referred also to the Divine Being when I conversed with him on Saturday evening.

25th.—I forgot to mention, that on Sunday morning, a nephew of the King met me as I was walking near the royal residence, and said, "We are very sorry you are going to leave us so soon. When you came to Kumási before, we were afraid of you; but we have no fears now, and are glad to see you here."

I met the same individual again on the very spot where the fire so fiercely raged and threatened our dwelling, when, providentially, the wind changed. He said, "God preserved you Christians from the fire." I answered, "Yes; and we feel thankful."

I am now busy packing up my things, and preparing to start for the coast on Monday next.

26th.—About half-past ten, A. M., the King came to our abode, to thank us personally for the exertions we made during the fire on Saturday. I said I was glad that we were able to afford any assistance, and wished we could have done more; and also, that we were much grieved that so sore a calamity had happened.

He said, "It pleased God that it should happen." To which I answered, "Yes, it is intended, as well as all other trials, to benefit by teaching us wisdom. God instructs sometimes by prosperity, and at others by adversity." He very patiently suffered this word of exhortation, and then left us, apparently well pleased. Before he came in, he went into the yard where the carpenter works, and was much gratified in seeing the workmen, at his request, sharpen some tools on our grinding-stone; a thing which he had never witnessed before.

27th.—I was unwell during the greater part of the day. Mr. Pell, the new Dutch Resident for Kumási, arrived here about noon.

Mr. Watson is again ill. O mystery of Providence! Bad news from the Niger expedition! Many of its brave men have fallen victims to the climate. How extraordinary! How mysterious! O God, shield, comfort, and support thy people! Let not the successive heavy news overwhelm them with too much grief.

28th.—I was busy transferring many articles of property, connected with the Mission to Kumási, into the hands of Mr. Brooking, preparatory to my departure for the coast.

29th.—I settled certain necessary affairs with Mr. Brooking; I also sent to the King, to remind him of my wish to leave Kumási on Monday next; and at eight, P. M., I went down to take leave, preparatory to my departure early on the morning of that day. He was surrounded by Apoko and other linguists and attendants, and appeared rather low-spirited. He expressed his thankfulness for the presents which Her Majesty the Queen of England, and the Wesleyan Missionary Society, had sent him; and said he was sorry that the distressing condition of the town, from the effects of the late fire, had hindered him from giving me the opportunity of seeing him in the carriage; but as soon as the streets were cleared, he would use it, and Mr. Brooking should have an opportunity of seeing him do so, and then he would write and tell me about it. I took my leave of him, and returned to our quarters.

Sunday, 30th.—At half-past six, A. M., I read prayers, and preached from Isai. xl. 25—31. The congregation was large and attentive. There were three Chiefs present, who paid deep attention to the word of grace. Shortly after the commencement of the service, the chief Moor entered the yard: we offered him a seat, and he remained during the whole of the service, and seemed much pleased, with what he both saw and heard. While I was speaking of the almighty power and goodness of God, his hard and care-worn features underwent an extraordinary change; his countenance beamed with delight and satisfaction, and he seemed carried away by the splendid idea and exhilarating facts contained in the text. Since my departure from the coast, I had seen many things which have filled me with astonishment; and which convinced me, that the Lord was blessing us in our work, and gradually preparing our way before us; but this seemed more than all others to astound me, to behold such conduct in so aged and venerable a follower of the false Prophet.*

* The Rev. Mr. Brooking, in writing to Mr. Freeman, several weeks after his return to the coast, remarks, "The Moors are

Early in the afternoon I walked out, to call on Apoko and others, to take leave of them. The last person on whom I called, was Osai Kujoh, the successor to the throne. He received me very kindly, and conversed with me, in a very gratifying manner, for several minutes. He expressed his satisfaction at the good understanding which now exists between Ashânti and England, and his wishes that it might always continue. He spoke of peace as a blessing, and of war as being very injurious and destructive; to which I answered, "Yes; war is injurious even to conquerors." To this he gave his full assent, and said, "We have, in days that are past, had but little friendly intercourse with the English; and consequently we have been deprived of many advantages. Our taste for European things in general is at present but small; yet I hope, as things become more settled, and we are better acquainted, affairs will undergo a steady change, which will be very beneficial to us." During our interview, he referred to my early departure from Kumâsi, and said, "You have now been with us some time; and we begin to know you, and are very sorry that you are going to leave us." I answered, "I am sorry, also, and should feel much pleasure in remaining longer, if I could; but my duties on the coast demand my immediate return. I must leave to-morrow; but I hope to have the pleasure of seeing you again. I have now visited you twice, which, I believe, no European has done before. I therefore consider myself in one sense an Ashânti, and must, if possible, come up at the usual season, with the Kabosirs,

---

exceedingly friendly with me; one of whom brings me a bottle of new milk every morning." Considering the usual hostility of Mahommedanism to the Christian faith, these are singular and interesting facts.—EDIT.

to pay my compliments to the King." This amused him very much; and he said, "Of course, you must come up as you have said, and we shall be happy to see you; and we believe you will come, according to your promise, because you have kept your word, ever since we have known you." I then took my leave of him, highly gratified that a man so near the throne was so well disposed towards us.

At four, P. M., I again preached, from 1 John iv. 8, to a very interesting congregation. The venerable Moor was present again, paying deep attention.

31st.—I rose at five, A. M., and began to prepare for my journey. Apoko came over to see me, and to deliver a message from the King, referring to some secular business on the coast. After breakfast the King again sent Apoko, to request that I would stop until he had taken his bath, and then he would send messengers to say, "Farewell." About half-past nine, Apoko and several persons arrived, bringing one golden tobacco-pipe, and another, made with silver, in an unfinished state. Apoko said, the golden pipe was for Her Majesty the Queen of England, and the silver pipe for the Wesleyan Missionary Committee, as tokens of thankfulness on the part of the King, for the handsome presents he had received.

Apoko also informed me, that the King would make me a present of a silver tobacco-pipe; and that the pipes should be sent to the coast, as soon as the former was finished.*

I then commenced my journey, accompanied as far as Karsi by the Princes and Mr. Brooking. I left Kumási

* In the course of Monday morning, the King sent me £9 gold-dust, and a slave, about twenty-five years of age, whom I, of course, set at liberty, as soon as I reached Karsi.

at half-past eleven, A. M., and reached Eduabin about half-past three, P. M.

The heat was intense; and as I was not fully supplied with men to carry my luggage, I was obliged to walk all the way, and let my hammock-men assist with the boxes, &c., so that I was very much fatigued on my arrival at Eduabin.

February 1st.—We started from Eduabin at six, A. M., and reached Fomunah at five-and-twenty minutes before six, P. M. We were welcomed by the Chief, and treated kindly. We rested at Fomunah for the night.

As I was leaving Eduabin in the morning, I met a messenger with letters from the coast, acquainting me with the arrival of Mr. Allen. How encouraging, after all our recent heavy losses, to find that our friends stagger not at our difficulties! to find that there are Christian Missionaries who dare to come, and friends who hesitate not to send them, to assist in filling up the breaches which death has made among us!

2d.—At half-past eight, A. M., I took my leave of the Chief of Fomunah, and resumed my journey. We halted a short time at Quisah, and again on the summit of the Adansi hills. We started from thence at half-past two, P. M., and reached Akrofrum at six. I was much troubled with a severe attack of tooth-ache accompanied with a swollen face: a trifling circumstance to talk about, but not a pleasant companion in the wilderness.

3d.—At four, A. M., we resumed our journey in the dark, and, travelling rapidly, reached the Prah about five, P. M. At six, a heavy tornado came on, and lasted some time. The rain was very heavy, and the thunder and lightning awfully grand: a mercy that it did not overtake me, with my swelled face, &c., in the forest. I felt thankful for a little hovel which sheltered me from the fury of the contending elements.

4th.—After making arrangements for raising a little school and resting-house at the Prah, at nine, A. M., we again resumed our journey. It was delightful travelling, the heavy rain having cooled the earth, and given a charming freshness to the forest. Late in the afternoon, feeling myself weary with walking, I was riding in my chair, when we passed a great tree, at the foot of which lay, coiled up, a large black snake, within three or four yards of us. I felt anxious to kill it, and preserve it; but the men were alarmed, and looked on it with horror, and seemed ready to take to their heels. Having my fowling-piece ready loaded, I killed it. Its length was about six feet six inches, the largest I had seen since I left Cape Coast. We stopped for the night at Apunsi Kwanta.

5th.—At half-past five, A. M., we started for Mansu. During the day, we passed some of the places where we had the greatest difficulties in conveying the carriage. I thought that, had I not seen the carriage taken through and over those places, I should hardly have believed it possible. We reached Mansu about half-past four, P. M.

Sunday, 6th.—At half-past ten, A. M., I conducted divine service. Several of the natives were present. At a quarter past four, P. M., I again preached to an attentive, though small, congregation. Gabri, the Chief, is at Cape Coast, with several of his people.

7th.—I was busy, attending to affairs relative to the Mission-house, school, &c.

8th.—At eight, A. M., I received letters, acquainting me with the arrival of Messrs. Rowland and Wyatt at the coast. Such a supply of Missionaries as this, exceeds all my expectations; and yet it falls far short of the number we require.

At two, P. M., I again resumed my journey, and

reached Yankumási about half-past five. I was very kindly received by Asín Chibbu, who seemed anxious to know the result of my visit to Kumási, and was pleased with the information I gave him.

9th.—I started from Yankumási at half-past six, A. M., and reached Cape Coast at six, P. M.; thankful to God for journeying mercies, and for so much success in our enterprise.

APPENDICES TO THE SECOND JOURNAL.

APPENDIX, A.

From the Journal it will be seen, that, before Mr. Freeman left Kumási on his return to the coast, regular public worship had been commenced, and that the services were attended by many of the Ashántis, including several persons of high rank; that the King had given land for the erection of a suitable Mission-house; that he had allotted a large native-house for the residence of the Missionaries, until the new building should be completed; and that the King had not given the Princes, his nephews, a separate establishment, but left them to reside with the Missionaries, on whom, of course, they are altogether dependent for Christian and civilized society. Having formed a religious community, consisting of converted Fantis connected with the Mission, and a few strangers, Mr. Freeman thus left the nucleus of a Christian church in Kumási; and, shortly after his return to the coast, he had the satisfaction to learn, that the King had consented to the establishment of a school, and that one had been actually commenced. The following extracts show the state and prospects of the Mission down to the latest date:—

Extract of a Letter from the Rev. T. B. Freeman to the Secretaries of the Wesleyan Missionary Society, dated Mission-House, Cape Coast, February 25th, 1842.

I rejoice to say, that the Lord has been mercifully pleased to crown our efforts in Ashánti with success. Our important negotiations with the King have been brought to so comfortable a close, that he has taken Mr. Brooking under his protection as a resident Christian Missionary in Kumási; given us land in a very healthy and airy part of the town on which to build a Mission-house; allows the people to attend divine service without restraint, and treats us with uniform kindness and attention. This great advantage having been gained, we humbly hope that all other arrangements will, under the blessing of God, follow in due order, and that an appearance of permanency will soon be given to the Ashánti Mission.

Many of the Chiefs and Captains occasionally attend divine service; and we may reasonably calculate on their hailing with pleasure the establishment of schools, &c., as they become better acquainted with us, and are able to form more correct ideas of the claims of scriptural Christianity. The King seems very anxious to introduce improvements into the country, as far as the prejudices of the people will admit of his doing so. His carpenters are sent to the Mission-house to work at the same bench with ours; and I expect that, by this time, he has sent men to our saw-pits, to learn to cut boards, &c. During my residence at Kumási, he often visited us at the Mission quarters, and gave many proofs that we have, by the blessing of God, secured his confidence. A short time before I left Kumási, a dreadful fire broke out, and destroyed, at least, half the town. Had such a catastrophe taken place during my former visit, they would probably have attributed it to the anger of their Fetish, on account of my being in the town; or to some baneful power which they imagined me to possess, and to have employed to their injury; but such a change has now taken place, that in the midst of the awful dangers with which they were surrounded, during the raging of the flames, when they saw us actively engaged at the most dangerous points, in endeavouring to check the progress of the devouring element, they recognised us as their friends; and the King himself called at our residence, a day or two afterwards, and personally expressed his thanks for our exertions.

From the same, dated April 17th, 1842.

All things are going on admirably well in Kumási. Mr. Brooking writes full of spirits, and big with hopes of abundant success. He is now engaged in building the new Mission-house: and I am as busy here, endeavouring to meet his wants; and they are not trifling ones, in a place so far distant from the coast. Prejudice, on the part of the Ashántis, seems to pass away as the morning cloud and the early dew; so that we are all astonished at the pleasing prospect of things in Ashánti. The King is now about to form a new street, in honour of the Mission; which will be a great convenience to the brethren there, as it will open a healthy communication with the market-place, and the principal parts of the town.

Mr. Brooking entreats me to send up a Missionary to Kumási without delay; stating it to be his opinion, that Kumási is far more healthy than the coast, in which opinion I entirely agree. I have long felt anxious to have another Missionary in Kumási; but as Mr. Watson's health is still delicate, I know not what steps to take. I durst not send Mr. Watson, and Mr. Allen certainly ought to go to Domonási. The only efficient person, therefore, is Mr. Rowland, whom I thought of sending to Badagry. After serious reflection for many days, I mentioned the matter to him, and he immediately expressed his willingness to go to Kumási, Badagry, or *anywhere else*. Judging our way to be clear, I have decided on Mr. Rowland's departure for Kumási on the 10th or 11th of May, and have written to Mr. Brooking to send down one of the young men to the Prah, with travelling conveniences, to conduct him. As Mr. Rowland does not understand the nature of travelling in this climate, I intend, by God's permission, to take him as far as the Prah myself. I am aware that you may perhaps blame me for risking my health by so much incessant labour; but what can I do in such a case? Go he *must*, and he *must not* go alone. He has had a thorough seasoning, and the medical men say that he may now go anywhere with safety: they recommend Kumási in preference to the coast. It is a cheering fact, that the climate improves as we advance into the interior. Mr. Allen is now preparing for Domonási. He is to go up with us to the Prah, by way of seasoning him, and on our return he will immediately occupy his proper post.

APPENDIX, B.

Extract of a Letter from Prince William Quantamissah, to the Rev. John Beecham, dated Kumási, May 1st, 1842.

I AM very glad to address you a few lines, which I hope will find you, Mrs. Beecham, and all your family and friends in the enjoyment of good health.

I write to return you my sincere and best thanks, for the very great kindness and attention we experienced from you, when in your favoured country.

I am happy to inform you, that, through the mercy of Heaven, we safely arrived here on Monday, the 13th of December, in the year of our blessed Lord 1841, and were honourably received by our uncle the King. Our much-respected friends, the Rev. Messrs. Freeman and Brooking, your Society's two able and worthy Missionaries, were with us; so our journey from Cape Coast up to Kumási was very comfortable. His Majesty is much pleased with the handsome carriage your honourable Society was kind enough to send him; and I do assure you, that your Society has done much for Ashánti, in sending him this carriage. For this I have two reasons; and I will explain them to you. First, the carriage will civilize and improve the town of Kumási. Instead of the old streets, which are narrow and dirty, now, on account of the carriage, the King has ordered new streets to be made, passable for the carriage; therefore the carriage indeed will improve and civilize our country; thank God to say. The second reason is plain and simple,—that the King, instead of being carried by men on their heads and shoulders, will now be carried by the carriage; and again, the carriage will take, in some measure, half of the distresses and hard labour from our fellow-neighbours' heads and shoulders; therefore permit me to say, your noble Society deserves all praise. Remember me kindly and affectionately to them all; more especially to Dr. Bunting and family, Dr. Alder, Mr. Hoole, and other leading members of the Society, whom I had the pleasure of seeing at your hospitable house.

I would have written to you seven or eight epistles before this, but I had to wait for opportunity to send what I was preparing. When we arrived at Cape-Coast Castle, we received, through the hands of the Rev. Thomas B. Freeman, volumes of books, which we have now with us, and for which we return you our thanks. I do assure you, that, though we are now parted, and perhaps we shall never see each other again, yet neither time nor place can obliterate from my memory the kindness of my well-wisher.

Pray never cease to help Ashánti, and poor Africa at large.

APPENDIX, C.

Extract of a Letter from the Rev. Robert Brooking, dated Kumási, April 6th, 1842, to the Rev. Thomas B. Freeman, Cape-Coast Castle.

ALL things around us are as promising as ever. I am still frequently visited by the principal Chiefs. Indeed it seems that I am exciting a greater interest among them. I am just now getting a few articles of furniture completed. A few days ago I had a side-board finished, and put up in its place; which circumstance has drawn numerous visiters hither. They are also greatly astonished at the wonders of the turning-lathe.

You will remember, in reading the adventures of that excellent Missionary, WILLIAMS, that the first thing he turned in the South-Sea Islands was the leg of a sofa. By a curious coincidence, quite undesigned on my part, that was also the first thing I turned in Kumási; nor did it occur to me, until after Degowar came in and saw it; who, after he had examined it, for upwards of half-an-hour, with the greatest attention, and placed it in twenty different positions, pronounced it to be a most beautiful thing. The King also paid me a visit to-day. He was here almost an hour; he, too, was much gratified with what I have done, and desired me to work the turning-lathe, with which he was greatly delighted. He expressed a degree of surprise, when, after he asked me how long I had had it, I informed him three weeks, that no one had told him I had got such a wonderful thing. He was also pleased with the side-board: and when he saw the stool, he pronounced it to be an excellent thing, and told Quantamissah that he should like to have one to be carried with him when he goes on a journey, but that he did not like to ask me to make him one. I shall set Kobri to make him a neat one, and send him down as soon as possible; and am glad that I have such an opportunity of doing him this favour.

One of the Chiefs told me the other day, that if he had been told that the side-board had been made on the coast and brought up here, he should not have believed it, but have concluded that it certainly came from England.

APPENDIX, D.

Extract of a Letter from the Rev. Thomas B. Freeman, to the General Secretaries, dated Mission-House, Cape-Coast Castle, May 9th, 1842.

To see a footing secured in Kumási, has been to me, so much as I have been identified with it, a source of joyous expectation, mercifully weighed in the balance against my severe sufferings, from various causes, during the past year: and should God, in his providence, be pleased to remove me from this scene of trial, this state of "pleasing, anxious being;" should He call me to follow my sainted friends into an invisible world before I begin my descent from the summit of life's meridian prime; I trust I shall be enabled to depart with something like the sentiments of old Simeon in holy writ,—"Lord, now lettest thou thy servant depart in peace: for mine eyes have seen" one of the most powerful Monarchs of interior, degraded Africa, become a nursing-father to the heralds of "thy salvation." To God most high, the loving Father, the redeeming Son, the convincing and sanctifying Spirit, be all the praise and all the glory! Amen and amen!

If time would permit, I have many things to say; but I am so hardly pressed, that I cannot do what I would. Yesterday I was sick in bed, I believe chiefly from the effects of incessant toil, and close application to business; and to-day I have to write several letters, and to close my papers for this vessel, independent of my being obliged to prepare for a fortnight's or three weeks' absence from home, to take Mr. Rowland to the Prah, (a distance of nearly ninety miles,) chiefly on foot, with an intention of visiting the interior parts of the station, before my return to Cape Coast. This labour is not of short duration, but it is nearly the same all the year round. I need great strength, both of body and spirit, to bear this. I bless God that I am enabled to do it.

APPENDIX, E.

THE following extracts describe various Missionary operations on the Gold Coast, and especially show the necessity which exists for greatly increased exertions to meet the spiritual wants of the native population:—

DIX-COVE.—*Extract of a Letter from the Rev. John Watson, dated Dix-Cove, July 13th, 1841.*

My inability to write to you on the return of Mr. Mycock—inability arising from the seasoning fever—will, I have no doubt, be deemed a sufficient excuse why you have not heard from me earlier. However, the revolution of another quarter brings with it the duty of "giving" you "an account of" the exercise of my ministerial "stewardship."

Our General Superintendent, deeming it necessary that a European Missionary should be stationed at this place, selected me for that purpose; and, as soon as my strength was sufficiently recruited, I accordingly repaired hither, at which place I arrived, April 7th, 1841. The estimated distance from Cape Coast to Dix-Cove is between sixty and seventy miles by land. The population of this town is computed at five thousand; though one-fifth or more of these are generally absent from home, either attending to their farms in the bush, or on trading excursions. Your Missionary has never been preceded in this part of the Mission-field by a messenger of peace, except by an American Episcopalian Missionary, who resided here but eight weeks. There is only one European merchant resident here. A boys' school was only commenced twelve months previous to my arrival; so that the facilities hitherto afforded to the inhabitants for acquiring a knowledge of divine truth having been limited, the darkness of Heathenism is consequently nearly unbroken, and "the god of this world" has hitherto reigned in this part of his dominions with almost undisputed sway. The limits of this communication, and my comparative inexperience, prohibit me from saying any thing respecting the religious opinions, superstitious practices, &c., of the natives, except that their principal tutelar deity is the alligator; which, being devoutly revered and suitably protected, has multiplied rather too rapidly, and having recently become injurious to men, and destructive to sheep, goats, fowls, &c., the authorities have deemed it necessary to demonstrate the mortality of their divinities, by shooting two of them.

During the first fortnight of my residence here, I

was hospitably entertained by John G. Sandeman, Esq., Commandant, (*pro tempore*,) at the expiration of which period no suitable house being obtainable, I was under the necessity of renting the one which I now occupy for six ackies of gold (£1. 10*s*. currency) per month. It consists of three rooms on a ground-floor, the respective sizes of which are seventeen feet by nine, eleven by nine, and nine by nine. It is situated on the beach, and the high-tides wash the foundations of the side and end-walls of my bed-room, and approach within four yards of the entire front of the house; so that your Missionary unavoidably lives in steam by day, and in dew by night. I trust, dear Sirs, you will perceive the indispensable necessity of immediately erecting a Mission-house, if you resolve to continue a European Missionary at Dix-Cove. At present a residence here is eminently perilous; and, indeed, that I am alive to write these lines is matter of grateful surprise to myself.

Our religious services were held in the open air until the commencement of the rainy season in the latter end of May, when we were compelled to retreat to the school-room, in which our services have subsequently been held. My congregations have varied from forty to two hundred; and many attend regularly now, who only attended casually at first. My reception among the people has been exceedingly kind and flattering. The principal head-men and merchants manifest an ardent desire for instruction; and, previous to my arrival anong them, they envied the privileges of the inhabitants of Cape Coast. They saw the full light of truth shining at a distance; and the few streaks of it which occasionally reached them were only sufficient to show them their destitute condition, and to excite the desire that the "Sun of righteousness" might arise on them, "with healing in his wings."

Twelve persons have been united in church-fellowship, some of whom, we trust, have entered into "the kingdom of God, which is not meat and drink, but righteousness, peace, and joy in the Holy Ghost;" and of others we have hope that they are not far from the same kingdom. The boys' school is now committed to our superintendence and direction: at present there are thirty-five boys in it, who display great aptitude in learning; and their progress is exceedingly creditable, considering the short time that the school has been established.

A girls' school was commenced on Monday, May 17th. Previous to this the whole town was canvassed by me; and the discouraging result was, only the promise of two girls. The female sex are so degraded here, and considered so much inferior, that the idea of educating them was ridiculed and laughed at as the greatest absurdity which the human mind could entertain. However, difficulties and discouragements are everyday occurrences with Missionaries; and notwithstanding the indifference of some, and the idiotic laughs of others, the school was opened at the time appointed; and when the people were satisfied as to the benevolent character of my intentions, by my furnishing the girls with frocks, work-bags, &c., their prejudices began to yield, and we succeeded in obtaining seven on the first day. The number has gradually increased since the commencement, and at present we have sixteen in the girls' school. For such a beginning, we "thank God, and take courage."

Apollonia.—*Extract of a Letter from the Rev. William Allen, dated Cape-Coast Castle, February 2d,* 1842.

I am happy to announce to you my safe arrival at Cape Coast. We were six weeks and two days before we made land. When we came to Apollonia,* the Captain went on shore to trade with the King, and met with a friendly reception. He told the King that he had a Missionary on board; whom he expressed a strong desire to see. The Captain wrote me a letter to that effect; and the King sent his large canoe, with twelve men, to conduct me on shore. I suppose I was the first Missionary that ever set a foot on the shores of Apollonia. I stopped at the King's house, and met with the kindest welcome. The Captain and I were together. We had not our meals with the King, but a most splendid entertainment was provided for us; and when we wanted to go, the King was unwilling that we should leave. He threw himself into a passion about our departure; and had placed round the court-yard not less than fifty men, armed with guns and swords, to prevent us from going; and in addition to these fifty men in the court-yard, he ordered all the workmen from a new house which he was building, not less than twenty, to come and stand also at a door-way through which we must pass, if we got out of the court-yard; some were armed with axes, others with adzes, each of them having a weapon of some kind. We stayed here two days, and even then it was not without trouble that we got away. At length the King, in a fit of passion, ordered the canoe-men to take us to the vessel immediately: this was what we wanted. In reference to the character of this King, I may remark, that he is supposed to be more barbarous than the King of Ashánti. A short time since, his mother died, and, to honour her, he caused twenty men, twenty women, and twenty young girls, to be sacrificed. They first killed a man,

* Near the western extremity of the Gold Coast. At this place the British formerly had a fort.—EDIT.

then a woman, and then a young girl; and continued their cruelties in this order, till they had killed the whole. The females were slain by striking them on the back of the head with clubs: they partly cut the throats of the men, and then tied ropes to their legs, and drew them round the town, their throats still bleeding, and men following them with clubs, striking them on their stomachs; and when they were brought back to the place from whence they started, they cut off the heads of those who were still living. The bodies of both male and female were thrown into a hole in the bush, to be food for beasts of prey. This King orders the head of a person to be cut off for a very trifling offence. I saw a large tree growing near to his house, in one of his court-yards, the trunk of which was lashed round with the skulls of human beings; there were not less than fifty human heads tied to that tree! I saw also several of his large drums, which were encircled with human skulls.

Akrah.—*Extract of a Letter from the Rev. Thomas B. Freeman, dated Cape-Coast Castle, April 17th,* 1842.

Our schools at Dix-Cove are doing well: they contain forty-five boys, and nineteen girls.

Our school at Cape Coast is rapidly advancing: it is now kept in the Mission-house, and contains sixty girls. I hope our friends at home will not forget us respecting clothes, needles, thread, &c.: we are sadly at a loss for these things.

Mr. and Mrs. Shipman have returned to their post at Akráh, and are busy in preparing to receive as many young men as we can obtain, to undergo a course of theological training and other preparation, for the more efficient discharge of their duty as teachers, &c. We have fixed upon Akráh as a proper place for this, because the Mission-house is large, and the society so small as to admit of Mr. Shipman's devoting much of his time in teaching and preparing the young men for usefulness.

Extract of a Letter from the Rev. Thomas B. Freeman, dated Cape-Coast Castle, June 25th, 1842.

Since I last wrote to you, I have accompanied Mr. Watson to Dix-Cove, to make arrangements for his permanent residence there. Alive to the importance of avoiding expenses as much as possible, I have tried by every means to hire a good habitation for him, but cannot succeed; and hence we are under the necessity of building a small house immediately. We have selected a piece of ground, of which we expect to obtain a "grant" from the Local Government; and are now purchasing materials, and preparing workmen to commence the house forthwith. As we have plenty of labourers at hand, I trust we shall succeed in getting it finished before the rainy season. I am glad to say that Mr. Watson's health seems to be fully restored; as a proof of which I need only tell you, that he has performed a journey of a hundred and forty miles along the coast, during the rainy season: a great part of which we had to walk, often climbing over rugged rocks, and sometimes wading through muddy paths, during the heat of the day, and the damps of the night: he has now proceeded to Anamabu, to pack up his things, and to prepare for his removal to Dix-Cove, in perfect health. This is encouraging amidst our heavy duties. I hope the new house at Dix-Cove will be built with greater rapidity, and with less expense, than we have accomplished such work before, on any part of the coast. We are thinking of slating the roof, as it will be the safest, as well as the most expeditious method. We can obtain slate from America, cheaper than we can from England; and I think I can procure it from thence, by the time that we shall be ready for it. Many of the merchants here are using slate for the roofs of their houses, and find it no more expensive than the ordinary method of terracing.

I hope these steps will meet with the approbation of the Committee, and that the result will prove our strict adherence to economy.

I am now preparing to proceed to Badagry, with Mr. and Mrs. De Graft, by the first opportunity; and hope, by the blessing of God, to be able to write to you from thence, in about two months from this date.

I bless God that our reports from all parts of the District are encouraging, both from the interior and along the coast. Some of us, either from hard labour, or from the exhausting effects of the rainy season, are not quite so strong in bodily health as we could wish: but we will not complain; for we know in whose glorious work we are engaged.

THIRD JOURNAL

OF THE

REV. THOMAS B. FREEMAN.

CHAPTER I.

INTRODUCTION—BADAGRY—YARIBA—DAHOMI—IMPORTANCE OF THESE STATIONS—MR. FREEMAN DEPARTS FROM CAPE-COAST—ARRIVES AT BADAGRY—PREPARATIONS FOR THE ERECTION OF A MISSION-HOUSE—SENDS A MESSENGER TO THE KING OF ABOKUTA—AN AWFUL CATASTROPHE—RETURN OF MESSENGER—PRESENT FROM SODAKA, THE KING—HIS LETTER—INTERVIEW WITH SOME MOORS—PROGRESS OF THE NEW MISSION-HOUSE—ARRIVAL OF MESSENGERS FROM SODAKA, TO CONDUCT MR. FREEMAN INTO THE INTERIOR.

THE Wesleyan Missionary Committee, aware of the expectation which has been awakened by the announcement of the visit of the Rev. Thomas B. Freeman to Badagry, Yariba, and Dahomi, embrace the earliest opportunity of laying before their friends his account of the journey; which, in point of general interest, equals at least the Journals of his two previous visits to Ashânti, and which is especially important, as descriptive of some of the most promising openings for the spread of Christianity, and the advancement of civilization in Africa, that have as yet been presented.

When it was first made known that the Committee had resolved to attempt the formation of a Mission at Badagry,* some of the friends of Africa, best acquainted

* For information respecting the circumstances by which the Committee were led to adopt the resolution here referred to, see "Missionary Notices" for December, 1841, and June, 1842, with the "Annual Report of the Society" for 1842, p. 101.

with the arduous nature of such an undertaking, declared that, should the attempt be attended with success, they should regard that success as furnishing *proof* that there is nothing too difficult for Missionary enterprise to achieve. The formidable task has, however, been accomplished; and Badagry, only known previously as the seat of the most sanguinary superstition,* and the

---

* "Badagry," Lander remarks, "being a general mart for the sale of slaves to the European merchants, it not unfrequently happens that the market is overstocked with human beings; in which case their maintenance devolves on the Government. Thieves, and other offenders, together with the remnant of unpurchased slaves, who are not drowned along with their companions in misfortune and misery, are reserved by them to be sacrificed to their gods; which horrid ceremony takes place at least once a month. Prisoners taken in war are also immolated, to appease the manes of the soldiers of Adoilee slain in battle; and of all atrocities, the manner in which these wretches are slain is the most barbarous. Each criminal being conducted to the fetish-tree, a flask of rum is given him to drink: whilst he is in the act of swallowing it, a fellow steals imperceptibly behind him with a heavy club inflicts a violent blow on the back of the head, and, as it often happens, dashes out his brains. The senseless being is then taken to the fetish-hut, and a calabash or gourd having been previously got ready, the head is severed from the trunk with an axe, and the smoking blood gurgles into it. While this is in hand, other wretches, furnished with knives, cut and mangle the body, in order to extract the heart entire from the breast; which being done, although it be yet warm and quivering with blood, it is presented to the King first, and afterwards to his wives and Generals, who always attend at the celebration of these sacrifices; and His Majesty and suite making an incision into it with their teeth, and partaking of the foamy blood which is likewise offered, the head is then exhibited to the surrounding multitude. It is afterwards affixed to the head of a tall spear, and with the calabash of blood, and the headless body, they are paraded through the town, followed by hundreds of spearmen, and a dense crowd of people. Whoever may express an inclination to bite the heart, or drink the blood, has it immediately presented to him for that purpose, the multi-

scene of the worst atrocities and cruelties of the slave-trade; where, such was the jealousy with which Europeans were regarded, that our countryman, Lander,

---

tude dancing and singing. What remains of the heart is flung to the dogs; and the body, cut in pieces, is stuck on the fetish-tree, where it is left till wholly devoured by birds of prey. Besides these butcheries, they make a grand sacrifice once a year, under their sacred fetish-tree, growing in a wood, a few miles from the city. These are offered to their malevolent demon, or spirit of evil, quartered, and hung on the gigantic branches of the venerable tree, and the skulls of the victims suffered to bleach in the sun around the trunk of it. By accident, I had an opportunity of seeing this much-talked-of tree, a day or two only after one of the yearly sacrifices. Its enormous branches were literally covered with fragments of human bodies, and its majestic trunk surrounded by irregular heaps of hideous skulls, which had been suffered to accumulate for many years previously. Thousands of vultures, which had been scared away by our unwelcome intrusion, were yet hovering round and over their disgusting food, and now and then pouncing fearlessly down upon a half-devoured arm or leg. I stood as if fascinated to the spot by the influence of a torpedo, and stupidly gazed on the ghastly spectacle before me. The huge branches of the fetish-teee groaning under their burden of human flesh and bones, and sluggishly waving in consequence of the hasty retreat of the birds of prey; the intense and almost insufferable heat of a vertical sun; the intolerable odour of the corrupt corpses; the heaps of human heads, many of them apparently staring at me from hollows which had once sparkled with living eyes; the awful stillness and solitude of the place, disturbed only at intervals by the frightful screamings of voracious vultures, as they flapped their sable wings almost in my face;—all tended to overpower me; my heart sickened within my bosom, a dimness came over my eyes, an inexpressible quivering agitated my whole frame; my legs refused to support me; and, turning my head, I fell senseless into the arms of Jowdie, my faithful slave."—*Lander*, pp. 260—268.

"March 24th, 1830.—We are most anxious to proceed on our journey; but the Chief, Adooley, evades our solicitations under the most frivolous and absurd pretences.... Meantime the rainy season is fast approaching, as is sufficiently announced by repeated

was compelled to drink the poisonous fetish-draught; has welcomed back the emigrants from Sierra-Leone, who have returned to the shores from whence they had been forcibly dragged, with no other protection or recommendation than the Christianity which, during their absence, they had received by means of British liberality; aud Christian Missionaries have been hailed there as friends and benefactors, and have made an encouraging commencement of their work.

The formation of this Mission has been attended with other important results.

1. It has opened the way into the Aku or Yariba country. On his arrival at Badagry, Mr. Freeman found that the greater number of the emigrants for whose benefit the Mission was primarily intended, had proceeded into the interior, and had settled at a town called, in the Aku language, *Abokuta,* from *aba,* "under," and *okuta,* "a stone," which was represented as the chief town of the Eba tribe. To this place, as soon as he had made the necessary arrangements for settling Mr. and Mrs. De Graft, he determined to repair; and was surprised to find, at a distance of about ninety geographical miles N.N.E. or N.E. by N. from Badagry, a large town, covering twice as much ground as the capital of Ashânti, and containing, according to his calculation, from forty thousand to fifty thousand inhabit-

---

showers and occasional tornadoes: and what makes us still more desirous to leave this abominable place, is the fact, as we have been told, that a sacrifice of no less than three hundred human beings, of both sexes and all ages, is shortly to take place. We often hear the cries of these poor wretches; and the heart sickens with horror at the bare contemplation of such a scene as awaits us, should we remain here much longer. We, therefore, can only wish that, if such is to be the case, we may not be compelled to witness this bloody abomination."—*Landers' Journal,* vol. i., p. 19.

ants. At this place, of which Clapperton makes no mention whatever, and which does not appear to have been previously visited by any European, he met with many emigrants who were united with our Mission at Sierra-Leone, as well as some others who had been attached to the Church Missionary Society, whose Christian conduct had produced such a favourable impression upon Sodaka, the King, that he granted them the peculiar privilege of entering his presence without prostrating themselves upon the ground; encouraged them to cultivate the civilized habits which they had acquired; and was prepared, by the good impression which they had made upon his mind, to receive Mr. Freeman as a Christian teacher with great cordiality.

The importance of this opening for Missionary and philanthropic effort can scarcely be overrated. Already commercial intercourse with the coast is established, as the emigrants come regularly down to the markets at Badagry; and, on the other hand, amicable intercourse is maintained between Abokuta, or Understone, and Hausa, the southern boundary of which is distant only about seven days' journey, and to whose King Mr. Freeman had the opportunity of sending a friendly message by an embassy, which arrived at Understone while he was there.

2. The commencement of the Mission at Badagry has led to friendly intercourse with Dahomi, and has afforded the opportunity for introducing the Gospel into that kingdom. Knowing the character of its Sovereign, and apprehensive that our proceedings at Badagry might probably be interrupted by his interference, Mr. Freeman determined, if possible, to see him, and endeavour to secure his acquiescence in our plans. He accordingly, on his return from Abokuta, proceeded, by way of Whydah, to the royal residence at Kanna, where he contra-

dicted the report which had been circulated, that the Missionary was building a fort at Badagry, and explained to the King the true nature and objects of the Missionary undertaking. A very favourable impression was evidently made upon the mind of this influential Monarch; for he intrusted to Mr. Freeman's care, for education, four children, selected from the royal household; and requested that Whydah, as well as Badagry, might also be favoured with a Missionary, who should go up once a year to visit the capital.

On the steps taken by Mr. Freeman for making the British authorities acquainted with the willingness of the King of Dahomi to abolish the slave-trade in his dominions, and his desire to maintain commercial intercourse with this country, and on the subsequent arrangements which were made, we are not at liberty at present to enter. We shall await the result with much solicitude; impressed as we are with the opinion of some, whose long acquaintance with Africa entitles their opinions to respect, that should Great Britain renew its friendly relations with the King of Dahomi; adopt the recommendation of the late Parliamentary Committee, on Western Africa, to re-establish the factory at Whydah, (which, it will be seen, is now desired by the King of Dahomi himself,) together with the one at Badagry; and give such protection to the emigrants from Sierra-Leone, as would be afforded by a decisive announcement on the coast that she would not allow them to be molested or oppressed; the accursed traffic in human beings would soon be brought to an end in the Bight of Benin, and the emigrants might be made the pioneers of Christianity and civilization in the countries extending from the coast to the Niger.

The perusal of the following document will not fail to call forth from many hearts, the grateful acknowledgment of the Psalmist: "This is the Lord's doing: it is marvellous in our eyes." The spirit of kindness and of religious inquiry which has manifested itself in countries where the worst passions of corrupt human nature have hitherto predominated without check or restraint, can only be accounted for on the principle, that a divine influence is preparing the minds of the people for an extensive and beneficial change. This conclusion is strengthened by the consideration, that at this very juncture, a large class of native agents have, by a series of providential arrangements, received a Christian training at Sierra-Leone; and are returning to their fatherland, where a spirit of inquiry and desire for instruction and improvement is now extensively elicited. This auspicious movement, however, cannot be regarded merely as matter for devout contemplation and grateful thanksgiving. It must be considered as a loud call to renewed exertion on the part of this Society. At least EIGHT additional English Missionaries, Mr. Freeman writes, are immediately wanted, to embrace the opportunities for usefulness which now present themselves, and to direct and superintend the efforts of the emigrants to do good. But the present state of the funds of the Society will not allow the Committee, as yet, to respond to this demand. Friends of Christian Missions, lend your aid! You have long been praying that the great Head of the church would providentially remove all obstacles, and open the way for the general spread of his Gospel, as well as that he would prepare the minds of the Heathen for its reception, by the outpouring of his Holy Spirit; and now that he is answering your prayers, will you dare to mock the Lord, by withholding the instrumentality which himself has rendered necessary for the conversion of the world? It cannot be. "Thy people shall be willing in the day of thy power," is the "sure word of prophecy." This is eminently the day of the Messiah's power; and shall not his people be found willing to contribute the appointed means for the extension of his peaceful reign over those African regions, to which his gracious providence now points the way?

SEPTEMBER 19th, Monday.—At noon I went on board the schooner "Spy," Captain L. Huquet, accompanied by Mr. and Mrs. De Graft. When we arrived on board, the vessel was under weigh. In the evening we anchored off Anamabu, and received some beams and planks for our intended Mission-house at Badagry. This being accomplished, we again took up anchor, and proceeded to Akrâh.

20th.—Heavy rains fell during the past night. The cabin was too small and confined to admit of our sleeping below; hence we were obliged to continue on deck in the rain. God be praised for strength to bear such exposure! About nine, A. M., I went on shore, and found Mr. and Mrs. Shipman well, and happy in their work, for which I feel thankful to God. At half-past two, P. M., I returned on board; and in the evening we weighed anchor, and sailed for Badagry.

22d.—We spoke Her Majesty's ship "Persian," from whence an officer came on board to inspect our vessel.

23d.—We passed Whydah, and spoke Her Majesty's ship "Cygnet," and in the evening anchored in Badagry Roads. As soon as we had let go our anchor, we sent a canoe on shore through the surf, with orders to the canoe-men to come off for us and convey us ashore, if they found the sea favourable. We anxiously waited, and watched them as they went on shore through a heavy sea; and finding that they hauled the canoe up on the beach, we concluded that they were afraid to venture, and consequently we remained on board for the night.

24th.—About eight, A. M., we perceived the canoe-men had come down to the beach, and were launching the boat; and at half-past nine, they came along-side, bringing with them Mr. Parsons, Mr. Hutton's trading agent at Badagry; from whom we learnt, that the surf was bad and dangerous. At half-past eleven, Mr. and Mrs. De Graft went on shore, by the mercy of God, perfectly safe and dry; and about half-past twelve o'clock, Mr. Parsons and I landed in safety. The roadstead at Badagry is open, and greatly exposed, in consequence of which, the surf often runs high. As it is generally most smooth in the morning, and becomes dangerous as the day advances, I felt very anxious to cause the luggage of Mr. and Mrs. De Graft, and of our servants, to be sent on shore as early as I could. When I landed, and found our little family, and all the luggage that we had ventured to send, safely collected on the beach, I felt grateful to the God of all grace for this fresh manifestation of his kindness. Having reached the shore, we proceeded from the beach over a sandy plain, about a mile in width, covered with a thin sward of grass. We arrived on the banks of the Lagoon, which communicates with the sea at Lagos, and stretches westward with few interruptions as far as Cape St. Paul's. At Badagry the Lagoon assumes the appearance of a fine broad river, with a current setting down towards Lagos. Directly opposite that part of Badagry called "the English Town," the breadth of the Lagoon is from half to three quarters of a mile. We crossed the river in a large canoe; and, between two and three o'clock in the afternoon, had the unspeakable satisfaction of placing our feet on shore at Badagry, where we were kindly received by Warru, the Chief or Headman of the English Town.

25th, Sunday.—Although we were only five days at sea, I very much enjoy the delightful change of walking on solid ground, amidst the ever-verdant scenery of this part of Africa. We are put to some little inconvenience, for want of quarters; but, after having been obliged to spend five days and nights on the unsheltered deck of a small vessel, we are not much disposed to complain of indifferent accommodation on shore. Mr. and Mrs. De Graft occupy part of one of Mr. Hutton's bamboo stores, and I live in my little tent. No place is to be obtained in which we can hold divine worship, which is a serious inconvenience; but I hope we shall soon do better.

26th.—Busily engaged landing our luggage, furniture, and timber for the intended Mission-house.

October 2d, Sunday.—In the afternoon Mr. De Graft conducted divine service in my tent, and preached from Psalm xcvi. 4. Our congregation was small, consisting of our own family and workmen. At present we have not been able to hold any regular public service, on account of having no convenient place; and it seems too early as yet to preach in the public streets. The Christian emigrants from Sierra-Leone are nearly all residing at Abokuta, or Understone, a large town upwards of one hundred miles from Badagry.

3d.—We finished landing our goods from the "Spy;" after which Captain Huquet went on board, and sailed for the island of St. Thomas.

4th.—Went into the bush to seek timber for piles for the new Mission-house. The soil of Badagry is very sandy; and as there is no stone in the neighbourhood, we must build a wooden frame-house on piles.

5th.—We proceeded up the Lagoon looking for

timber, and found some that will suit us, about four miles from Badagry. The brig "Oscar," from England, anchored in the roads to take in palm-oil from Mr. Hutton's factory.

6th.—The schooner "New Times," from England and Cape-Coast, &c., anchored in the roads. Brought our large canoe from the beach to the Lagoon, for the purpose of transporting timber down to Badagry. Found it hard work to take the canoe across the plain, on account of its great weight: it is very strong, and so large as to require twenty-one men to work it at sea. To effect this purpose, we were toiling in the heat of the day for several hours.

8th.—Sent a messenger to the King at Understone.

9th, Sunday.—Preached in the afternoon, under an awning prepared for the occasion. At the conclusion of the service, I met Warru, and Akia, and Jinji, the other Chiefs of the town, to explain to them more fully my object in visiting Badagry. They appeared pleased and satisfied with my explanations, and thanked me for the visit.

11th.—Commenced building a temporary bamboo cottage for the use of the Mission, until we are able to provide something more substantial.

13th.—An eventful day! About one, P. M., heard a report of a tremendous explosion in the direction of the beach, and saw an immense volume of black smoke rise immediately over the place where the "New Times" was anchored. Though the town of Badagry is situated about two miles and a half from the sea, and the ground so low, that the hull of a vessel in the roads cannot be seen; yet the masts of the "New Times" could be observed from the most elevated ground: to this spot we ran, and found that the masts of the vessel had disappeared. Knowing that she had a quantity of powder on board, we began to suspect the destruction both of the vessel and her cargo. A party immediately started for the beach; and, alas! not a vestige of the ship could be seen, nor any person to give the least information respecting her; whence they concluded, that the vessel was blown up, and that the whole of the crew had perished! In the course of the afternoon, a canoe which was floating astern, with part of the hawser by which it was secured to the vessel, was found with the head-boards torn off. Two mattrasses, part of a seaman's chest, and a Bible, with a few pieces of damaged cloth, were also discovered. Every succeeding hour has tended to confirm us in our fears, that the Captain and all the crew have perished. How solemn, how awful the reflection, that, without (in all probability) a minute's warning, the ill-fated company were launched into eternity! O my God,

"Arm me with jealous care,
As in thy sight to live!
And O thy servant, Lord, prepare
A strict account to give!"

We have all been deeply affected at this painful catastrophe. May it quicken our souls!

In the afternoon our bamboo cottage was in a state sufficiently forward to admit of our removal into it; for which we feel especially thankful, as the tornado season is just now beginning, and tents are too frail for such rough weather. That, with a piece of painted canvass over the top, under which I have slept every night since our arrival, has withstood several heavy showers of rain. For several days and nights past, Mr. and Mrs. De Graft have occupied a temporary tent, in preference to the store, because the latter is infested with a dangerous kind of snake.

16th, Sunday.—At eleven, A.M., Mr. De Graft read

prayers and preached in the cottage; and at half-past three, P. M., I officiated. Many of the pagan natives were present in the afternoon, who appeared interested and attentive. Thank God for a convenient room in which to worship; the want of this has made me feel very uncomfortable since our arrival at Badagry.

17th.—Busy in directing the workmen on the new Mission-premises.

18th.—Attending to numerous secular duties.

20th.—Went up the Lagoon with the workmen, to cut down timber for the Mission-house.

21st.—I felt poorly. Mr. De Graft went up the Lagoon for timber. My messenger, James Ferguson, an emigrant from Sierra-Leone, returned from Understone, bringing me a strong useful pony as a present from Sodaka, the King, also a Moorish saddle and bridle. At such an act of kindness on the part of a perfect stranger, I was agreeably surprised. Ferguson brings also a pressing invitation to me, from Sodaka, to visit him at Understone. The following copy of a note which I received from the King, and written, I suppose, by one of the Sierra-Leone emigrants, is a gratifying proof of the favourable state of his mind respecting a visit from a Christian Missionary:—

"To the Englishman at Badagry,

"I thank you for your kind promise, that you will visit us in this country. I shall be glad to receive you; and, by the blessing of God, nothing shall harm you.

"I remain,
"Yours truly,
"Sodaka,
"King of Understone.

"*Understone, October*, 1842."

On receiving these strong and cheering tokens of Sodaka's kindness and good feeling, I determined on visiting Understone as soon as the work on the Mission-premises in Badagry should be sufficiently forward to admit of our leaving it for a week or two without sustaining injury.

22d.—Busy in directing the workmen.

23d, Sunday.—At half-past ten, A. M., I read prayers and preached; and at half-past three, P. M., Mr. De Graft conducted the service. Many of the natives were present, and behaved well.

24th.—Mr. De Graft went up the Lagoon for more timber, while I made preparation for putting down piles for the Mission-house.

25th.—We commenced driving the piles. They are each fourteen feet in length, and nearly a ton in weight. The labour of cutting them, and bringing them the distance of a quarter to three quarters of a mile down the plain to the banks of the Lagoon, lifting them into the canoe, taking them out, and placing them on the Mission-premises, has been very great.

27th.—Employed with the workmen. In the evening we held a prayer-meeting; after which I took down the names of several who were in church-fellowship with us at Sierra-Leone, preparatory to their examination, and formation into a class.

28th.—Sent across the Lagoon for more timber for the Mission-house. Some rain fell in the night.

29th.—Went up the river to look for timber; but were compelled to leave our work unfinished, and hasten home, to escape a heavy tornado. Rain fell during the greater part of the night.

30th, Sunday.—At eleven, A. M., I read prayers and preached to an attentive congregation; and at four,

P. M., Mr. De Graft. The congregations were attentive. It has been a very fine day.

31st.—Went up the river again for timber; and returned at two, P. M., with a good supply. Some rain fell in the night.

November 1st.—Mr. De Graft went up the river for more timber. I have felt slightly indisposed all day. We had rain, with heavy thunder. The heat was very great, the thermometer standing at 80° at eight o'clock, A. M., and during the day from 80° to 85°.

2d.—Mr. De Graft went up the river for more timber. Feeling unwell, I remained at home. Surprised by a tornado, with heavy rain, in the afternoon. Her Majesty's ship "Persian" arrived in the roads, in company with the "Queen Victoria," from Sierra-Leone. The "Victoria" has one hundred and fifty emigrants on board, many of whom are members of the Wesleyan society.

3d.—Busy in fixing the piles for the remainder of the new Mission-house. Several of the emigrants landed from the "Victoria." We had rain in the night.

4th.—Many emigrants have landed. Rain again in the night, with thunder and lightning. A Captain, ship's crew, and passengers, taken from a slave-ship, captured by Her Majesty's ship "Rabbit," have been brought here by the "Victoria." The greater number of them are on shore, intending to go down to Lagos in a day or two. They are chiefly Portuguese.

5th.—We have been engaged in preparing a temporary screen from the sun, for divine worship to-morrow. The schooner "Spy" returned this evening from Prince's and St. Thomas's islands.

6th, Sunday.—Mr. De Graft conducted divine service at eleven, A. M. At four, P. M., I felt much better, and preached to a large and attentive congregation. From thirty to forty Moors were present, and behaved in a very respectful manner. After the sermon I addressed them for a few minutes, and told them my object in visiting Badagry, and my wish to be on terms of friendly intercourse with them: they seemed pleased with what I said. A tornado visited us between one and two o'clock in the afternoon.

7th.—Marked out the ground preparatory to the building of a bamboo chapel; dimensions, forty feet by eighteen.

8th.—I feel some bodily indisposition. Rain fell between one and two, P. M.

9th.—Still poorly, but busily employed in building the bamboo chapel. The weather very fine.

10th.—I am in better health. Went up the river in a boat in the afternoon, to examine the skirts of the forest on the banks, about six miles from the town of Badagry. We saw some good timber, which will be of great use in building. The weather continues very fine, though the sky is occasionally cloudy.

11th.—Mr. De Graft went up the river for more timber. Feeling rather poorly, I remained at home, and read Park's "Travels in Africa."

12th.—We have been busy in putting down the four last heavy cocoa-nut tree piles for the Mission-House, and finishing our little bamboo chapel for divine worship.

13th, Sunday.—At eleven, A. M., I read prayers and preached to a very interesting congregation, consisting chiefly of Christian emigrants from Sierra-Leone. Just as I was about to engage in prayer at the conclusion of the service, a fine snake, about four feet and a half in length, came into the chapel. The people were of course alarmed, and many of them ran out of the chapel; but, through mercy, no person sustained injury. They succeeded in killing it, and I have preserved it in spirits as a curiosity. In the afternoon Mr. De Graft preached to an attentive congregation.

14th.—I drew bills on the Committee, and wrote six letters; one to the Committee, and the others to parties on the Coast and in the interior. About three, P. M., Captain L. Huquet, of the schooner "Spy," left us to go on board his vessel, to proceed to Akwa, and thence to London. We had a happy prayer-meeting in the evening.

15th.—Busy in directing the workmen at the new house. The weather is fine and dry. We saw some messengers, who have come down from the King of Dahomi. They say, they are glad to see us here; but I doubt their sincerity.

16th.—Attending to the workmen at the house and the chapel. This is the first religious evening-service which we have had since our arrival. The weather hot and dry.

18th.—Employed in directing the workmen at the Mission-house. Early in the morning we had very heavy rain. I felt poorly and fatigued in the evening, on account of having been out in the heat, while suffering from a cold.

19th.—Engaged with the workmen.

20th, Sunday.—At eleven, A. M., I read prayers and preached. In the afternoon Mr. De Graft conducted the service. The heat is oppressive.

21st.—Commenced putting up the timber for the roof of the house. I felt unwell, from so much exposure to the heat of the sun. We held a prayer-meeting in the evening.

22d.—Busy with the roof of the house.

27th, Sunday.—At eleven, A. M., Mr. De Graft

preached; and at half-past three, P. M., I conducted public worship. Very few of the emigrants were present, many of them having gone into the interior to visit their friends. After the morning service I met some of them in class, and was much pleased with the artless and simple account which they gave of the Lord's dealings with them. May He bless them with grace to live to his glory amidst these scenes of superstition, vice, and folly! We had an interesting prayer-meeting in the evening.

28th.—Occupied with the work at the new house, though feeling poorly from a violent cold.

29th.—Too ill to attend to my duties.

30th.—Still indisposed, but improving.

December 2d.—God be praised! my health is rapidly recovering. I have been busy at the new house, and in making preparations for a journey into the interior. The roof of the Mission-house is now thatched.

3d.—We gave the labourers a dinner, to reward them for their steady and laborious attention to the heavy work of building the shell of the new Mission-house. While looking at the men regaling themselves with a good dinner, I felt thankful to God that so much toilsome work had been accomplished in so short a time without any serious accident; while, with very inadequate means, we had to raise and fix so much heavy timber. Blessed be God, who has thus prospered the work of our hands!

4th, Sunday.—At eleven, A. M., I read prayers and preached to an attentive congregation. Warru attended divine service, to my great satisfaction. I was indeed delighted to see him set such an example to his people. In the afternoon fourteen men belonging to Sodaka, King of the Akus, arrived, to conduct me into the interior.

CHAPTER II.

MR. FREEMAN DEPARTS FOR THE INTERIOR—AMOWU—ATONGA—TROOP OF HORSEMEN, AS AN ESCORT, IS SENT BY THE KING SODAKA—ADDO—MILITARY ENCAMPMENT—SHUMAI, THE KING'S BROTHER AND CAPTAIN OF WAR—APPEARANCE OF THE COUNTRY—CONVERSATION WITH THE CAPTAIN RELATING TO THE WAR—DEPARTS FROM THE ENCAMPMENT—MOJIBA—MOWO—GRASSFIELD—ALLOWAGU—AWAYADI—OWAYADI—APPROACH TO ABOKUTA, OR UNDERSTONE—OKWARU—MESSENGER SENT TO THE KING—ENTRANCE INTO THE TOWN—DESCRIPTION OF ABOKUTA—INTRODUCTION TO THE KING—CORDIAL RECEPTION—MEETS WITH CHRISTIAN EMIGRANTS FROM SIERRA-LEONE.

DECEMBER 5th.—We prepared to start for the interior, at nine, A. M., but found such difficulty in obtaining carriers, (that kind of work being strange and new to the people of Badagry,) that we were not ready to set off until two, P. M. When we commenced the journey, Warru accompanied us about two miles on the path, and then sent a messenger to conduct us on our way to Understone.

We travelled for two hours through a flat country, diversified with open plains and small tracts of forest; when we arrived on the banks of a deep and extensive marsh, which we had to cross in canoes. I think the marsh could not be less than three quarters of a mile or a mile in width, with from ten to fifteen feet depth of water in the deepest part. We made the horses swim by the side of the canoes. It was between seven and eight o'clock before the whole party landed on the opposite side. We took up our quarters at Amowu, a small village close to the marsh. The houses were nothing but low sheds; and, as it was quite dark before we entered the village, I pitched my tent, in which I slept. Mr. and Mrs. De Graft reposed in a shed close to me. For some time I was disturbed by the natives, who, not understanding the nature of a tent, kept running against the lines, inducing me every minute to expect that the tent would come down about my ears. At length things became quiet; and I enjoyed sound sleep, and a good night's rest. From Badagry to the marsh we passed through two small villages, Aladagu and Adelafom. The distance from Badagry to Amowu is, I think, about nine miles N.N.E.

6th.—Some little differences taking place between the guide and the carriers, we did not leave Amowu until a quarter past nine, A. M. We travelled through a country similar to that through which we passed yesterday, the tracts of forests becoming rather more numerous as we proceeded further into the interior. At noon we arrived at Atonga, a small village, where we were met by a troop of horsemen, twelve in number, belonging to Sodaka; who came to conduct us through the forest to an encampment which he had formed to protect his people, when travelling to the coast, from the outrages and depredations of a hostile tribe in the neighbourhood, who had often laid violent hands on the Akus, while passing singly or in small parties through the forest, and had taken them to the slave-marts, where they sold them into foreign countries.

At two, P. M., we reached Addo, the encampment; and were received in a very handsome manner by Shumai, Sodaka's brother, a War-Captain, who has the command of the troops at that station. This military post consists of a great number of small huts or sheds, surrounded by a mud-wall about five feet high, and a ditch about four feet deep. It is nearly within musket-shot of the wall and out-works of the hostile tribe. Each party has small places or seats erected in the trees near the walls, from whence the sentinels watch and report each other's movements. After we had rested ourselves, we walked almost within musket-shot of the enemy before we were aware of our danger. Many of the Akus from the encampment were around us; and several shots were fired at our party, without doing any mischief. Some of the Akus carefully approached the walls of the enemy, and returned the fire, sheltering themselves under a mound of earth. Both parties seemed to enjoy this *playing at soldiers.* As we passed along the market-place in the encampment, while the parties outside were skirmishing, many of the Akus were amusing themselves by dancing to the sound of their rude native music, consisting of a drum and castanets; apparently as much unconcerned as though they had been at a fair, instead of nearly within musket-shot of their enemies. As soon as we reached the encampment, I found myself an object of general curiosity. My little tent was surrounded on every hand; and to see us sit and take dinner in the European fashion, filled them with astonishment.

On our way from Amowu to Addo we passed through two small villages, Bumrus and Rus, beside Atonga.

7th.—Yesterday I expressed a wish to proceed on our journey early this morning; but Shumai said, he should not be able to obtain for me a fresh supply of men so soon; and, beside this obstacle, he particularly begged that I would stop a day with him. I therefore very reluctantly made up my mind to spend one whole day at the encampment.

In the morning, after breakfast, we had family prayers in the tent, surrounded by a great number of the natives. During our devotion, they were quiet and attentive; and appeared much interested with the accordion, which I played when we sung a hymn.

The aspect of the country around the encampment is

flat and open, much of it being in a state of temporary cultivation. As I walked out, I saw corn, millet, yams, kidney-beans, and other vegetables, in full growth. The millet is used chiefly for their war-horses; which they take care to feed well, and keep in good condition for active service.

The hostile tribe occupy no part of the open country, but seem to have taken refuge in an adjoining forest.

In the course of the day Shumai called me aside, and spoke to me concerning the war. He stated, that it had now lasted three years without intermission; that they had, in the course of that time, lost a thousand men, and their enemies a still greater number. He had himself received several wounds from musket-balls, but his life had been preserved. He said, they had long been trying to bring the war to a close, and the hostile tribe to obedience, but their efforts had been unavailing; and he asked me what advice I could give in the affair. I told him, I was a man of peace, and had never been engaged in war; but I thought, as there appeared no chance of bringing them to submission by the means they had adopted, and as they would always require a considerable force in the camp, to protect their people on the path, unless they were reduced to subjection, they had better bring against them a force sufficient to do away with the possibility of their risking a general engagement even-handed; and when their enemies saw a force which they could not resist, they would, in all probability, submit, and behave better for the future: thus peace and safety would be secured without bloodshed. He seemed pleased with my remarks, and said, the King, his brother, was so annoyed at the conduct of the hostile tribe, that he had instructed him (Shumai) to destroy their town, and entirely disperse them; but he agreed with me, that it would be better to try every means to bring them to submission without bloodshed, if possible; and begged that I would, on my arrival at Understone, converse with his brother on the subject.

8th.—At half-past seven, A. M., we were provided with a number of new carriers, and proceeded on our journey. We travelled in a N.N.E. direction, through a large extent of forest. Shumai and one of his Captains accompanied us on horseback, about four or five miles on our way. We then rested in the forest, and took some refreshment; and, having taken leave of our escort, we proceeded. About noon we crossed a marshy place a quarter of a mile wide, with about three feet depth of water; and then reached Mojiba, a very small village, the only one we had seen since we left the encampment. I calculate the distance between the camp and Mojiba to be from eighteen to twenty miles. Here we drank some delicious palm-wine, rested the people and the horses a short time, and then resumed the journey. Our path still lay through the forest, and we reached no village until five, P. M., when we came to Alawagu, where resting a few minutes, we proceeded to Mowo; at which place we arrived about a quarter past six, and halted for the night. The village was so small, and so full of people, that we were obliged to pitch our tent, and many of our company had to sleep in the open air. Our road to-day leading through the thick jungle, was not one of the best: many trees lay across the path, over which the horses had to step or leap with great care; and many ravines on the way were so steep and dangerous, that we were obliged to alight, and, giving the horses their reins, compel them to get down the best way they could. Fortunately, no accident happened. The distance we travelled to-day may be from twenty-eight to thirty-two miles.

9th.—We took breakfast before we started; and at half-past seven, A. M., resumed our journey. We travelled until half-past twelve, P. M., when we arrived at Grass-field, a very small village, where we found several of the carriers, who had gone before, resting and refreshing themselves with a draught of water. I felt hot and thirsty, and would have taken some water; but I found it so thick and bad, that nothing but extreme thirst would have compelled me to drink it. I washed my mouth, and proceeded. Shortly after this we came up to the men who carried our provisions: we halted, and took refreshment. We then travelled until half-past five, and reached Alowagu, and another small village containing nothing in the way of houses, but a few open sheds. This little place, not more than a hundred yards square, was literally crammed with people, chiefly traders and travellers. The small street was so filled with packages, large calabashes full of food for sale, and with the people themselves, that I was obliged to ride round by the skirts of the forest, to get into the path on the opposite side. We then proceeded to Great Alowagu, where we arrived at six, and pitched our tent for the night. The carriers were so fatigued with their journey, through the intense heat of the day, that we had difficulty in causing our luggage to be carefully put up for the night. Though Great Alowagu is larger than several of the villages through which we have passed, yet it is so small that many of our people were obliged to sleep in the open air. During the course of two days' journey, the features of the country have materially altered. In the early part of the day we passed through several ruined villages in the forest, formerly inhabited by the hostile tribe, the shattered remains of which are now driven below the encampment at Addo. Judging from the extent of the ruins and sites of these villages, some of them must have been large and populous, when flourishing and in a state of prosperity. Though at so great a distance from the coast, these places contain beautiful cocoa-nut trees heavily laden with fruit. I felt anxious to drink some of their delicious milk; but the fear of being benighted in the wilderness, hindered me from stopping to gratify my wishes. On every hand, the beautiful Palm-tree rises to invite the attention of the traveller, who often finds himself on the banks of streams and rills of excellent water. The open plains are ornamented with a fine species of *Budlæa*, and some handsome varieties of *Hibiscus*. The grass is not so large and coarse as that in the neighbourhood of Kumási and Jabin: it does not exceed from eight to ten feet in height. I calculate the distance which we travelled to-day to be from thirty to thirty-five miles.

10th.—We took breakfast, and at a quarter past seven, A. M., resumed our journey. We soon came into a country still more open and undulating; the shrubs, grass, &c., of the same character as those which we saw yesterday. In passing over the hills, some extensive and beautiful prospects presented themselves. We passed through several fine plantations of corn, yams, and cotton, and through a pretty little village named Awayadi, where we remained to rest a few minutes. The villagers were much surprised and agreeably excited at our appearance; and during our short stay, they loaded us with presents of beautiful bananas, as a token of their pleasure and satisfaction at seeing us. As we passed along, I saw several small villages on the hills and in the valleys, surrounded by plantations of yams, corn, millet, &c. They were so near to the road that they could be seen distinctly. The general aspect of the country now began to indicate our approach to an African metropolis: many people were met in the path, and here and there a well-mounted horseman. About eleven, A. M., we met a few of the Sierra-Leone emigrants, who accosted us in the English language. To hear my native language spoken by strangers in the interior of Africa, was grateful to my feelings. We crossed a beautiful stream of water: and about noon reached Owayadi, a small village on a hill, whence we had a splendid prospect of the surrounding district. The general features of the country now appeared quite different from that through which we had passed from thirty to fifty miles nearer the coast. In the neighbourhood of Badagry, and for many miles into the interior, not a piece of stone a pound in weight can be seen; but we saw, this morning, several lumps of granite, and all the usual indications of the country having a rocky bed.

At Awayadi we pitched our tent, and took some refreshment; and, as we found ourselves within a few miles of Understone, we changed our clothes, expecting to make our entry in the course of the afternoon. Here we were informed, that the King, fully expecting us yesterday, had sent out a party of horsemen to meet us; but the messenger who had been sent forward from the camp had arrived, and informed the King that we were travelling leisurely along, and that he need not expect us for two or three days. This erroneous information caused some confusion, and our near approach took the King by surprise. After obtaining a fresh supply of carriers, we resumed our journey, and soon gazed on a prospect which filled us with admiration. Understone, the metropolis, appeared in the distance, stretching over hill and dale, the houses mingled with immense blocks of stone, which, under the powerful rays of the sun, looked as white as snow. Understone, with its fine hills covered with huge blocks of granite, reminded me very forcibly of Free-Town at Sierra-Leone, when approaching it from the sea. We started from Owayadi about three, P. M.; and at five, we reached Okwaru, a small village only a short distance from Understone. Here we halted, and sent our guide forward to inform the King that we had reached Okwaru, instructing him to try to make arrangements for our immediate entry, on account of the approaching Sabbath. Night soon closed in, and I saw it would be impossible to make our entry this evening; we therefore pitched our tent, and prepared to compose ourselves for the night. Presently our guide returned with a kind and complimentary message from Sodaka, and stated that he (Sodaka the King) would send people for us very early in the morning.

11th, Sunday,—At six, A. M., some horsemen arrived to conduct us to the capital; and about seven, we resumed our journey. In half an hour we reached the outskirts of the town, after crossing the Ogu, a considerable river about seventy yards wide, running S.S.W., and falling into the sea at Lagos, about thirty miles below Badagry. The river is very low, as it is now the height of the dry season; but, during the rainy period, I should think it would have from fifteen to twenty-five feet of water in the deepest part. This morning we crossed it on horseback. As we entered the town, I found it to be a much larger place than I had expected. The streets were lined with the natives, who had collected together in great numbers to witness the extraordinary scene of an English Missionary visiting Understone. Their excitement was great, and they testified the pleasure and satisfaction which they felt, by the constant cry on every hand of, *Aku!* "Welcome!" We passed through several streets, narrow and confined, and at length reached the King's residence, nearly in the centre of the town. We rode on horseback into a large court-yard, surrounded with houses having clay walls from six to ten feet high, with sloping thatched roofs extending from six to ten or twelve feet over the walls, and reaching to within three feet of the ground, forming a kind of verandah; with an earthen floor raised from six to eighteen inches above the level of the ground. Under a large verandah of the above-mentioned description, Sodaka was seated, surrounded by many of his people. We alighted from our horses, and paid our respects to him. He bade us welcome to Understone, and expressed his great satisfaction at my paying him a visit. He was seated on the floor, on a large native mat, supporting himself against a beautiful leather-covered cushion of native manufacture. He wore a handsome damask cloth, thrown lightly over his shoulder, and a scarlet cloth cap with a blue tassel on the crown of it. Before him stood a large glass bowl of European manufacture, well supplied with gora-nuts. Seats were placed for us in the yard, close to the verandah; and we rested ourselves for a short time, and then repaired to our own quarters. The scenes which I have witnessed this morning will never be erased from my memory. Among the horsemen who came to Okwaru to conduct us to Understone, were several of the Christian emigrants from Sierra-Leone. After a long absence from their father-land, they had returned, bringing the grace of God in their hearts, and had for some time been anxiously looking for a visit from a Christian Missionary. I shall never forget the joy which beamed in their countenances as they seized me by the hand, and bade me welcome. "Ah!" said they, in the course of our conversation, "we told our King, that the English people loved us, and that Missionaries would be sure to follow us to Understone: but he could hardly believe that any one would come so very far, to do us good. Now," said they, "what we told our King is really come to pass! O master! you are welcome, welcome, welcome!"

Sodaka seemed quite overjoyed; and, as we were walking across the court-yard to our own quarters, he clasped me in his arms before all the people, and thus testified his extreme satisfaction. Shortly afterwards he came to our apartments, and talked with me for some time in a free and familiar manner. "My people," said he, "told me they were sure their friends in England would not neglect them; but I feared you would not venture to come so far. Now I see you, and my heart rejoices; and as you have now come to visit us, I hope the English will never leave us." Thus did this noble-spirited Chieftain pour out the warm effusions of his heart. My feelings were of the most intense character. I saw in Sodaka's open and manly countenance, something which gave the seal of truth to all that he said. His remarks were not vain, empty compliments; I believe they came from his heart, and were spoken in sincerity and truth.

CHAPTER III.

FIRST RELIGIOUS SERVICE AT ABOKUTA, ATTENDED BY SODAKA, THE KING—DESCRIPTION OF ABOKUTA—ITS MERCHANDISE—HAUSA—IS VISITED BY MESSENGERS FROM THE KING OF HAUSA—SIERRA-LEONE EMIGRANTS—HISTORY OF THEIR VISIT TO, AND SUBSEQUENT SETTLEMENT AT ABOKUTA—CRUELTY OF THE NATIVES OF LAGOS—GENEROUS CONDUCT OF SODAKA TOWARDS THE EMIGRANTS—THEIR EMPLOYMENT—CONVERSATION WITH SODAKA—CIRCULATING MEDIUM OF ABOKUTA—PREPARATIONS FOR DEPARTING FROM ABOKUTA—RETURN TO BADAGRY—OKWARU—OWAYADI—GREAT ALOWAGU—MOWO—MOJIBA—ADDO—AMOWU—AFRICAN SOUP—REACHES BADAGRY—ANXIETY OF THE BADAGRIS CONCERNING THE JOURNEY TO ABOKUTA.

In the afternoon, having been refreshed with food and rest, we held a public prayer-meeting in the court-yard. We placed our travelling-table opposite the King's verandah, as a kind of desk on which to lay our books; and, to my astonishment, Sodaka came, and seated himself by me at the table. Nearly all the Christian emigrants were present, dressed in European clothes: we had an interesting service. I gave a brief address, which was explained to the King in the vernacular tongue. The child-like simplicity of Sodaka, a powerful King reigning over a numerous people, is truly astonishing. To view him as a party in the scene already described, and then to remember that it took place in the midst of his capital, where he is surrounded by at least fifty thousand of his people, one cannot but admire his noble spirit.

These pleasing prospects are chiefly the results of Missionary enterprise, in seconding the efforts of the British Government to suppress slavery. These Christian emigrants have acted the part of the Israelitish maid, in the beautiful history of Naaman the Syrian. (2 Kings v. 2.) They have brought with them a good report of the God of Israel, the happy effects of which are strikingly visible. Let the friends of Africa rejoice! They have not laboured in vain, nor spent their strength for nought. Many of those who preached the Gospel to these emigrants, and, by the grace of God, were the means of bringing them into the way everlasting, have fallen victims to a deadly climate, and their happy spirits are passed into the heavens; and here in Understone are the seals of their ministry; here are their "epistles" to be "known and read" by thousands of Africa's sons, while the blessed results of their Herculean labours will pass down to generations yet unborn. "Let the people praise thee, O God! yea, let all the people praise thee!" Let the cold-hearted sceptic complain of the sacrifice of the lives of Missionaries and their wives, in burning climes and a tainted air. The true philanthropist cannot but rejoice, though his heart may lament over the solitary grave of the Missionary in a distant land. As for myself, I bless God that I live to see this day. I rejoice that I am, under any circumstances, permitted to see these wonders, which will appear in all their vital and important character in the great day of eternity. Then religion, that child of heaven, will have her due estimation; and the feeblest efforts to advance the moral well-being of our fellow-men, will rank among the noblest works in which man has been employed in every age of the world.

12th.—We walked out to see part of the town. Abokuta, or Understone, is by far the largest that I have seen in Africa; and from what I can judge, I think it is nearly if not quite double the size of Kumási. The houses are constructed on the same plan as the King's house, already described, with the exception of being smaller in proportion. There is no order or regularity in the streets; the houses being built without attention to beauty or uniformity. In this respect, there is no comparison between Understone and Kumási, the latter being far superior; but Understone is capable of great improvement. The beautiful vales and hills which the site occupies, and the noble blocks of granite* rising above the houses in every direction, give it an appearance at once bold, romantic, and beautiful. There are no public buildings, market-places, &c., of any importance; each principal street seems of itself to be a market-place, in which native productions are exhibited for sale, such as rich cotton cloths, Moorish caps, gunpowder, knives, cutlasses of native manufacture, bowls, dishes, calabashes, reels of cotton, rope and line of various sizes, fresh meat, beef, pork, and mutton, rats, (of which the natives seem very fond,) ready-made soup, palm-oil, palm-wine, a kind of beer made from maize, some from millet, plantains, bananas, pine-apples, papaws, limes, oranges, ground-nuts, corn, yams raw and ready-cooked, kidney-beans, sweet potatoes, roll-tobacco, &c., &c.

The appearance of an English Missionary in the town was so extraordinary a circumstance, that the moment we walked out into the streets we were followed and even surrounded by scores of people, whose curiosity was excited in a very singular manner. It seems to be the first time that any European has visited Understone.

---

* Clapperton also speaks of the immense masses of granite which he met with on the line by which he went up from Badagry to Eyeo or Katunga. On leaving Bendekka, for instance, which cannot be at any great distance from Abokuta, he says, "Our road lay through winding and beautiful valleys formed by rugged and gigantic blocks of granite, which in some places rose to the height of six or seven hundred feet above the valleys in which we travelled. Sometimes the valley is not a hundred yards broad, at other times it may widen out to half a mile."—EDIT.

Busy in adjusting ourselves in our new quarters, and preparing an open shed in the King's yard, under which to take our food, and to sit during the heat of the day.

13th.—Rode out on horseback a short distance on the Hausa road. I learn that Hausa is only seven days' journey on horseback from Understone. We also examined another part of the town. Had a heavy shower of rain in the afternoon.

14th.—Occupied in trying to buy a horse or two, to take down to the coast, and in taking a sketch of a part of the town. Had rain again in the afternoon.

15th.—I have been engaged during this day in various matters; writing in my journal, sketching part of the town, &c. I have been also visited by messengers from the King of Hausa. These ride on the finest horses that I have seen in Africa; are armed with bows and arrows, and are well dressed in Moorish habits. They were sent by their master, with a message to Sodaka, who seems to be on very friendly terms with the King. I am glad that they called upon me, as it may serve as an introduction at some future day. I regret that circumstances will not admit of my proceeding to Hausa during this visit, as the way seems to be open.

Had some pleasing conversation with Sodaka, and requested him to tell the King of Hausa's messengers every thing which he could respecting my visit to Understone.

16th.—Met all the principal men among the emigrants from Sierra-Leone, and had a long conversation with them respecting their proceedings and circumstances since they left that colony. The following is the information which I received from them:—

About three years ago, the first emigrants landed at Badagry and Lagos. The people of the former place received them kindly, and allowed them to pass through into their native towns and villages. Not so the inhabitants of Lagos: instead of following the example of the Badagry people, they laid violent hands on the property of the emigrants, and in many cases deprived them of everything except the clothes which they wore. Even the Chief of Lagos, who is since dead, did not scruple to violate all the principles of humanity; he deprived them, by force, of all their savings, with which they intended to greet their long-lost families on their return to their father-land; and even had the cruelty to tell them, that they might think themselves well off, and be well satisfied, that they were allowed in this forlorn and helpless manner to proceed into the interior. I heard of this conduct at Badagry; and to-day the sufferers themselves have confirmed all that I had previously learnt. Out of about two hundred and sixty-five emigrants, the passengers of three vessels, who landed at Lagos, it appears that not one escaped with any of their property, save the clothes in which they were clad. So much for the liberated Africans returning to their native land, landing among an unprincipled people on the Coast, unprotected! In this distressed condition, many of them had to travel four days' journey into the interior, before they could reach their long-lost families; and when they did at last gaze on their native rocks at Understone, instead of appearing before their friends in that respectable manner in which the benevolent Government that had saved them from the iron grasp of slavery desired they should appear, they stood at the entrance of their native habitations without a farthing to purchase food for the day.

Altogether from two to three hundred emigrants have landed at Badagry during the past three years, and have, with their property, passed safely to their native homes. This is a pleasing fact, which stands in striking contrast with the conduct of the people of Lagos. Sodaka, the King of the Akus, has manifested a generous spirit. He has received his injured people kindly; makes a striking difference between them and their countrymen in general, by allowing them to approach him on their feet standing; (the national custom requiring that the people should prostrate themselves when they first appear in the presence of their King;) and by encouraging all, both men and women, to wear European clothes, and to cultivate the manners and customs of that country, which they brought with them from Sierra-Leone. He is pleased with their appearance and conduct, and wishes his subjects to follow their example. This is honourable to both parties; and will surely be gratifying intelligence for the British Government, and all who are interested in the regeneration of Africa.

Those emigrants who have some knowledge of any mechanical profession or business, have, since their arrival at Understone, endeavoured to work at their respective trades and callings, whenever an opportunity has offered; but as such opportunities have been rare, they have been chiefly employed in trading, and in agricultural pursuits, such as the cultivation of corn, yams, cotton, &c. Coffee is unknown here; and perhaps the distance from the coast is too great to render it a profitable article of culture for exportation. Cotton is in considerable demand in the native markets.

Sodaka was much amused with my pocket-compass, and astonished at the inclination of the needle to the north.

17th.—Occupied in obtaining horses for different parts of the coast, and hastening forward all business, preparatory to our departure for Badagry, on Tuesday next.

Had conversation with Sodaka on subjects connected with geography and astronomy, and explained to him the use of a pocket-sextant which he saw me using. I succeeded in showing him the sun on an artificial horizon, brought down to an arch of 90°; and he appeared much astonished and delighted.

In the evening Sodaka undertook to pay for the horses which I have chosen, and to send the people down with me to Badagry to bring the money back. The mode of payment for everything in cowries, makes travelling in this part of the interior difficult, because they are such a heavy kind of cash. The average price of a good horse here is from thirty to fifty dollars; and ten dollars' worth of cowries are a fair load for one man; thus it would require three or four men to transport cowries sufficient to purchase one. Seeing such fine, strong, and small horses here, I am attempting to take a few of them down to the coast; for, if we can use them in travelling from the coast into the interior, it will much reduce our expenses.

18th, Sunday.—The heat has been intense. We had a prayer-meeting in the morning. In the afternoon I preached in our quarters; but the closeness and smallness of the place hindered us from having a large congregation.

19th.—I rose with a fixed determination to prepare for returning towards Badagry to-morrow, although I know Sodaka is anxious to detain me a few days longer. Certainly I should wish to spend a longer time at Understone; but the near approach of Christmas, and the importance of my reaching Whydah as early as possible, compel me to act in opposition to my own feelings. Sodaka's eldest son arrived, after an absence of three years at a place nine days' journey distant from Understone. He appears to be about eighteen years of age.

At five, P.M., Sodaka and a few members of his family, and the principal men among the emigrants, dined with me. We fixed a temporary table under the shed in Sodaka's yard, and all things passed off well. Our party amounted, to the best of my recollection, to about twenty-five persons. Sodaka seemed much delighted; it was the first time he had ever eaten food after the manner and custom of Europeans.

20th.—At four, P.M., after considerable difficulty to induce Sodaka to consent to my early departure, we turned our faces towards Badagry. Sodaka accompanied us to the extreme outskirts of the town, in a temporary hammock, consisting of a large damask cloth tied to a piece of bamboo. As we passed through the streets, it appeared as though nearly the whole town had collected to bid us farewell, which I believe they did under the influence of the best of feelings. "Good bye," said many of them as they waved their hands, "come again soon! come again soon!" Sodaka parted with us with considerable emotion, and was, I think, sorry that we had left him.

At forty-five minutes past five, P.M., we reached Okwaru, and took up our quarters for the night.

21st.—At six, A.M., we proceeded on our way, having obtained a fresh supply of carriers for three days' journey. At half-past eight, we reached Owayadi, where we halted to breakfast. At half-past nine, we resumed our journey, and travelled until half-past two, P.M., when we arrived at Great Alowagu, and took up our quarters for the night. This day's journey has been trying, inasmuch as our way lay through extensive plains, with scarcely any shelter from the intense rays of the sun. Though we had finished our day's work early in the afternoon, I felt so exhausted as to be unfit for any thing: I therefore lay down to rest soon after our arrival.

22d.—At six, A.M., we proceeded on our route, and at a quarter past four, P.M., after a long and hard ride, reached Mowo, pitched our tent, and halted for the night.

23d.—At a quarter past six, A.M., we resumed our journey, and travelled until eleven, when we reached Mojiba, and stopped to breakfast. At half-past twelve, we again proceeded, travelling rapidly. At forty-five minutes past two, P.M., we reached Addo, the encampment. In about an hour our carriers came up with the luggage, and we rested for the evening.

24th.—At four, A.M., I rose, called up the people, and prepared for an early departure.

At half-past five, we started for Badagry. The forest was so wet with the heavy dews of the night, that we were soon as wet around our legs and knees, as though we had walked through a river. At ten, we reached Amowu. On our arrival, after so long a ride before breakfast, wet and tired, I longed for some refreshment; but our canteens and carriers were far behind, as we had pushed on rapidly to get the horses over a deep marsh about three quarters of a mile in width, before the luggage came up. My clothes on the upper part of my body were wet with profuse perspiration, while my feet and legs were of an almost icy coldness from the dew of the forest. In this state I was obliged to wait until my portmanteau arrived; and, fearing the consequences, I gladly and thankfully partook of some native soup, which I found for sale in the street, made with pork and palm-oil. A muscle-shell supplied the place of a spoon; and though I could scarcely fancy taking palm-oil in such a wholesale manner, I found the soup to have a refreshing and invigorating effect. In due time the luggage came; and after taking a hasty breakfast, and changing my wet clothes, I crossed the marsh in a canoe, mounted my horse, and, accompanied by one of our men on horseback, pushed on to Badagry. At half-past twelve I reached the Mission-house in safety, thankful to God for his many, many mercies.

On my approaching the outside of the town of Badagry, I perceived that the people, as they saw me enter the town, looked upon me with mingled feelings of surprise and pleasure; and I said, "The people seem surprised to see us." "Yes," said my attendant, "a great many of the Badagris said, before we started, that if you did go, you would never return; thinking that you would be killed by some people of the interior. Warru came to me one night, just before we set off, and said, 'It is not good for your master to go into the interior: the people are not to be trusted: perhaps they will kill him. Try and persuade him not to go.' But I said, 'My master does not care for that; his work is just now in the interior, and he will therefore go. If he live, it will be well; if he die, it will be well; he does not care: he has a good home to go to when he dies.'" This was the language of a Christian convert from Cape Coast, and conveys to us, in words too plain to be misunderstood, what a great moral change Christianity has produced in his country. I was deeply affected with this remark; it breathed the true sustaining principle of a real Christian. It also proved the existence of deep and sincere affection towards me. I discovered in it the touching sentiment of Ruth:—Maugre all danger, "whither thou goest, I will go, and where thou lodgest I will lodge; thy people shall be my people, and thy God my God; where thou diest will I die, and there will I be buried." These were not the feelings of a single individual; they pertained to others who were travelling with me. How merciful was the Lord to us as a party! Though perhaps there was danger from the hostile tribe in the neighbourhood of the Aku encampment, yet we returned in safety; not a hair of our head has been injured.

In the course of the next two hours, Mr. De Graft and all the party arrived.

25th, Sunday, Christmas-Day.—I am suffering too much from fatigue and excitement to enjoy this day as my heart could wish. Our people also were tired and worn out with fatigue. At four, P.M., Mr. Townsend read prayers, and I preached to an interesting though small congregation on the incarnation of the Redeemer of mankind.

26th.—Engaged during the day in closing the business of the Mission, and preparing for my departure from Badagry.

27th.—Sick in bed, the effect of my recent toils in the interior.

28th.—Health is improving. I have been busy packing up. During the day my hands were fully occupied, and my mind exercised with a multiplicity of business. About seven, P.M., unable to sit up any longer, I went to bed. Warru came and sat down, and talked with Mr De Graft and myself until between nine and ten o'clock. This long conference was on the subject of our present prospects and future proceedings. Warru seems to enter into all our views and feelings, as far as he is capable of doing so, promising us encouragement and support to the utmost of his power, and expressing an anxious hope that Badagry will have its due share in the benevolent intentions of Britain, towards the natives of the west-coast of Africa. Gratified with the result of this long interview, I soon fell asleep.

CHAPTER IV.

MR FREEMAN EMBARKS FOR WHYDAH — NEW-YEAR'S-DAY — VISITS THE CHIEF, TO WHOM HE INTIMATES A WISH TO SEE THE KING OF DAHOMI — MR. DE SOUZA — HOSTILE COMMOTION IN THE COUNTRY—INJURIOUS REPORTS CONCERNING THE WESLEYAN MISSION, AND OBJECT—ACCIDENT IN THE SURF AT WHYDAH—HARMATTAN—KINDNESS OF THE CHIEF OF WHYDAH—SABBATH SERVICES—ANTICIPATED MOVEMENT OF THE BRITISH COMMODORE, FOR THE TOTAL DESTRUCTION OF THE SLAVE-TRADE AT WHYDAH—MR. FREEMAN CONTENDS WITH PREJUDICES—REAL POSITION OF MR. DE SOUZA AT WHYDAH—EXTRACTS FROM MINUTES OF EVIDENCE BEFORE COMMITTEE OF PARLIAMENT—PRINCE DE JOINVILLE —DEATH OF MR. SHIPMAN AT AKRAH—MR. FREEMAN EXPECTS SPEEDILY TO VISIT THE KING OF DAHOMI.

DECEMBER 29th.—At a quarter past five, A. M., I arose and prepared for joining the brig "Queen Victoria," to proceed to Whydah. All things being ready for my departure, I rode round the town, and took my leave of Akia and Jinji, the French and Portuguese Chiefs, or Headmen, parted with my kind friend Captain Parsons, and then returned to the Mission-house, where Mr. and Mrs. De Graft and myself committed ourselves into the hands of our gracious God, and parted at his footstool. Warru accompanied me down to the banks of the Lagoon, where I took my leave of him, and proceeded across the river, accompanied by several of Sodaka's men who wished to go down to the beach and look at the sea, which they had never seen before, and to see me go through the surf in our canoe.

On reaching the other side of the Lagoon, our first work was to convey the luggage over the plain to the beach, a distance of about a mile, and to transport the large canoe by the same route. The task of pulling the boat over the heavy sand during the burning heat of noon, was no trifle; it occupied the men from two to three hours. At length it was ready to be launched on the ocean; which we immediately commenced doing, though the surf was rolling awfully high, and thundering on the sand. I had sent some of my luggage in another canoe, among which was a basket of fowls, but the canoe had upset among the breakers. When, therefore, I arrived on the beach, I saw part of my luggage (which had been all saved) spread on the sand to dry. The only damage done was the death of the fowls. All the canoe-men, and one of my servants who was going to the vessel, reached the shore in safety. At length I entered the canoe, and we put off among the breakers: they seemed to threaten us, and of course broke into the canoe, giving me a good wetting. Sodaka's people, with several others, remained on the beach till they saw us safely through the breakers, when they waved their hands, testifying their joy at seeing me safe out of danger, and then left the beach. We soon reached the vessel, and remained at anchor all night.

30th.—At eleven, A. M., we weighed anchor, and stood out to sea.

31st.—We have been beating to windward within sight of land. At a quarter past seven, P. M., we arrived in Whydah roads; and let go our anchor, when it was so dark that we could but just distinguish two vessels which were at anchor close by.

January 1st, 1843, Sunday.—Another eventful year has rolled into the vast ocean of eternity, carrying with it all my joys and all my sorrows. I lament that I have not more abundantly improved my precious time, and done more to promote the glory of the Greatest and Best of Beings. O Lord, let thy mercy be showed unto me, and give me great spiritual and physical strength, that the year on which I am now entered may be one of great exertion in my noble employment! and while I labour to benefit others, bless me with a large increase of personal piety.

At seven, A. M., the thick fog which hung over the land broke away before the powerful rays of the sun, and we found that we were pretty close in shore. As the vessel is small and uncomfortable, and several of my people felt sick, I thought it right to land at once, as we could not conveniently hold divine service on board. To my great disappointment, I found the town of Whydah so far from the beach, that it took us a long time to carry the luggage which it was necessary to bring on shore, and the sacred day passed away without our being able to hold public worship.

In the course of the day I visited the Chief, who received me kindly. I briefly told him my object in visiting Whydah, and in wishing to see the King of Dahomi. He did not, of course, at first fully understand me, and appeared to look on me with suspicion: for this, however, past experience had prepared me, I felt no discouragement, resting assured that the Lord would aid me, and make my way plain before me.

After by no means an unpleasant interview, we postponed any further conversation to a future opportunity; and I left the Chief, pleased with my reception. The weather to-day has been dry, and the heat intense.

3d.—Early in the afternoon I had a long interview with the Chief, when I more fully explained my object in visiting Whydah. I spoke of our new Mission at Badagry, and my anxiety to see the King of Dahomi, to explain to him the nature of that Mission, and our object in commencing it at this critical juncture, when many parts of the interior are in a state of hostile commotion. I dwelt at length on the anxiety of the

British Government, and a great portion of the British public, to confer real and lasting benefits on the natives of Africa, by the introduction of Christianity and civilization; and asked him whether he did not consider such sentiments honourable and good on the part of England, and worthy the attention of those whom they were intended to benefit. He said, in answer to this, that my palaver was good, and that I could go up and see the King of Dahomi his master, and speak this palaver to him. From the Chief's residence I then repaired to Mr. De Souza, and had a long conversation with him. I explained to him the nature of my Mission; and he said he would render me every assistance in his power.

Mr. De Souza informed me, that the King of Dahomi is engaged in war; but he thought, that if I could wait a fortnight, the King might then have returned to Abomi, when I could pay him a visit. He further said, that in about six weeks he was going up himself; and if I could make it convenient to wait so long, or to go to Cape Coast and return to Whydah at that time, he should be glad of my company. I thanked him for his kind offer; but as I feel extremely anxious to get back to Cape Coast as early as possible, I decided on waiting for the King's return from the theatre of war, and then hastening to see him without delay.

My interview with Mr. De Souza was a pleasing one, and I left him with feelings of thankfulness to God for his mercy in thus making my way plain. In the course of conversation, I learnt from Mr. De Souza, that a false report had been brought from Lagos to Whydah respecting my proceedings at Badagry. It had been stated, that I was engaged in building a fort at that place, and that when I visited the interior, I actually took with me two pieces of artillery. That they should call our Mission-house now building at Badagry "a fort," does not surprise me; for before I left that place, a large airy dwelling-house, fit for an European family, raised from ten to twelve feet from the ground, on twenty-two stout cocoa-nut pillars, averaging about three-quarters of a ton each in weight, appeared a thing so novel and extraordinary, that the people were often seen standing in groups at a short distance, gazing on it with astonishment. But what could give rise to the report of my taking artillery into the interior, I cannot understand. This information made me feel increasingly anxious to see the King of Dahomi at once, lest he should give credence to these reports, and look with an unfavourable aspect on our Mission at Badagry.

4th.—Having decided on remaining to see the King of Dahomi, I have been busily engaged in arranging matters with the owners of the Sierra-Leone vessel, which brought me from Badagry. They must not wait for me, as my detention here may be from six weeks to two months. The expense of detaining the vessel would be too great for the Mission, on the one hand; and, on the other, the owners of the vessel could not spare so much time. The weather continues dry, and the heat as great as usual.

5th.—I closed all business with the owners of the "Queen Victoria" in such good time, that she sailed in the afternoon for Cape Coast and Sierra-Leone. While in Understone I bought four young horses for our stations in the interior of Fantee. Although horses will not thrive at Cape Coast, yet there seems every chance of their doing well in the interior. If we can succeed with them, they will assist us much in our work, and tend to reduce our ordinary travelling expenses considerably. These horses I have sent to Cape

Coast in the vessel, and landed my own horse at Whydah to assist me in my journey to Abomi. The Aku horses are much larger and stronger than those which I have seen in Ashánti. Just before the "Queen Victoria" sailed, I sent off the canoe to bring some things on shore; and as the vessel was about to sail, the men overloaded the boat, in order to save time. The consequence of this was, that as the canoe was coming on shore through a tremendous surf, it was raised so high on the broken wave, and being too much loaded, was dashed with such violence on the sand, that it went to pieces, and I not only lost the boat, but had twenty dollars' worth of property completely destroyed. The canoe has been a good servant, and has had much hard work. It was not new when I bought it; and has performed many trips through the surfs of Badagry, and brought a great deal of heavy timber several miles down the river for building the Mission-house. I felt thankful that the accident did not occur yesterday; for if it had, I should certainly have lost a valuable horse, as he never could have survived such a shock, even if he had not been drowned.

6th.—The Chief came to pay me a visit, and behaved in a very familiar and friendly manner.

7th.—Went down to the beach, and landed various articles of provisions, &c., from an American vessel.

8th, Sunday.—At eleven, A. M., I conducted divine service in the hall of the English Fort, and preached to an interesting little congregation, consisting of our own people, a few of the natives, and some emigrants from Sierra-Leone, who, I find, have been residing here for two or three years. Some of the latter were accustomed to worship in our chapels at Free-town; and, though they have been so long absent from the means of grace, they still retain a relish for divine things.

I suppose this is the first time that the Gospel has been preached in Whydah for many years past. May the Lord bless his word, and commence a great and glorious work among this people.

In the afternoon I felt unwell, through extreme reaction after so many weeks of toil and excitement.

9th.—Went down to the beach to land some articles, and to examine a new canoe.

10th.—Bought a new canoe, which is a great relief to my mind, as I should feel uncomfortable to be in such a place as Whydah, where nearly all the Europeans are Portuguese, strangers to me, and naturally inimical to my proceedings as a Christian Missionary.

12th.—I have been busy in making up accounts relative to the Badagry Mission.

13th.—Spent part of the day on the beach, attending the fitting up our new canoe. We were visited by a strong *harmattan;* when the air became so thick with fine particles of sand, that I could scarcely discern the distant horizon at sea.

14th.—In the course of this afternoon Mr. De Souza paid us a visit in the Fort; and entered into a long conversation respecting Dahomi and Ashánti. The interview was pleasing; and he again assured me, that he was ready to render any assistance in his power during my intended visit to the King of Dahomi.

Late in the evening one of my canoe-men arrived from Popo, to which place I had sent him several days since, to try to procure a new boat for our Mission at Badagry. Through the kindness of Lawson, one of the head-men of Popo, I am glad he has succeeded. This is gratifying to my feelings, as Mr. De Graft, or any other brother residing at Badagry, would be put to many painful inconveniences, without a good canoe for landing articles through the heavy surf from vessels in the roads.

15th, Sunday.—At eleven, A. M., I conducted divine service, and preached to all our people travelling with me, and to several of the natives of Whydah. I felt unwell in the afternoon, the day being extremely sultry, and trying to an European constitution.

17th.—I am still employed about fitting up the canoes. We had another strong *harmattan*. Wrote numerous letters to different parts of the District.

18th.—Went to the beach, and saw Captain Groves, from whom I obtained some cash. He sails for Akráh and Cape Coast to-morrow. I closed a number of letters, and drew bills on the Committee.

19th.—Captain Groves, of the "Robert Heddle," sailed early this morning. I went down to the lake, and took my large canoe, recently brought from Popo, from the lake to the beach. Felt indisposed in the morning; but a journey to the beach afforded me relief.

21st.—Prepared to take extracts from my journal to forward to London. The weather is fine and dry.

22d, Sunday.—At eleven, A.M., I conducted divine service, and preached in the Fort to our attendants and a few of the natives. The little congregation was attentive. O God! give success to the word of truth.

23d.—Another strong *harmattan* wind visited us. I have been occupied in taking extracts from my journal.

26th.—Went down to the beach to look at the canoes, now fitted up, painted, and ready for service.

27th.—Early in the morning the Chief sent to inquire after my health, which he has regularly done for many days past. When I consider the changes which are daily taking place, all having a tendency to make my way more plain, I am truly astonished. On the 1st of this month I landed here in the midst of strong prejudices against an English Missionary; now I find I am daily gaining ground in the confidence of the Chief, which is strikingly manifested in his respect for me, and anxiety for my welfare. "This is the Lord's doing; it is marvellous in our eyes." Blessed be his holy name! He does not send me to engage in a warfare at my own charge. Have faith, O my soul! have faith in God, and thou shalt see greater things than these!

In the evening I saw some vessels at sea through the thick atmosphere, occasioned by a strong *harmattan*. We could not well distinguish what they were; but as the British Commodore has threatened to land at Whydah, and destroy the slave-barracoons, and to take other measures for the total suppression of the slave-trade in this place, we thought it likely that the vessels were British cruisers destined for that object.

28th.—Saw a large three-masted vessel in the roads, which we thought to be Her Majesty's ship "Iris;" but the thickness of the atmosphere hindered us from distinguishing correctly. Under a strong impression that the vessel in question was the "Iris," and that the Commander might wish to communicate with the shore, I went down to the beach to send off my canoe to the vessel. On our arrival, I perceived that we were under a mistake. The vessel proved to be the "———," from Hamburgh. The day was hot and dry.

29th, Sunday.—At four, P.M., I preached to a small congregation, consisting chiefly of our own people.

30th.—I have had strong palavers, in consequence of the opposition of some parties to myself as an English Missionary. I fear nothing: my cause is the cause of God, and must ultimately prevail, though the combined powers of earth and hell oppose it.

31st.—I am determined to leave Whydah to-morrow, and proceed to Cape Coast, without seeing the King of Dahomi, unless the true cause of the events of the last two days is satisfactorily explained. I sent to the Chief, who begs me to stop. I saw Mr. De Souza;* who explained every thing in such a satisfactory manner,

---

* The following extract from a parliamentary publication will sufficiently inform our readers who Mr. De Souza is, and what is his position at Whydah.—EDIT.

"MINUTES OF EVIDENCE TAKEN BEFORE THE SELECT COMMITTEE ON WEST COAST OF AFRICA.—*Martis*, 10° *die Maii*, 1842.

"CAPTAIN HENRY SEWARD called in, and examined:

"*Question* 2271. You have been at Whydah?

"*Answer*. Yes.

"*Q*. 2272. When?

"*A*. In 1837.

"*Q*. 2274. Did you see a person there of the name of De Souza?

"*A*. Yes.

"*Q*. 2275. Did you do any business with him?

"*A*. A little; he was not in want of goods at the time.

"*Q*. 2276. Are you aware whether he deals in produce as well as in slaves?

"*A*. I heard him offer to get palm-oil when I was down there.

"*Q*. 2277. Offer to whom?

"*A*. To Captain Mormon, that he would take goods from him, and get him palm-oil in exchange, as the slave-trade was so bad.

"*Q*. 2278. If you had offered him, as a condition of bringing him goods, and taking his palm-oil, that he should discontinue selling slaves, do you think that would have tended to discourage his continuance in the slave-trade?

"*A*. It might, to a certain extent: but De Souza is not considered as a freeman; he is a subject of the King of Dahomi altogether: he cannot go off that beach unless by the sanction of the King of Dahomi; he cannot go from his house to the beach without the King of Dahomi's people following him; he cannot go round the town without them.

"*Q*. 2279. How has the King of Dahomi got this authority over De Souza?

"*A*. That must have been arranged formerly upon his settlement upon the coast. The King of Dahomi's territory is very great, and the Dahomi tribe is a powerful tribe.

"*Q*. 2280. Does De Souza exercise any authority in the place?

"*A*. He is the Headman there.

and exonerated himself so fully from all blame in the affair, that I have laid aside my determination of leaving the town to-morrow. I was pleased with Mr. De Souza's frank and manly behaviour, feeling my mind more at rest than it has been for several days. God be praised! "The wrath of man shall praise thee; the remainder of wrath shalt thou restrain."

The French frigate, the "Belle Poule," with the

"*Q.* 2281. He holds office, as it were, under the King of Dahomi?

"*A.* Yes; but if a Portuguese or Spaniard wanted to remain at Whydah, I should say that De Souza must ask the King of Dahomi before he could allow him.

"*Q.* 2282. Were there any Portuguese or Spaniards with De Souza there at that time?

"*A.* Yes; and there was an American there, but I forget his name now, that was engaged in the slave-trade.

"*Q.* 2283. Did you understand that the King of Dahomi was anxious to encourage the oil-trade?

"*A.* I do not know; I never heard that.

"*Q.* 2284. Did you ever hear that he discouraged it?

"*A.* I only judge from one case: when Captain Mormon started a factory at Badagry, De Souza got him leave from the King of Dahomi to open trade there for palm-oil. He collected a large quantity; and lately I have heard that he has had to leave Badagry. I can only attribute it to the jealousy of the King of Dahomi on the natives being employed in getting palm-oil instead of collecting slaves for the King of Dahomi.

"*Q.* 2285. Supposing an English settlement were formed at Whydah, do you think that would have the effect of putting down the slave-trade in Dahomi?

"*A.* There would be great difficulty in getting a fort there. If you get the sanction of the King of Dahomi you might do it; but without that, if you sent a hundred men, he might send two hundred men to annoy you....

"*Q.* 2287. Do you know the history of De Souza's settlement there?

"*A.* I believe he was a Spanish nobleman, and he was banished his country."

Prince De Joinville, arrived in the roads. The Prince came on shore, attended by several officers.

February 1st.—The Prince De Joinville went on board the frigate early this morning.

3d.—Mr. Zangronies, one of the principal slave-dealers in Whydah, died this evening.

4th.—At nine, A.M., Mr. Zangronies's remains were interred in the Portuguese burial-ground.

5th, Sunday.—Found myself indisposed this morning, At eleven, A.M., I met our little family for prayer, and exposition of a portion of Scripture. I intended to preach in the afternoon; but was hindered by the arrival of vessels, which rendered it necessary for me to proceed to the beach. These things are trying, but unavoidable. "How amiable are thy tabernacles, O Lord of hosts! My soul longeth, yea, even fainteth, for the courts of the Lord."

The schooner "Dolly Varden" arrived from Akrâh, Cape Coast, Cape-Palmas, and Sierra-Leone, bringing the painful intelligence of my excellent brother Shipman's decease at Akrâh, on the 2d ultimo. O God, how mysterious are thy judgments! We have indeed need of faith. How merciful is the Lord to me! On the very day that I hear of the death of one of my valuable colleagues, my heart is cheered by the intelligence of the arrival of new Missionaries at Cape Coast. May they long be spared to labour in this part of the Lord's African vineyard!

6th.—Received letters from Akrâh, dated January 30th, containing information of Mr. Shipman's illness; but I have already heard of his death. O mystery of Providence! We had rain about noon, preceded by a strong wind, and a considerable fall of the thermometer. This is the first shower which I have seen since I came to Whydah.

7th.—Wrote to Mr. De Graft at Badagry, and sent him some cash, &c. We had rain in the night.

8th.—The "Dolly Varden" sailed for Badagry. The *harmattan* season appears to be at a close. I am writing to Akrâh and to England.

9th.—Closed my letters, and started messengers for Akrâh.

11th.—In the morning Mr. Akhurst arrived from Akwa.

12th, Sunday.—At eleven, A.M., met my servants for prayers and scriptural conversation. At half-past three, P.M., conducted divine service, and preached to a congregation consisting chiefly of Fanti canoe-men, &c., who are travelling with me. In the course of the morning I paid a short visit to the Chief, in company with Messrs. Akhurst and Pugh.

13th.—Accompanied Messrs. Akhurst and Pugh to visit Mr. De Souza. He received us kindly, and told me he thought the King would send for me in three days. The heat is very great.

14th.—I feel unwell, with considerable weariness of body; which I judge to be the effects of the changes now taking place in the weather, from the *harmattan* to the tornado season.

March 2d.—During the past fortnight, indisposition and several trying circumstances have hindered me from writing in my journal. The weather has undergone a great change, the tornado season having arrived. I went out in the afternoon, intending to visit some plantations at a distance, but was hindered by a heavy tornado, and obliged to take shelter for about a hour.

CHAPTER V.

MR. FREEMAN DEPARTS FROM WHYDAH TO VISIT THE KING OF DAHOMI —DIFFICULTY IN ARRANGING FOR THE JOURNEY—SALWI—TORRI—APPEARANCE OF THE COUNTRY—ASOWA—ALADA—COUNTRY PALACE OF THE KING OF DAHOMI—DESCRIPTION OF THE TOWN—ENORMOUS FLOCK OF BATS—APPA—APPEARANCE OF A COMET—AVADI—AGREMI—MESSAGE FROM THE KING—KWO—ARRIVES AT KANNA, THE ROYAL RESIDENCE—APPALLING SIGHT—CEREMONIES UPON ENTERING THE TOWN—MR. FREEMAN'S OFFICIAL ATTENDANTS—PERSONAL INTRODUCTION TO THE KING—NATIVE CEREMONIES ON ENTERING THE ROYAL PRESENCE—ENCOURAGING CONVERSATION WITH GUZZU, KING OF DAHOMI, ON THE SUBJECT OF CHRISTIAN MISSIONS—HIS FAVOURABLE OPINION AND EARNEST WISHES RESPECTING SUCH OPERATIONS.

MARCH 6th.—At twenty minutes past nine, A.M., I proceeded from Whydah for Abomi. It was my intention to start early in the morning; but I found, as usual, great difficulty in collecting the carriers together. Some of them came, looked at their loads, and then went away, as they said, to obtain food, &c., for the journey; but I soon found that they did not intend to return any more. Others took the packages, and made as though they were actually setting off on the proper path; but as soon as they were out of sight, they turned aside, and put down their loads. When, therefore, I mounted my horse to proceed, I found that I must stay, and look closely after the carriers, otherwise some of my luggage would be left behind. Having at length sent all the people before me, I commenced my journey, accompanied by Madaka and Niawi, two of the most intelligent natives of what is called "the English Town," in Whydah, who were appointed by the Chief to act as guides and interpreters; also by some of the Whydah people, and my own little party of Fantis.

We travelled through a flat, open country, and at ten minutes to eleven, reached Salwi, a small village, containing a number of huts of a circular form, built with sticks and dried grass, and intermixed with small plantations of corn, &c. About midway between Whydah and Salwi, we crossed a marsh about two hundred yards wide, over which a rude bridge had been constructed, by placing a number of stout bantlings, each about eight feet long, one above the other, until the top ones were sufficiently high above the mud and water to obtain a dry footing. The bottom of this marsh appeared to be a kind of white clay.

Having rested at Salwi, at a quarter past eleven, we resumed our journey; and at half-past two, P.M., we reached Torri, where we took up our quarters for the night. Although we had only travelled about fourteen miles, the heat was so great, and the sun so powerful, that many of the people appeared exhausted, while others were so far behind on the path, that they were not able to reach Torri until nightfall.

The general character of the country through which we passed to-day was rather monotonous, it being flat, and consisting chiefly of large savannahs, broken here and there with small clumps of trees. This description of country is far more trying to the traveller than large tracts of forest, on account of the great exposure to the sun which cannot be avoided. Some pretty varieties of *Hibiscus*, and several fine papilionaceous plants, were flowering on the sides of the path, and inviting the attention of the admirers of the beauties of Flora. As we approached Torri, some very dark clouds and heavy thunder seemed to threaten us with a tornado; but it wore away without troubling us, for which I was thankful, as several of the carriers were far behind with the luggage.

7th.—At half-past six, A.M., we left Torri, and at forty minutes past eight, reached Asowa, where we breakfasted under some beautiful shady trees. The morning was cool and pleasant; and as we approached nearer and nearer to Asowa, we found the earth moistened by a heavy shower of rain, which had fallen during the night. The road being rather less open than that of yesterday, as we passed through among the low brush-wood, the parrots, and many varieties of birds of the most exquisite plumage, were hopping from spray to spray, and warbling their Creator's praise.

At a quarter past nine, A.M., we resumed our journey, and at a quarter past twelve reached Alada, where we decided on remaining for the night; the heat being so intense that the carriers were unable to proceed further without great difficulty. During the journey of to-day one of my Fanti carriers was so much overcome by the heat, that he nearly fainted. I gave him some pills of extract of gentian, and also a glass of ale; and he speedily revived so as to be able to proceed on his route without difficulty.

Alada is the largest place I have seen since I left Whydah. Many of the houses are built with clay; but they are generally so small and confined, that it is almost impossible for an European to remain in them during the heat of the day. Alada boasts of a royal residence, occupied occasionally by the King of Dahomi when he visits these parts. I did not see the interior of the palace; but as a country-seat for a monarch of Western Africa, I think it respectable in outward appearance. It consists of a large house, two stories high, of rather an European aspect, built with clay, surrounded by a wall of the same material, about two feet thick and ten feet high. The space of ground enclosed, would be from six to ten acres. In front of the palace are several splendid Silk-cotton trees, and other giants of the forest, throwing a grateful shade over a large space of ground, where the Captains and Chiefs assemble with their people, when the King remains in Alada. The area is kept very clean. It is swept every morning. I heard of a venomous kind of snake, common in this neighbourhood, the bite of which is certain death; but I did not see one. The town contains several large trees, which are covered during the day with tens of thousands of bats, about the size of a thrush or blackbird. The trees are so heavily laden with them, that the branches are often broken off by the weight. About six o'clock in the evening they leave the trees, and throng the air to such a degree, that it is almost darkened with them, while they betake themselves to the neighbouring forest to obtain food.

8th.—At forty-five minutes past five, A.M., we started from Alada, and at eight, halted to breakfast at Hair. At twenty minutes past nine, we proceeded on our way, and at noon reached Appa. The heat being great, and the people much fatigued, we decided on remaining there that night. The place being small, and the houses nothing but sheds, I was glad to pitch my tent to sleep in. As the shades of evening closed in, and the moon was throwing her silvery light over the dark foliage of the forest in the distance, one of my people came to tell me that he saw a strange sight in the heavens. I came out of my tent; and, to my great delight, I saw the comet with the nucleus just above the tops of the trees, and its enormous tail in length equal to the chord of an arc of 45°. The people seemed much excited at this (*to them*) strange appearance; and I amused myself for several minutes in attempting to explain its nature and its revolutions.

Appa contains a royal residence, inferior however to that in Alada.

9th.—We proceeded from Appa at forty-five minutes after five, A.M., and at nine rested for breakfast at Avadi. We crossed a tract of country, which, I am informed, is nearly overflowed with water during the rainy season. It has a marshy appearance, and is from eight to ten miles wide, covered chiefly with low brush-wood. I rode my horse part of the way over; but some portions of the road were so very rugged, that I was obliged to walk, and to allow the horse to travel by himself as well as he could. We started from Avadi at ten minutes after ten, and in the course of forty minutes afterwards, we reached Agremi, where there is another royal residence, but inferior to the preceding. Here a messenger met me from the King, requesting me, with his master's compliments, to proceed a few miles farther and rest the people, and remain for the night at Kwo; and that he would receive me early the following morning. We consequently proceeded, and arrived at Kwo at thirty minutes after twelve, P.M., where we took up our lodgings for the night. As we advance into the interior, the country becomes even more open than it is forty miles from the coast. I found it trying to travel through the heat of the day, exposed to the full rays of the sun for so many hours together; but, thanks be to God, my health is still good, and though I often feel fatigued in the evening, a bath, and a good night's rest, which through mercy I generally enjoy, make me vigorous for the toils of the ensuing day.

10th.—At six, A.M., we proceeded on our journey, and in about one hour came within sight of Kanna, where the King is residing. Fine savannahs, stretching several miles in different directions, with here and there a large forest-tree, and the clay walls of some of the houses in the distance peeping out from among the dark green foliage of the Banyan, Locust and other trees, formed altogether an interesting scene. The country is also less flat and dull in the neighbourhood of Kanna than any I have seen since I left Whydah. As we were entering the outskirts of the town, we passed within five or six yards of a gibbet, from which was suspended the body of a man. The gibbet was from eighteen to twenty feet high, and consisted of two rough posts and a beam fastened across the top. The body was hanging with its head downwards, the legs being lashed to the beam just above the ankles. One hand appeared to be dropping off; having probably been partly severed by some sharp instrument. Two or three turkey-buzzards were feeding underneath the gibbet. On inquiry, I found, that the man had been guilty of some crime which had thus rendered him obnoxious to the laws of the country. It was indeed a frightful sight.

A little after seven o'clock we halted in the outskirts of the town, under the shade of a large tree, and took breakfast. Just as I had finished, a messenger arrived, requesting me to proceed. Accordingly we went about a quarter of a mile farther, and again stopped under the shade of another tree. While waiting here some of the women from the King's household passed us, with pots of water on their heads; the people were obliged to show respect to the King, by stepping back a few paces while the women passed. After we had rested but a short time, we heard the drums begin to play, and soon saw a party of native soldiers at a distance approaching us, with arms, flags, and native music. As they advanced towards us, we moved nearer to the tree, and collected more closely together, allowing room for the soldiers to march around. They then drew near. I could perceive their Captain among them, who was riding on a mule under the shade of a large umbrella. When they arrived opposite our position, they halted a moment, and the Chief saluted me as he sat on his mule, by taking off his hat, and gently inclining his head towards me. The hat was low-crowned and coarse, something like those worn by waggoners in some parts of England. They then made a circuit, singing as they went; after which, the Chief dismounted, and danced before me for a few minutes. This was succeeded by several of the soldiers firing a salute with muskets and blunderbusses; and then, the Chief's stool being placed near me, he came and shook hands with me, and joined our party.

The streets were filled with companies of soldiers, for a considerable distance; each party having its respective flags, banners, and umbrellas. They presented a gay and exciting appearance. Some of their flags were European, others American. I saw Spanish, Portuguese, English, and French flags. Several of them also were native. One of the latter displayed a lion, cut in a rude form, out of black or blue cloth, and then stitched to the flag, which appeared to be a kind of straw-coloured bunting. This rude figure represented a lion with its mouth open; and, to give redness to the inside of the mouth, cloth of that colour was used. The eye was also shown by cloth of another hue: altogether considerable ingenuity was displayed. Another of the royal flags had several black spots on a white or palish ground, and several of the flag-staffs were decorated with a human skull fastened on the top.

The first party of soldiers having joined us with their Chief, another, and a second, and a third party succeeded, until we were surrounded by several Captains and a large number of soldiers. When all had joined us, we prepared to proceed into the town, the Chiefs' and the soldiers leading the way. In about twenty minutes we arrived opposite the King's gate, where, in an extensive area of several acres, beneath the shade of some fine Banyan-trees, a great number of Captains, Chiefs, and Headmen were seated under large umbrellas, surrounded by numerous attendants. At the King's gate, the Chiefs of his household were seated, with messengers and domestics. Under the grateful shade of the Banyan-trees the people formed two circles, one within another, with sufficient space between them for our party to walk comfortably round: we proceeded to traverse this circle nine times, saluting the numerous Chiefs and Captains as we passed them. When we passed the King's gate the first time, his messengers, and one of the Whydah interpreters, with his people, knelt down on their knees, and took a quantity of dust, and threw it on their heads; they then stretched themselves nearly prostrate on the dust, and touched the earth with their foreheads, chins, and cheek-bones, to testify their humble submission to their master, whom they believe to be the greatest King in Africa.

After we had traversed the circle nine times, I took my seat under a tree nearly opposite the King's gate, where I received the salutations of the Chiefs and Captains. First came Mewo, who, I afterwards learnt, had been appointed by the King to take care of me, and attend to my wants. Mewo was introduced to me as my father; a lady, Yawa, of the King's household, was also brought forward as my mother. Kabada, another Chief, was introduced as my House-Master, on whose premises I was to take up my temporary residence in Kanna. About thirty persons were introduced in this manner.

Although it seems customary among them that a

stranger should not see the King at the time he makes his first entry, I have no doubt that the King saw me by a kind of secret *reconnoitre*. The public entry of a stranger appears entirely managed by the Chiefs. When we had gone through the usual ceremonies opposite the King's gate, Mewo and Kabada accompanied me on the way to my lodgings. In proceeding thither, we had to go round a part of the royal premises; and, as we passed the different gates, we found a Chief and a party of soldiers at each, waiting to salute me by discharging forty muskets. After passing three gates in this manner, we reached our quarters; which I was delighted to find were roomy and comfortable. After all the excitement of the day, I felt weary, and was glad to obtain a little quiet.

Shortly after my arrival at my apartments, the King sent a present, consisting of twenty-five calabashes of native food, ready-cooked and prepared for my people, and six large basins full of stew, hashes, roast fowls, yams, &c., &c., for my own use. Thus we were regaled with a plentiful supply of fresh and wholesome food at a seasonable time; for we were all exceedingly fatigued with the tedious ceremonies of our entry. Such attention was a great kindness on the part of the King, and proved that he wished to make me feel that I was among friends.

In the cool of the evening, Kabada came and talked with me for more than half an hour; and I could easily perceive that he wished to ascertain the object which I had in view in visiting Dahomi, that he might immediately carry information to the King. I consequently talked very freely with him; and when I had told him all that I had to say, he left me, to attend His Majesty.

11th.—Early in the morning the House-Master Kabada came to inquire after my health. A short time afterwards, the King sent to bid me good morning, and to ask how I did.

In the forenoon, the King sent to inform me, that he would see me at his residence to-morrow. The messenger said, "The King says, you and all your people must be tired after your long journey; and he thinks it will be good for you to rest to-day. To-morrow he will see you." I felt quite satisfied with this arrangement, and even thankful for it. A day's rest is grateful, after long journeys and great excitement.

12th.—About eleven, A. M., the King sent messengers to inform me that he was ready to see me; and I consequently proceeded to the royal residence, accompanied by my interpreters and a few of my people. When we arrived at the gate, we found Mewo seated outside, under his umbrella, smoking his pipe, and waiting to receive us. After I had been seated a short time under one of the Banyan-trees, Mewo went in to the King; and a messenger came, requesting me to proceed. We passed through the gate, and entered a large enclosed space, from eighty to ninety yards square. I again took my seat under the shade of a tree to await another invitation.

In three or four minutes the messengers returned, requesting me again to proceed. We then advanced towards another gate on the opposite side, the messengers continually saying in a low voice in the native tongue, "May we come? May we come?" as they walked along in a stooping position. We then passed through the gate, and entered another yard about the same size as the former; and, on the opposite side, under a thatched verandah of considerable dimensions, sat His Majesty Guzzu, King of Dahomi, surrounded by a great number of the ladies of his household, and several hundreds of female soldiers armed with muskets and cutlasses, doing duty as his body-guard. The rude verandah seemed to be decorated for the occasion with pieces of damask, and handsome cloths of native manufacture bound round the pillars. The King was seated on an European chair, covered with cloth; and before him was placed a small European table, containing several decanters filled with different kinds of liquor, also tumblers and wine-glasses, and a supply of water. As we approached nearer and nearer, the messengers prostrated themselves on their hands and knees; and in this posture advanced several yards, until they came close to the place where the King was seated. Then they threw dust on their heads, and prostrated themselves, touching the dust with their foreheads, chins, and cheek-bones. Mewo and Kabada were kneeling on the ground immediately opposite the King. The King rose from his seat to receive me, as I entered the verandah, took me very cordially by the hand, and bade me welcome to Dahomi. My travelling camp-stool was then placed on the other side of the table directly opposite the King, and I was requested to sit down. His Majesty also seated himself, and seemed pleased to see me. After asking me how I liked my journey, and giving me an opportunity of informing him what I thought of the country through which I had passed, he asked me to drink with him; and while I was doing so, I heard heavy guns firing at a short distance from the place where we were seated, and was informed by the King, that he was firing a salute in honour of the Queen of England. When twenty-one guns had been fired, he showed me in his hand twenty-one cowrie-shells, and said they were equal in number to the guns he had fired in honour of the Queen of

England. I of course returned thanks. He then fired a salute of nine guns to welcome me to Kanna. To object to this would, in such a case, have been wrong, as he would not have understood my motive for so doing. I therefore endeavoured to put a good face upon it, and even thanked him for his kindness. We then entered into conversation, when I explained to him the real object of my visit, entered at length into the subject of the Badagry Mission; acquainting him with our objects and intentions, contradicting the false rumour respecting our building a fort at Badagry, and assuring him that our operations there were of a strictly religious, and not of a political, nature. He seemed very well satisfied with the explanations I gave, and immediately said, "Cannot you do something at Whydah also?" to which I answered, "My particular business with your Majesty is concerning our Mission at Badagry; but if you wish us to commence one at Whydah, we will try and attend to your request as early as possible." In answer to which he said he wished us to do so. I then spoke to him of the anxiety manifested by Her Majesty the Queen of England, and her people, to do good to Africa by every possible means. Referring again to the Badagry Mission, I stated that a great number of Aku people, who had been taken from slave-ships by British cruisers, had been landed at Sierra-Leone, where they had lived many years under the protection of the British government; that they had expressed a wish to return to their native land; that they had done so; and that, as many of them had been under the instruction of English Missionaries at Sierra-Leone, I had, while at Cape-Coast, received instructions to proceed to Badagry, and try to make some arrangement for their being taken care of; but that we did not wish to confine our operations to Badagry, or any particular place, but to act as the friends of all. I further stated that we had recently commenced a Mission in Ashânti, and had great demands for Missionaries all around us at Cape Coast; but, notwithstanding, I was sure that every effort would be made in England to do something for Whydah. I also added that the Queen of England had been recently turning her attention very much towards Africa, and several times the question had lately been asked, "What can be done for the good of Africa?" that measures were now being adopted for promoting this benevolent object; and I thought it probable, that the Queen of England would soon send to him about the re-occupying of the English Fort at Whydah, and opening friendly communications with him. He was evidently highly pleased with what I said, and replied, "I hope the Queen will send to me, and send a Governor for the Fort directly."* I then acquainted him of my extreme anxiety to return to the coast without delay, on account of my long absence from Cape Coast, where business of an important nature demanded my speedy return; and he assured me that he would not detain me, but make me ready very soon. Our long interview was then brought to a close; he rose up and accompanied me across the two yards, and out at the door into the area in front of the gate. On our arrival outside, accompanied by several hundred female soldiers,† the King ordered them to fire their muskets and blunderbusses;—thus I was taken unawares with more firing which lasted from ten to twenty

* The importance of the King of Dahomi's consent to the re-establishment of the British Fort or Factory at Whydah, as recommended by the "Select Committee on the West Coast of Africa." may be seen by a reference to the extract from the "Minutes of Evidence," in a note on page 247 of this Journal.—Edit.

† There is a plate in Dalzel's "History of Dahomi," representing the King at the head of his armed women going to war.—Edit.

minutes. I was sorry it took place on the Sabbath; but I could not hinder it. This little brigade of soldiers presented a very singular appearance. They were dressed so much like men, that a stranger would not have supposed that they were women. The King's soldiers wear a loose shirt without sleeves, which comes nearly down to their knees, and is fastened round the waist by their cartouch-belt: a musket, a small heavy cutlass, and a poniard complete their armour. The brigade of women fired their muskets and blunderbusses remarkably well, and appeared totally void of fear.

The interpreter and messenger having intimated to me that I could see Abomi if I wished, I told the King, before we broke up our conference, that I should like to see that place. He seemed pleased, and readily consented to it. Arrangements were consequently made for my visiting Abomi on Tuesday next.

The King of Dahomi is a man of fine personal appearance, about six feet high, and rather stout, but not at all corpulent. His countenance is open and manly; and he appears of a mild and pacific disposition.

13th.—I visited the King again. I found him prepared to receive me in the same place where I met him yesterday; but as our interview was strictly private, only two or three attendants were present.

I was highly pleased with this proof of the King's confidence, as meeting and conversing with me, for a long time, under such circumstances. During this interview, I went over the same subject on which we conversed yesterday; so that I had another opportunity of bringing Missionary operations before him. Lest I should be mistaken as to his former remarks concerning a Mission at Whydah, I determined to make sure by referring again to that particular; and asked him if he really wished us to commence one in that place; to which question he freely answered, "Yes:" and thus removed all doubt from my mind. He further said that he would be glad for the Missionary who might reside at Whydah, to pay him a visit once a year in Abomi.

Some conception of my feelings, in the midst of all these important negotiations, may be formed by kindred minds, much better than I can describe them.

CHAPTER VI.

MR. FREEMAN VISITS ABOMI, THE CAPITAL OF DAHOMI—PROCESSION—FETISHMAN—KUMASI—RECEPTION—THE KING'S RESIDENCE—ENTRANCE INTO ABOMI—ADANGERAKADI, THE KING'S RESIDENCE—BARBAROUS EMBELLISHMENT OF THE BUILDING—DALZEL'S ACCOUNT OF THAT CRUEL PROCEEDING—CULPRIT ON A GIBBET—WALL OF HUMAN SKULLS—ABOMI DESCRIBED—RETURNS TO ABOKUTA—PRESENTS FROM THE KING—PREPARES TO RETURN—AUDIENCE WITH THE KING ON DEPARTURE—ARRIVES AT AGREMI—ALADA—TORRI—ARRIVES AT WHYDAH—FRIENDLY DISPOSITION OF THE CHIEF OF WHYDAH—PROCEEDS TO AKWA—APPEARANCE OF THE COUNTRY BETWEEN WHYDAH AND AKWA—THE LAGOON—AKRAH—CAPE COAST.

March 14th.—About fifteen minutes past seven, A. M., Mewo arrived at my quarters, and joined my House-Master Kabada, to take me to Abomi. The people in number about two or three hundred, with native drums and other instruments of music, their banners and large umbrellas, with Kabada, started first, and led the way; Mewo went next; and I, with my carriers, followed in the rear. Both Mewo and Kabada rode on their mules. We proceeded on a fine level road, varying in breadth from ten to forty feet. When we had proceeded about two miles and a half, we passed one of the King's Fetish-houses; from whence a Fetishman came and pronounced a blessing, begging of the Fetish a safe journey for us to Abomi. Though I pitied the people on account of their superstitions, yet I could not help admiring their apparent sincerity. Having rested here two or three seconds, we again went forward over a fine open country, flat, but still interesting. The two great ornaments of these sylvan scenes, are the Monkey Bread-tree, *Adansonia digitata*, and the Locust-tree, *Inga lugubrosa*. The Guinea-peach, *Sarco-cephalus esculentus*, with its beautiful globular blossoms, is another ornament of this part of Africa. The Palm-tree, *Elais Guineensis*, is also seen luxuriating in great abundance. The natives use the pulp of the nut for oil and soup; but the use of the wine is prohibited by the King. On inquiring into the cause of this prohibition, I was informed that many of the natives had used it to very great excess, and had become noisy and riotous in their houses: the King had therefore prohibited the use of the liquor, to check this growing evil. After proceeding on the Abomi path about six miles, we turned to the left, and proceeded to Kumási, the King's new palace, situated about two miles from Abomi. On our arrival at the palace several Chiefs were seated at the gate to receive us; and after having gone through the usual ceremonies of reception, I passed into the large court-yard, and saw part of the interior of the royal residence. The King being from home, I did not see the rooms, but the interior has a very respectable appearance. It is built in the European style, and appears strong and durable. The materials are of red clay. The roof is thatched with grass. The house has one large wing, which seems to contain some of the principal apartments. While I was seated in the interior court-yard, at a small table covered with some refreshments, the King's wives, residing at Kumasi, sent an abundant supply of food for my people, and sat at a distance as spectators, while I was taking a rough sketch of the premises.

From Kumási we then proceeded to Abomi. As we were entering the outskirts of the town, I saw among the crowd a countenance differing somewhat from the mass of faces around me, and thought there was something about it familiar to me. On inquiring if the man in question were an Ashánti, he answered in the affirmative, and appeared to look upon me as an old friend, though I could not have seen him before, because he had been in Dahomi, as I understood, more than six years. He seemed to know that I was acquainted with Kumási, the capital of Ashánti, very well, and would have entered into conversation with me, but I was afraid of exciting jealousy. There are, in fact, several Ashántis in Dahomi; but how they came there I cannot tell, and was afraid to make much inquiry. One, however, stated, that when the Ashántis fought the battle of Dodowah,* he was taken prisoner, and sold from Akráh to Whydah, and from thence went up to Abomi. This story seems likely to be true. Soon after I recognised the Ashánti, we reached Kabada's house in Abomi, where we lunched, and refreshed the people. An abundant supply of native provisions, ready prepared for my attendants, with soup and stews, &c., for myself, were sent over from Kanna, a distance of about eight miles, by order of the King; and, after resting about an hour and a half during the heat of the day, we proceeded to Adangerakadi, the King's palace in Abomi. We passed through several streets, rather confined and irregular, with nothing striking in their appearance, and then found ourselves in front of the royal residence. The entrance, and the area in front of it, were like all the others I have seen; but Adangerakadi is larger than any. After going through the usual form, I passed into the interior yard, saw some of the King's wives, and was treated in the same manner as at Kumási. In the yard I saw suspended from a tree, or from some sticks, (I forget which,) about from twenty to thirty pairs of Moorish stirrup-irons; trophies taken in some former engagement with the Akus, or probably with some of the

* This was the decisive battle which terminated the war between the British and the Ashántis, in the year 1826. Dodowah is twenty-four miles north-east of British Akráh.—Edit.

Moorish tribes immediately behind Dahomi. On leaving the palace, I was introduced to all the members of the King's household as the English Fetishman, the King of Dahomi's friend. The whole premises of Adangerakadi are very extensive, and enclosed within a clay wall from three to four feet thick, and about twelve or fourteen feet high. The area within must be at least from six to ten acres. As we passed along, outside the walls, I saw that they were decorated with human skulls, stuck on small sticks. The sticks were about fifteen inches high above the tops of the walls, and placed at regular distances from each other all round the premises. I should say that the distance from stick to stick, and consequently from skull to skull, would be about from twenty to thirty feet.*

---

* Dalzel, in his "History of Dahomi," narrates the circumstances which led to this horrid embellishment of the palace; and we give the substance of his narrative for the purpose of showing the importance of Mr. Freeman's visiting Dahomi, with the view of securing the acquiescence of the King in the establishment of a Christian Mission at Badagry. Adahunzu, a former Sovereign of Dahomi, having been successful in several wars, resolved to attack the neighbouring state of Badagry. His army, however, experienced a signal defeat, the greater part having been cut off by the Badagris; and he was so greatly affected by the disaster, that "at the celebration of the customs," the historian says, "he would not suffer his singing-men to touch on Badagry in their songs; the subject was, according to Dahomi idiom, *too strong for him.*" He had lost many brave officers and men, and denounced eternal vengeance against those who had been the occasion of his disgrace. He called together the Agaow, and all his Captains; and, while he watered his mother's grave, made a public speech of three hours; in the course of which he stooped down, and taking up a portion of earth in his fingers three times, he as often sware by his mother, that "if he did not make a total conquest of Badagry, he was unworthy to be called her and Ahadi's son."

About two months after this, he collected another army, with

From Adangerakadi we went to visit the King's mother. As we passed along the street, still near the walls of the royal premises, one of the Whydah people

---

which the Agaow again encountered the Badagris; six thousands of whose heads, delivered by the warriors of Dahomi to their King, were the sad proofs of the overthrow which Badagry had at length experienced. The proceedings of the King after this victory are thus described:—

"Great rejoicings followed this conquest. Adahunzu and his Captains danced round the place for several successive days; a profusion of victuals was expended in feasting; and a vast quantity of brandy was consumed; while the heads of the vanquished Badagris were daily exhibited for the gratification of the astonished multitude....

"1785. At the succeeding customs, the singing-men had a fine opportunity of flattering the vainglorious Monarch. Badagry was no longer a disagreeable theme. The air resounded with the notable exploits performed by the victorious army; and echo, from the adjacent woods, reverberated the *strong names* of the *Male Oyster*, (a phrase, according to the Dahomi idiom, meaning his titles and exploits,) till hoarseness and fatigue overpowered the vocal band. The officers and soldiers were liberally rewarded by the distribution of cowries and cloth; and the skulls of the vanquished enemy were ordered to be applied to the decoration of the royal walls.

"The person to whom the management of this business had been committed, having neglected to make a proper calculation of his materials, had proceeded too far in the work, when he found that there would not be a sufficient number of skulls to adorn the whole palace. He therefore requested permission to begin the work anew, that he might, by placing them farther apart, complete the design in a regular manner. But the King would by no means give his consent to this proposal; observing, that he should soon find a sufficient quantity of Badagry heads to render the plan perfectly uniform.

"The operators, therefore, proceeded with the work till the skulls were all expended, when the defective part of the walls were measured, and a calculation made, by which it appeared that *one hundred and twenty-seven* was the number wanted to finish this extraordinary embellishment. The prisons, where the wretched

said to me, "Do you see that man?" and on looking up, I saw, close to the wall on the outside, a kind of gibbet, on a pole, fixed in the ground; and about twenty feet high above the ground, was secured the body of a man, seated upright on the top of the pole. The body seemed to be in a good state of preservation. I could perceive that the abdomen had been opened, and sewed up; and I found, on inquiry, that the bowels had been taken out, and the body salted, and partially dried, before it was placed in its present position. I asked how long the man had been killed and placed there; and they told me, "About nine months." The man was a public offender, and had been guilty of a great crime. The walls, from top to bottom, on either side of the door, leading to one part of the royal premises which we passed, were decorated with a vertical row of human skull-bones, built into the clay, with the faces outward, level with the wall. After visiting the King's mother, we went to Mewo's house, and rested ourselves. All the principal men have both town and country houses. The Chief of Whydah has his town-house in Abomi. These houses are built with clay, and are in many respects not unlike an ordinary low

---

captives had been confined, were accordingly thrown open, and the requisite number of devoted victims dragged forth to be slaughtered in cold blood for this hellish purpose. Previous to their execution, they were informed that the heads brought home by the Agaow had not been found sufficient to garnish the palace, and that theirs were required to supply the deficiency. This act of barbarity was greatly applauded by all present."—*Dalzel*, p. 190.

To mark more strikingly the strength of the ruling passion in this transaction, Dalzel adds a note, stating that at the very time when those wretched captives were murdered, there were six slave-ships in the road of Whydah, with a great scarcity of trade; and that the price of a prime slave was little short of thirty pounds sterling.—Edit.

English cottage. The principal difference is, that the Abomi houses are nearly all surrounded with a rude, low, thatched verandah, with its eaves in front, not more than from three to five feet high, very much like many of the Aku houses in Abokuta, or Understone, described in the former part of my Journal. On entering Mewo's premises, I was conducted to a small table in a court-yard, where Mewo joined me, and refreshed me with some cherry-brandy and water. After resting ourselves for some time, we started, about seven o'clock in the evening, on our way back to Kanna. Just as we were leaving the outskirts of Abomi, Kabada, who was again leading the way, stopped, and directed my attention to a number of guns, some brass, others of iron, some of heavy, and others of light, calibre. There were all together thirty in number; one, I think the largest of brass, had been taken from Badagry, many years before; others had been obtained, in all probability, from vessels on the coast. Under the beautiful, soft shades of the twilight, we then proceeded on our way back to Kanna. It was a splendid evening:

"The moon, refulgent lamp of night,
On heaven's pure azure spreads her sacred light;
While not a breath disturbs the deep serene,
And not a cloud obscures the solemn scene."

I rode thoughtfully along, sometimes gazing on the starry heavens above me, now admiring the silvery rays of the moon, as they played on the soft and elegant foliage of the Locust-tree, and the different varieties of *Mimosa* and *Acacia*, which in some places lined the road. Kabada, with his people, his umbrella, and his banner, were just near enough to be distinguished through the shades of the evening; and though Mewo, who now came behind, bringing up the rear, was out of sight, I could faintly hear the sounds of his drums as they died away in the distance. All around me the scene was too romantic and exciting to admit of anything like a just description from my pen; but though I cannot fairly describe it, the impression of it thrilled through my soul, and while feeling so weary from the peculiar excitements of the day, that it was a hard task to keep my place on the saddle, yet I admired, and continued to admire, until I reached my lodgings, when I speedily sunk into the arms of sleep.

Abomi is a large town; but, from the peculiar manner in which the people build, there is nothing in the appearance of the houses and streets particularly striking. The houses of all the Chiefs and Captains are closely immured; so that, in passing through many of the streets, nothing can be seen but heavy clay walls on either side. In size, I should think it nearly or quite equal to Kumási; and perhaps the population about the same in number. The soil is red clay, mixed with sand; and, generally speaking, free from stones. There is, however, some granite in the neighbourhood; for on my way to Kanna from Whydah, I met a man carrying on his head a large piece of granite, about sixty pounds weight, which I understood he was taking to Whydah for sale. The most striking objects in Abomi, next to the royal premises, are splendid specimens of the Baabah, or *Adansonia digitata*. In almost every street, and at every turning, these vegetable monsters may be seen rising above the walls and houses.

15th.—Early in the morning I sent to the King, to request that he would soon make me ready to start for the coast. He sent me word that I must be tired after going to Abomi yesterday: I must therefore rest to-day, and to-morrow he would make me ready.

16th.—This morning the King sent to say that he

wished to see me, in order to make me ready to return; and, on entering the royal premises, I found him seated in the same place where he had received me before. His brigade of female soldiers were present, as on my first interview. After conversing with him for some time on various subjects, he presented, for Her Majesty the Queen of England, two handsome cloths of native manufacture, and two little slave-girls. I thought it would be unwise to refuse the slaves: as, by taking them to Cape Coast, educating them, and then sending them back to their own country, Aku, we might save their lives, and benefit that country. I felt satisfied that he could not so misunderstand anything of this kind, as to consider us countenancing slavery in any way; because I had told him already, that England could not and would not sanction it, in the least degree. He then presented a cloth of native manufacture, and a slave-girl, for President Maclean; and gave me a cloth, and a little slave-girl, for myself. Nearly all my own people were with me, and he made them presents of cowries and other little things to help them along the path. For all these things I returned thanks. The King also placed under my care two boys and two girls from his household, requesting me to take them to Cape Coast, and give them an English education; and, when they were prepared for it, to return them to him. This was to me an extraordinary mark of confidence on the part of the King, and proves at once that he really wishes to cultivate a good understanding with England. All these matters being arranged, he then called my Fanti carriers forward, and asked them several questions through an interpreter. After having for some time amused himself with the Fantis, he rose and accompanied me to the area outside of the gate, and ordered his female solders to fire their guns and blunderbusses.

I then obtained permission to return, and as soon as I reached my quarters, I informed the little Aku slave-girls that they were now all free; that they should go with me to Cape Coast for education, and afterwards be sent home to their own country. When the little creatures fully understood me, their tears, which had for some minutes been flowing apace, were all dried up, their countenances beamed with joy, and they became so noisy and riotous, that I was obliged to scold them. The little Dahomi children seemed alarmed at first; but when they knew their destination and prospects, they soon ceased to grieve. I now began to pack up my things, and prepare for returning to the coast early in the morning.

In the evening, my father Mewo, and Kabada came to present me with a piece of cloth each, as a token of their friendship and good feeling.

17th.—Early in the morning, about seven, A.M., the King sent me and my people a bountiful supply of food ready cooked and prepared; and about nine, he sent again to inquire if I were ready to start; and when he found all was ready, he sent for me. I left my lodgings with my people, luggage, &c., and we all repaired to the King's residence. We found him seated outside of the outer gate, surrounded by his female soldiers, and several hundreds of the other sex; with many Chiefs and Captains, and all the principal ladies of his household. He, as usual, received me kindly, and requested me to sit down opposite to him. Soon after my arrival, a salute of twenty-one guns was fired in honour of the Queen of England. I returned thanks. He then amused himself a short time by conversing with my Fanti people. The soldiers, male and female, then fired their small arms; after which, some of them came forward, and, in the name of their respective divisions, bade me farewell. Several of the Chiefs also did the same. I was then reminded of a message given to me the previous day, for Her Majesty the Queen of England; and, having received the King's compliments to Her Majesty, and to the Governor of Cape Coast, I was ready to depart. The drums then began to beat, and the King, surrounded by hundreds of the people, walked with me about one hundred yards on the path, and then said, "Farewell!" Kabada and Mewo now joined me, and we mounted our horses and proceeded. They accompanied me about a mile from the town, and then we all halted, while two Fetishmen ran with their utmost speed about a hundred yards along the path, made a full stop, and spread abroad their hands towards heaven, invoking a blessing on my journey down to the coast. When they returned, I was given to understand that the path was open before me; and I shook hands with Mewo, Kabada, and the Fetishmen, and proceeded on my way. As I left, Mewo and Kabada's people saluted me by firing their muskets and blunderbusses. We travelled for a few hours, and rested for the night at Agremi.

As soon as we arrived, I looked around for a place in which to sleep; but, as I could find nothing equal to a common English shed, I pitched my tent under the shelter of a large Banyan-tree, and took some refreshment with a good appetite, about half-past five, P.M., having travelled under a burning sun nearly all the day, and taken nothing to eat since seven o'clock in the morning. In our native land this would be nothing; but in an exhausting climate, like Western Africa, while engaged in the active exercise of travelling, it is no trifle.

18th.—At forty-five minutes past five, we resumed our journey, and reached Alada about five, P.M., where we halted for the night.

19th, Sunday.—We spent this day at Alada. The people, worn out with the fatigues of the last two or three days, were heavy and sleepy, and unfit in a great measure for religious duty. I intended, however, to hold divine service in the afternoon; but was hindered by an unexpected visit from the Chief and Captains of Alada.

Extremely anxious to reach the coast; and remembering how much many of my people had suffered from journeying through the intense heat of the day, I decided on travelling during the night. Consequently, about half-past seven, P.M., instead of retiring to rest, we resumed our journey: at half-past twelve we stopped at Torri, and took some refreshment. Having rested about three quarters of an hour at Torri, we again proceeded, and reached Whydah at half-past four, A.M. We stopped on the outskirts of the town at a small house, until six o'clock, and then proceeded to the house of the Chief. He met me at his gate, and bade me welcome. He was delighted at the account which I gave of my reception by the King, and seemed pleased with the results of my journey to Dahomi. I took my leave of him, and went to my quarters in the old English Fort. Shortly after my arrival, many of the natives came to welcome me back to Whydah, with every possible demonstration of good feeling.

In the course of the day I visited Mr. De Souza, and acquainted him with the handsome manner in which the King had received me.

Although I had been riding on horseback nearly all the previous night, I felt but little weariness: my physical strength was equal to the work I had to do; for which I thank God.

27th.—During the past week I have been busy in preparing to leave for Cape Coast. While engaged in these preparations, messengers came down from the King to inquire after my health, and how I succeeded in my journey to the coast. The Chief of Whydah, Yovaga, made me a present of a bullock and a country cloth: one of the interpreters also presented me with a country cloth. During the week I have attended to some important business connected with Whydah and Lagos, and our Badagry Mission. A slave, it was reported, had taken refuge on the Mission premises; which circumstance placed us in danger of coming into unpleasant collision with the people. These are delicate and trying matters, demanding prudent care and attention.

The schooner "Medora" having come from Badagry, bound for Cape Coast, calling at Akwa on her passage, I prepared to embark on board that vessel at Akwa, and consequently sent some of my luggage with her from Whydah. The "Medora" then proceeded to Akwa, a distance of about from twenty-five to thirty miles to windward of Whydah; to which place I proceeded by the Lagoon in a canoe. This morning Mr. De Souza had promised me his travelling-canoe, in which to go up the Lagoon; and about seven, A.M., he came to the English Fort, accompanied by one of his sons, to conduct us thither, a distance of from two to three miles. On reaching the Lagoon, Mr. De Souza and his son assisted in arranging and starting the four canoes containing my people and luggage. I then took my leave, heartily thankful for their great kindness to me. I owe Mr. De Souza my best thanks for his steady, uniform kindness during my stay at Whydah. Although I frankly opened my mind to him on various matters connected with the slave-trade, and told him that my business in seeing the King of Dahomi was that of placing on a firm basis a Mission intended to protect and benefit those very people who had been shipped off from Whydah and other places near at hand, and afterwards captured and liberated by British cruisers; yet he still continued to assist me, and to pay every kind attention to my wants. I scruple not to state, that he by his influence in many instances made my path easy, and saved me from many annoyances which I might otherwise have received.

We proceeded at a steady pace up the Lagoon. The canoe-men did not use paddles, but long pieces of bamboo, with which they forced the canoes along by resting the ends on the ground at the bottom of the river; in the same manner as an English waterman would push a boat along a creek too narrow for the use of oars. The appearance of the Lagoon between Whydah and Akwa is not so beautiful as it is in the neighbourhood of Badagry. In the former part, the banks are low and marshy, with no striking object in view; in many places, also, it is narrow and confined, and the depth of water not more than from two to four feet. We passed several crooms, the most important of which were Afailkakia and Grand Popo. A little after midnight, we reached Akwa, where I was kindly received and entertained by Mr. Akhurst.

28th.—About half-past nine, A.M., we went up the Lagoon to Little Popo, a distance of about eight miles from Akwa. We travelled about four miles in an hour. The appearance of the river between Akwa and Popo is much like what we saw yesterday. When, however, we approached within two or three miles of Popo, the town wore a pretty appearance. Standing on several little islands rising out of the glassy bosom of the water, decorated with a few white houses with painted jalousies and small uncovered galleries, it wears a more pleasing aspect than any other second-class town along this part of the coast.

I called on Lawson, one of the most influential and respectable natives, who visited England many years since, when he obtained a little knowledge of the language. He received me kindly, and made me welcome. What surprised me most was to find that the old gentleman was trying to raise a small school, in which to teach young children the first rudiments of an English education. I inquired whether he would like us to send a Teacher or Missionary to Popo or not; he said he should be very glad if we would do something for that town, in the same manner as we were doing in other places. I promised to supply the school with books immediately, and to do more as soon as possible. After remaining from two to three hours at Popo, we returned to Akwa.

On Thursday, March 30th, I embarked from Akwa on board the "Medora," Captain Hayward: on the following Monday I landed at Akrâh, where I stopped a few days; and on Monday, April 9th, I reached Cape Coast, deeply affected with feelings of gratitude to that gracious Providence which had preserved me through so many dangers, and brought me home in safety.

(Signed) T. B. Freeman.

APPENDICES TO THE THIRD JOURNAL.

APPENDIX, A.

Extract of a Letter from the Rev. S. A. Shipman to his Father the Rev. John Shipman, dated British Akrah, Dec. 16*th*, 1842.

I AM very happy to say, that we are both in the enjoyment of good health, and have been so, I think, since I wrote last. Surrounded as we are by sickness and death, this is great cause of thankfulness. Hearing that a vessel was in sight, and coming into the roads, which was likely to sail for England direct, I walked to to the Fort a few minutes ago to learn the truth, and on approaching it perceived, to my astonishment, the flag half-mast high. On inquiring, I find that another of the Danish gentlemen is dead, Mr. Wulff, the Secretary of the Fort. He has been out on the coast six years, and has been carried off by dysentery. How thankful we ought to be for God's continued mercies to us! As I was walking to the Fort I received a letter from Mr. Freeman, dated Badagry, November 14th: "Every thing concerning this Mission promises, and is still going on remarkably well. I cannot but admire the gracious providence of God, in sending us down here just at this important point of time. One hundred and fifty emigrants from Sierra-Leone have just arrived; and I hope we shall be able to obtain for them parcels of land from the Chiefs, so that they may settle at Badagry. I hope to get the roof on the house during the course of the next fortnight, and then proceed to the Orkŭ country. I shall then return, (if I do not see my way open to proceed to Senne,) and go to Whydah and Abomi, and make the best of my way home to Cape Coast, by way of Akrah. We have built a small bamboo chapel, that will contain about two hundred persons: we opened it yesterday for divine worship. The King of the Orkus has made me a handsome present of a beautiful little pony, with a Moorish saddle and bridle, all complete."

This is very encouraging; and I do not think that any interruption will be offered to the Mission and emigrants, unless it be by the King of Dahomi. He has a very great spite against the Badagry people; and as a jealous, powerful, and very savage Monarch, I think there is still great reason to beware of him, if not to fear him.

I am endeavouring to compile a vocabulary of the Fanti language, and have also got translations made of the Commandments, the Lord's Prayer, and part of the Catechism: I cannot, however, proceed so rapidly as you imagine. My interpreter is a very good one, though I have been deprived of his services for the last three months, he being called to supply Mr. De Graft's place at Winnebah: I have had to employ the young man whom I am instructing in that capacity."

APPENDIX, B.

DAHOMI.—*Extract of a Letter from the Rev. T. B. Freeman, dated Kanna, Kingdom of Dahomi, Western Africa, March 11th,* 1843.

As I understand that a vessel will sail from Whydah or Badagry for England in the course of a few days, I hasten to inform you that I have, by the kind providence of God, safely arrived at Kanna, the present temporary residence of the King of Dahomi. I left Whydah on Monday last, and reached Kanna yesterday morning. His Majesty has given me a very kind and handsome reception, and has appointed to-morrow for my seeing him on the important subject of Christian Missions. I trust that the Lord has in his providence sent me here, and I hope that my visit to this powerful Monarch will be productive, in the end, of important moral results. By the close of next week I hope to reach Whydah, on my way to Cape Coast.

I have not yet received any letters from the Centenary-Hall since my departure from Cape Coast in September last; and as the means of communication between Cape Coast and Whydah and Badagry are not at all times frequent and easy, I hear but little from the Gold Coast. Nothing but a courtesy towards the King of Dahomi, indispensably necessary, when considered in connexion with our Badagry Mission, would have kept me so long absent from Cape Coast. For several weeks past I have felt very uncomfortable on account of my being so long from the centre of our important Missions on the Gold Coast; but I am sure the Committee will not blame me, when they know the cause of my absence. If I had not gone down to Badagry, that Mission could not have yet been properly commenced: and I feared that if it were delayed longer than September last, the Committee would have blamed me. From the rapid extension of our work in this part of the western coast of Africa, during the past two years, notwithstanding our mighty troubles, the Committee are doubtless satisfied that the God of Missions is with us, and that while our faith is keenly tried, the labour of our hands is blessed.

Judging from the general aspect of things in this part of Africa, I conclude that there will continue to be an increasing demand for Missionaries. Can the places be supplied? Ten or twelve well-seasoned, effective men would be little enough for this extensive district. At present, I thank God, my health is steady and good; and my heart is as much in this good work now, or even more so, that it was when I first entered into it. Our numerous trials, both public and private, have not abated any of my original ardour in the good work. Blessed be God, I can say with my heart,—and I say it with humility,—I still rejoice to struggle on in the great conflict.

Time forbids me saying much that I would wish to say. I beg a constant interest in your prayers.

APPENDIX, C.

BADAGRY.—We are happy to have it in our power to report (say the Secretaries of the Wesleyan Missionary Society) the satisfactory progress of the work at the recently-formed Mission at this place. Badagry is represented by Lander as divided into several towns or districts, four of which are called English Town, French Town, Spanish Town, and Portuguese Town. The Chiefs, or Headmen, of the former two are now favourable to the Mission; and Mr. De Graft mentions another very influential Chief as having become decidedly friendly, whom he speaks of as the Dutch Chief, or Headman. The perusal of the following letter will afford fresh cause for gratitude to Almighty God, who is so graciously preparing the way of his servant, and crowning his endeavours with success. Our readers, we are sure, will make due allowance for any peculiarity or defect of style and idiom, when they consider the circumstance of Mr. De Graft's comparatively recent, and of course as yet imperfect, acquaintance with the English language.

Extract of a Letter from the Rev. William De Graft, (Native Assistant Missionary,) dated Wesleyan Mission-House, Badagry, July 10*th*, 1843.

Being sensible of the anxious interest you indulge for the welfare and prosperity of this newly-taken post, in the very heart of the enemy's strong-hold, I cannot let this opportunity, which now offers itself for sending letters, go without once more addressing you, in the doing of which I am exceedingly thankful, and feel the most heartfelt gratitude, that I am enabled by the great Head of the church to send you something cheering.

Since my last communication, per the "Traveller," by the grace of God I have not withheld my hand from scattering the precious seed of the word of life. I have cast the living bread upon the waters. Of the poor who are perishing in these dark places of the earth, full of the habitations of cruelty, for lack of knowledge, even the knowledge of our Lord and Saviour Jesus Christ, many have heard the joyful sound. We have endeavoured to sow beside all waters. To the Akus, and to the Ogus, or the Popos, we have divided portions with an impartial hand, that every one of them might have a little. Not observing the winds of difficulties and trials which seem to thwart and to blow adversely; neither regarding the clouds which appear to envelop the bright designs of our Lord; but with an eye of living faith to Christ Jesus, the victorious Captain of our salvation; we have urged our way in the thorny path of duty, knowing that both winds and clouds are in his hands, and under the indisputable control of him who hath engaged us in the warfare, and who hath said, "And, lo, I am with you alway, even unto the end of the world." And, I am happy to say, our labours have not been in vain in the Lord. Blessed be God! his holy word hath not returned void unto him, but it hath accomplished that which he pleases,—the the salvation of immortal souls; giving us reason to triumph, and to hope that the word "shall prosper in the thing whereunto he hath sent it," even the filling of "the earth with the knowledge of the glory of the Lord, as the waters cover the sea."

In the discharge of our arduous, but very delightful, duties, we have experienced much of the cheering influences of Jehovah's aiding arm. He, in the battle, hath covered our defenceless heads; wrought all our works for us, in owning, ratifying, blessing, and defending his own work; so that while we preached Jesus, and him crucified, to the people's ears, the Holy Spirit preached to the hearts of the people, insomuch that some of the dead in trespasses and sin have heard the voice of the Son of God echoing in the Gospel word:—

"Come, ye weary sinners, come,
All who groan beneath your load;
Jesus call his wanderers home,
Hasten to your pardoning God.
Come, ye guilty spirits oppress'd,
Answer to the Saviour's call;
Come, and I will give you rest,
Come, and I will save you all."

Yea, "dying" they "have heard the welcome sound;" several have come forth and joined themselves to this infant church in the wilderness, breathing praise and thanks to the God of love, and seeking to be ever blessed. Among them there is an elderly man, a native of

Obohou, with his wife. Obohou, by this person's description of it, is about four hundred miles from this, inland. He is about fifty years of age. He tells me, that he is the eldest son of Ageza Lakunde, King of that country, who reigned some time there till 1835, and, by right, he was the person who was to succeed his father, who died in the above-mentioned year; but, owing to the disputes that followed his father's death, his uncle, who was a very ambitious man, making claims to the throne contrary to the laws of their country, and the will of the populace, by forcible means took the throne, and drove him out of their country by threatening his life. He, of course, fled into this country, and has been sojourning here ever since, about eight years. Some time ago he received messengers from Obohou, informing him, that his tyrannical uncle was dead, and all the people wished him to return home, and take the throne and the government of the country. But he did not feel disposed to go, and returned a message home to the effect, that what he was wishing for he had not yet found nor obtained, therefore the time for his return appointed by God Almighty was not yet come. But since our arrival here, about five months ago, he has attended and sat under the preaching of the word of God. Immediately after he heard the word, it proved like a balm to his wounds, it healed up his sorrows and troubles, his heart felt very glad, and concluded, "If God is so good, the soul of man immortal, and happiness insured for ever and ever to all those who believe in Christ, the Son of God, then this is exactly what I want. Begone my sorrows, and all earthly good, with all my fears, for God is become my friend!" Since he heard the Gospel he has compared it with the Moors' religion, prevalent in these countries; but he still found the religion of Jesus Christ to be more excellent. His sincere desire, he tells me, is eternal happiness after death; for he is now an aged man already: and when he thinks of his approaching dissolution, he desires his last end to be peace; and therefore wishes to know what he must do to be saved.

This man sincerely inquires his way to Zion with his face thitherward. The interesting accounts he gives of his motives for coming to God, with the connecting circumstances, have induced me to give him the name of "Simeon." For this man's expressions, the whole of which I cannot conveniently insert herein, approximate pretty near to the devout Simeon of old, who, after he saw the promised Messiah in the temple, proclaimed, "Now lettest thou thy servant depart in peace, according to thy word, for mine eyes have seen thy salvation." And his wife, who is also advanced in years, between forty and fifty, we have named "Anna." This man tells me that he is endeavouring to learn all about this holy religion, and to acquire a little knowledge of the English language; and that, if it pleases God to spare his life, and open his way to his own country, he would take a Teacher with him to tell them what the Lord has done for him, and to instruct his countrymen in the ways of God. Now this is certainly very encouraging. Well did the poet write those beautiful lines:—

"Nor shall thy spreading Gospel rest,
Till through the world thy truth has run:
Till Christ has all the nations blest,
That see the light or feel the sun."

Notwithstanding the darkness that still covers this part of the earth, and the gross darkness that covers this people, yet, agreeably to the sure word of promise, "But the Lord shall arise upon thee, and his glory shall be seen among thee," our prospects at present, with joy

I say, are getting more cheering; for the glimmering rays of a glorious day-spring from on high are visiting this shadow of death. The glorious Sun of Righteousness begins to arise with healing in his wings. Since my last, our society has increased from twenty to forty-five, out of which number there are ten emigrants, who, when in Sierra-Leone, did not know God, but have found him, on their own shores (after their return) to be their Redeemer,

"Nor slow to hear, nor weak to save."

Two Fantis also have found their Saviour here, and two natives of Obohou. The society is much improving both in grace and in the knowledge of our Lord and Saviour Jesus Christ. This I observe clearly in our class-meetings, which are indeed times of spiritual refreshing.

We have also large and increasing mixed congregations, consisting of Akus, emigrants, and Popos, or the natives of this place, every Sabbath-day, both in the forenoon and afternoon. I have been glad several times to observe some of the respectable natives of this town attending in our chapel, sitting calmly down, and their countenances beaming with amazement mixed with delight, while we have been declaring unto the people the wonderful plan of our redemption. It is true, that we have no Badagry converts at present; but, as I have mentioned above, a glorious day-spring just begins to adorn and illumine the hitherto dark, grossly dark, horizon. Many who would not come within the precincts of the Mission-premises before, now do not scruple to step comfortably into the chapel on a Sunday morning and afternoon, and hear the word of God for themselves; and there is a rumour of the wonderful works of God for man now among the people, and there will be a shaking among the "dry bones" by and by. This we sincerely believe; and after the shaking, &c., there will be "an army" (Ezek. xxxvii. 1—10) to praise God in this land.

God is working; but it is in his own way, and according to the instructive parable of our blessed Saviour. His way seems often to be that of a gradual diffusion of divine truth into the minds of the people without immediate and visible good: and this is another encouragement for sowers of the precious seed.

"Through all his mighty works
  Amazing wisdom shines;
Confounds the powers of hell,
  And breaks their dark designs
Strong is his arm, and shall fulfil
His great decrees and sovereign will."

The day-school which I opened here last January is very promising: we have now already between forty and fifty children (boys and girls) in it, who are getting on very well indeed, to our great satisfaction and joy. Hence you see another point is carried; a nursery is founded for the infant church in this wilderness, and it is here we look with an expectant eye to see many to grow as tender plants in the house of God; for, by taking the rising generation into your schools, you rid and deliver them from the hands of strange children, and from treading in the footsteps of their parents; (especially if a better provision can be made for them, to stop on the Mission-premises entirely;) and by being thus taken from their native soil, of ignorance and superstition, planted in the house of God, by the Bible, that ever-precious stream which makes glad the city of our God, and sheltered from all the baneful effects of ignorance and superstition, many (if not all) shall bring forth fruit, that good fruit of usefulness, in their day and generation, even in old age, such as Samuel did, and Timothy proved, and "show that the Lord," the God of the Christians, "is upright, and that there is no unrighteousness in him."

Another piece of good news I have to announce is, that the prejudices of the people here have assumed rather a declining attitude with respect to the school and work at large; and their wish to have their children taught in our school greatly increases. Some of the Chiefs of the different parts of the town, who at first did not wish their children to attend, have sent me several. This certainly secures us two important objects at once, —that of increasing the numbers of our children in the school, and admitting us into open doors of usefulness among the divided districts of the town at large, and thus benefitting the whole. For at present, besides our old friend the Chief, Warru, the Governor of the English Badagry, we have the Dutch and the French Chiefs or Headmen on our side. The latter two also are now our cordial friends; and to afford them opportunity to manifest their sincere friendship, we had them to attend in the chapel and to partake tea with the children of our school and us, on the 4th instant; and as, perhaps, you would like to know more about this sort of tea-meeting, I give you an extract from my journal.

4th, Tuesday.—I was employed for the most part of the morning in gardening, transplanting pine-apples and cocoa-roots, trimming down our guinea-corn, and setting seeds of apples, (sour sop,) &c.,

This evening, about half-past six, P.M., having got every thing ready, agreeable to promise, I gave the children of the Mission-school tea in the chapel. The friends I invited, to witness and to partake of the same, made their prompt attendance, in a handsome manner, in proper time: among whom were the two native Chiefs, with their numerous retinue; namely, Warru, the English Headman, and Posu, the Dutch Headman. The French Chief being sick, was not with us. Posu is a very influential man, and a great warrior, a man of good judgment and friendly disposition, and one who, since I had the pleasure to become his personal acquaintance, has embraced us as his cordial friends, and is apparently very much attached to us and our good cause. We have now, six children from his house, and he still candidly promises to do all he can for the school, by sending more into it, as he sees it will be very beneficial to his people. This Chief has been a long time absent from this town in the Aku encampment,* to aid King Sodaka in putting down the men-stealers. He is King Sodaka's great and good friend; and he is just returned, on some public business, and expects to go back again soon into the camp; but he assures us of his friendship by offering a constant communication between us: and I beg to let you know, that the person who was introduced to me as the Dutch Headman, when I went round on the first canvassing of the town for children to attend the school, was one of the two French Chiefs, and not this man. The thing was a misunderstanding; but Posu, the above-mentioned, is the right Headman for the Dutch district. The chapel was crowded, and wore, on the whole, a very cheerful aspect. The children, about forty in number, both of Sierra-Leone and this place, were neatly dressed in their European clothes, and the members of the society who attended were all in their best; the Chiefs also wore their neat country costume. The crowded meeting and the chapel, nicely arranged and well-lighted up, gave a very

---

* See the Rev. Mr. Freeman's Third Journal.

delightful appearance. I opened the meeting with singing and prayer, and then had the tea, cakes, and bread shared out to the children, to the Chiefs, and to the members of our society present, &c.; and while the children were drinking their tea, we had eight of our principal men in society, by turns, to improve the time by short and appropriate addresses to the children, and to the meeting at large, in the English tongue, as well as in the vernacular language. This occupied about two hours; when I concluded the meeting by addressing the people principally on the subject of our Mission, the object of the good people in England in sending the Gospel unto them, and undertaking the instruction of the rising generation, and the extent of the good they want to bestow on these countries, as co-workers with our gracious Creator and our God. I then called the attention of our people to the due encouragement which they ought to give us, for the good of their country, by sending the rising generation to this school, (and others which, we trust, will hereafter be established in this country,) as well as by directing the attention of their people to the house of God, to have the Gospel preached unto them, and by taking the lead at their head as ensamples in appearing first in the house of God.

The Chiefs and people paid very deep and serious attention to the speeches addressed to the assembly throughout, with countenances displaying heartfelt pleasure and gratitude. On the whole, the little meeting appeared to excite much of interest and much of astonishment. We all sang the doxology, and came away with the blessing of God.

Never did I observe, since our beloved Superintendent left us, such a coincidence of events to make my way pleasant and prosperous. To God be all the praise!

Warru is still very friendly, and strives to serve us as usual.

I beg to inform you of the arrival of more emigrants, on the 13th of May last: one hundred and eighty more were brought down here by the brig "Victoria," belonging to some of our members in society; but, painful to relate, in endeavouring to cross the bar, which at this part of the coast is very dangerous, one canoe was upset, and eight lives were lost, three women and five children. One of the women was a member of our society in Sierra-Leone. Of course, to all the bodies we recovered, we gave Christian burial.

But the most part of the one hundred and seventy-two in last June left this for Understone, or Abokuta, where they are going to fix their permanent residence. I do not believe that, out of the one hundred and seventy-two, there are now left in the town fifty; hence Understone claims your attention, where the opening still exists; the King and people urging their sincere desire for Missionaries to dwell among them. The people from Sierra-Leone, in passing up to Understone, have no molestation at all offered them; they pass up safe and unmolested. All this is to be attributed to King Sodaka's influence and protection: he is very anxious to have his places civilized by these people; and his constant cry is, "Come up to help us."

I am obliged reluctantly to abandon the idea of sending any further accounts at present relative to this country and people, as I promised and sincerely wished to fulfil, on account of the additional encroachment of various employments on my time. But this is still my ardent wish; and I hope I shall, if all is well, serve you better at some future opportunity. I wish to send you a detailed account, as far as I have been enabled to ascertain, of the bloody superstitions now existing in this place, as well as an account of that low moral degradation into which this people are fallen. And now I recommend ourselves, along with your infant cause in this country, to your favourable notice; and as I said in my former letter, so I say again, that if any people need the Gospel, the Popo people specially need it. Requesting, above all, a special interest in your prayers, I beg leave to subscribe myself,

Yours in the Gospel,

William De Graft.

APPENDIX, D.

Kumasi.—*Extract of a Letter from the Rev. Thomas B. Freeman, dated Kumasi, September 7th,* 1843.

I am happy to acquaint you with my safe arrival here with Mr. Chapman, on Saturday last, the 2d ult. Mr. Chapman has borne the journey very well indeed, and the King of Ashánti has received us in a very handsome manner.

I am much pleased with the present aspect of the Mission. Although we have at present no Ashánti converts, a gracious influence seems to be resting on the people. Last Sunday was one of the high days of the great annual yam-custom; and I rejoice to say, that while the town was in a state of extreme excitement, we had many of the natives present at divine service, paying deep and serious attention.

We are living in the new Mission-house, though it is still in an unfinished state. When thoroughly completed, it will be a very comfortable residence, an ornament to Kumási, and the means of producing a great moral effect.

I have many things to say, but time, as usual, presses me sore. My life is one continued scene of physical and mental toil; but I am ready to spend and be spent for God. Mr. De Graft's accounts from Badagry are very encouraging. I need not dwell on them, as he tells me he has written to Mr. Beecham.

A few days before I started for Kumási, I visited Dix-Cove; and I am glad to report, that our work there is beginning to assume a more cheerful character. The labours of a good Missionary there would, I am persuaded, be speedily productive of great good. I am surprised at the wonderful change which has taken place at Dix-Cove during the last two months. When I was there I not only met the society, but all the Headmen of the town; and they have promised to countenance and aid the Mission by all means in their power.

APPENDIX, E.

DOMONASI.—*Extract of a Letter from the Rev. William Allen, dated Mission-House, Domonasi, September 1st*, 1843.

HEARING that the "Governor Maclean" is about to sail for England, I embrace the opportunity of writing you a few lines. You would be happy to learn from the District-Minutes, that the number of communicants is gradually increasing, and that the work of God, in this part of the world, continues to wear a pleasing aspect.

It is a source of grief to your Missionaries, that the funds of the Society will not allow more Missionaries in this interesting part of the Mission field. The cries and entreaties of the people for us to go and preach to them, &c., are enough to break the heart of any Christian, because we are obliged to turn a deaf ear to them. Not only are we solicited by the people in this neighbourhood, but they are coming hundreds of miles, and making use of all arguments possible, to induce us to teach them the way to heaven; but we have already taken in more places than we can attend to.

An influential Chief was begging of me, the other day, to establish a school in his krum; and because I could not give him any encouragement, he said he thought it was a very hard thing that so much food was cooked in England, and he and his people were not allowed to taste of it; intending, by that expression, to convey the idea, that the Gospel was prepared in England, and they were not allowed to hear it.

The Committee need not be surprised, if the Missionaries (who have a burning zeal for the salvation of their fellow mortals) do over-exert themselves among a people who are thirsty to hear words whereby they may be saved.

The length of our District is from Dix-Cove to Badagry, the distance of five hundred miles, and in the interior as far as Kumási, the distance of one hundred and eighty or two hundred miles from the coast; and in that whole range of country we can have access to the people, and only four Missionaries! May I not ask, in Scripture language, "What are we among so many?" And may not those people, to whom we are obliged to turn a deaf ear, say, "No man careth for my soul?"

It is unnecessary for me to enter into any particulars respecting this Circuit; for you would learn from my report for the Anamabu Circuit, which I presented at our District-Meeting, how I am getting on.

Since our District-Meeting, we have established a

school at Donasi, the distance of eight miles from Domanasi, under very pleasing circumstances. We have already fourteen children in the day-school, and thirteen young men in the evening-school, who are very anxious to learn to read the Scriptures; and Kwasi Ankai, the Chief of the place, who is, with the exception of old Otu, the most influential Chief in the Fanti country, is, I believe, seriously disposed, and very anxious to learn to read; and can already, notwithstanding the short time he has had an opportunity, read an easy chapter in the New Testament. He very simply asked me, the last time I saw him, if I thought he was too old to learn the way to heaven. He is only about thirty-five years of age. "This is the Lord's doing, and it is marvellous in our eyes." Whatever may be our trials and discouragements in this part of the Mission field, our encouragements more than counterbalance them. I am more than ever persuaded, if our kind friends in Europe could only see the degradation of this people, and their willingness to receive the Gospel, they would stretch every nerve in order that they might have it. I am afraid but few do their duty in this respect. I, as an individual, reflecting on my past life, and especially for these last two years, have received much of the goodness of God: as a mark of gratitude to Almighty God for preserving my life in this unhealthy climate, and for the success with which my feeble efforts have been crowned, you will please to make my subscription to the Mission cause, for the year 1843, two guineas instead of one; with a promise on my part, if the Lord preserve my life two more years to labour among these people, that, as a token of renewed gratitude to God, I will then raise my subscription to four guineas annually.

Messrs. Freeman and Chapman, who were on their

way to Kumási, arrived at Domanasi on the 23d of August. As duty called me to Mansu, I accompanied them thither the next day, and on the 25th, they left Mansu, and proceeded on to Kumási, both in excellent spirits.

ROCHE, PRINTER, 25, HOXTON-SQUARE, LONDON.

For EU product safety concerns, contact us at Calle de José Abascal, 56–1°, 28003 Madrid, Spain or eugpsr@cambridge.org.

www.ingramcontent.com/pod-product-compliance
Ingram Content Group UK Ltd.
Pitfield, Milton Keynes, MK11 3LW, UK
UKHW010349140625
459647UK00010B/955